Environmental Law in Mexico

Environmental Law in Mexico

Third Edition

José Juan González Márquez

This book was originally published as a monograph in the International Encyclopaedia of Laws/Environmental Law.

Founding Editor: Roger Blanpain
General Editor: Frank Hendrickx
Volume Editor: Kurt Deketelaere

Wolters Kluwer

Published by:
Kluwer Law International B.V.
PO Box 316
2400 AH Alphen aan den Rijn
The Netherlands
E-mail: lrs-sales@wolterskluwer.com
Website: www.wolterskluwer.com/en/solutions/kluwerlawinternational

Sold and distributed by:
Wolters Kluwer Legal & Regulatory U.S.
7201 McKinney Circle
Frederick, MD 21704
United States of America
E-mail: customer.service@wolterskluwer.com

ISBN 978-94-035-0256-4

e-Book: ISBN 978-94-035-0496-4
web-PDF: ISBN 978-94-035-0506-0

The Author

José Juan González Márquez (b. 1959), who holds a Juris Doctor Degree (Mexico, 1981), an LLM in Economic Law (Mexico, 1984) and a PhD in Environmental Law (Spain, 1999), is a Full-time Professor and Researcher at the Metropolitan Autonomous University in Mexico and head of the Environmental Law PhD Programme administered by the Metropolitan Autonomous University in cooperation with the University of Alicante, Spain. In addition to his research and scientific service, he teaches the courses Property of Natural Resources, Tax Law, and Environmental Law. He is also the chairman of the Mexican Institute for Environmental Law Research and Director of the *Mexican Environmental Law Journal.* Gonzalez is a fellow of the National Research System of the Mexican Council of Science and Technology. He was also a member of the Governing Council of the UICN Academy of Environmental Law during the period 2005–2013 and of the Academic Advisory Group of the International Bar Association, Energy Section, Environment and Infrastructure Law.

In the past, he was Director of the Legal Division of the Attorney General's Office for Environmental Protection.

Gonzalez is the author of several books and articles in the field of Latin American and Mexican Environmental Law, Tax Law and Energy Law. Besides his academic activities, he is the adviser for a number of Federal and local governmental agencies in the field of environmental enforcement and compliance. In 1999, he drafted the currently in force Environmental Act of Mexico City.

Gonzalez is also a member of the editorial boards of the *Energy and Natural Resources Law Journal* and the *Macquarie Journal of International and Comparative Environmental Law.* In 2008, he organized the Sixth Annual Colloquium of the UICN Academy of Environmental Law.

The Author

Table of Contents

List of Abbreviations

Agencies

AIE	International Agency of Energy
CBD	Convention on Biological Diversity
Environmental Agency for Energy Sector	National Agency for Industrial Safety and Environmental Protection of the Hydrocarbon Sector
Ministry of the Environment	Secretary of the Environment and Natural Resources
NCPNA	National Commission of Protected Natural Areas
NIE	National Institute of Ecology
NWC	National Waters Commission
Office of Environmental Prosecutor	Federal Attorney General's Office for Environmental Protection
PEMEX	Mexican Petroleum Company
PGEOT	Program of General Ecological Ordinance of the Territory
SCJN	National Supreme Court of Justice
SGD	Sustainable Development Goals
UNEP	United Nations Environment Programme
US	United States

Legislation

AA	Agrarian Act
Access to Information Act	Federal Act of Transparency and Access to Information
ASRD	Act for Sustainable Rural Development

List of Abbreviations

Civil Code	Civil Code of the Federal District as Regards the Common Jurisdiction and for the Whole Republic as Regards the Federal Jurisdiction
DOF	Official Gazette of the Federation
Environmental Act	Ecological Equilibrium and Environmental Protection General Act
FAAP	Federal Act of Administrative Procedure
FAS	Federal Act of the Sea
FDA	Federal Duties Act
Fishing Act	General Act for Sustainable Fishing and Aquaculture
Forest Act	General Act for Sustainable Forest Development
LH	Hydrocarbons Law
MA	Mining Act
Mexican Constitution	Constitution of the Mexican United States
OMNs	Official Mexican Norms
MNs	Mexican Norms
RACNM	Regulatory Act of Article 27 of the Constitution on Nuclear Matters
Regulation on EIA	Regulation under the Environmental Act in Regard to Environmental Impact Assessment
Standardization Act	Federal Act of Metrology and Standardization
TENs	Technical Official Ecological Norms
Urban Act	General Act of Human Settlements
Waste Act	General Act of Prevention and Integral Management of Waste
Waters Act	National Waters Act
Wildlife Act	General Act of Wildlife
Quality Infrastructure Act	Quality Infrastructure Act

General Introduction

§1. GENERAL BACKGROUND

I. Geography and Population

A. Geography

1. Mexico is located in the North American Continent. Its official name is the United Mexican States. The country has a territory of 1,972,547 km^2, placing it fourteenth in geographical size among all countries.

2. In the north, the Mexican Republic has a border of 3,152 km with the United States (US); to the south, it borders Guatemala and Belize along 956 km and 193 km, respectively.

3. Its geographic position has favoured Mexico. It is located between two great oceans that bathe its coasts, 70% of which border the Pacific Ocean and 30% of which border the Gulf of Mexico and the Sea of the Antilles.

4. The main rivers crossing Mexican territory are the Usumacinta, Papaloapan, Grijalva, Coatzacoalcos, Balsas, Bravo, Pánuco, Honda, Lerma-Santiago, Tecolutla and Fuerte. Four of these rivers flow into the Gulf of Mexico and discharge a total of 2.2 million litres of water per second. The Usumacinta discharges about 900,000 litres of water per second, Grijalva 700,000, Coatzacoalcos 400,000, and the Papaloapan 200,000. The Bravo is one of the longest rivers in the world, with a length of 2,800 km, as well as a maximum volume average of close to 120,000 litres per second.[1]

5. Mexico has great climate diversity. Climates range from warm, with annual average temperatures of 26°C, to cold, with annual average temperatures of 10°C. Nevertheless, 93% of the national territory oscillates between temperatures of 10°C and 26°C; this figure includes a hot, sub-humid climate for 23% of the national territory, dry for 28%, very dry for 21% and temperate, sub-humid for 21%.

1. Para todo México, 'Ríos de México: Ríos más importantes de México y su ubicación'. Available at: https://www.paratodomexico.com/geografia-de-mexico/hidrografia-de-mexico/rios-de-mexico.html 28 Oct. 2019.

6. The geology in Mexico is also diverse; the country is located on the edge of the North American Plate; the country is part of the Pacific fire belt so seismic and volcanic activity is frequent. In the centre and north of the country, we find plateaus surrounded by the main mountain ranges of the country, the Sierra Madre Oriental and the Sierra Madre Occidental, to the south, the Sierra Madre del Sur and in the centre, the Eje Neovolcánico integrated by eleven volcanoes, between which are the Popocatepetl and the Iztaccíhuatl, two of the most famous volcanoes of Mexico. To the south of the republic is the Yucatan Peninsula, integrated by Yucatan, Quintana Roo and Campeche; it is a region of lowlands, mostly limestone and hard land where the water runs through the subsoil forming interior rivers and bodies of water called cenotes.

7. Thus, because of its geographical location, form, climate, topography and geology, Mexico presents a wide variety of ecological conditions unique in the world that give it a great wealth of soils, mineral resources, and biodiversity. As reported by the World Bank, natural resources in Mexico are among the most bounteous in the world. With only 1.4% of the world's surface, Mexico ranks fourth in biological diversity, first in number of species of pine trees, second in reptiles and fifth in mammals and plants. Mexico is home to an estimated 10% of all known species, many of them endemic, found nowhere else on Earth (63% of endemic flora and 30% of endemic vertebrates).

8. Due to the variety of ecosystems found in Mexico, the country is the major producer of multiple agricultural products. Many areas of the country are dedicated to planting, both irrigated and seasonal. At the same time, the great variety of natural resources found in the country favours the generation of renewable energies. As they are: the potential generation of wind energy estimated at 40,268 megawatts, the potential generation of hydroelectric energy estimated at 53,000 megawatts and the potential generation of geothermal energy estimated at 10,664 megawatts.

9. At the same time, mining production in Mexico is a traditional economic activity. Mexico stands out worldwide in the production of minerals such as silver, copper, bismuth, arsenic, lead and zinc. The country is considered the first producer of silver worldwide and one of the first copper-producing countries in the world.

B. Population

10. Mexico is the eleventh most populated country in the world and third in the Americas (after the US and Brazil). Conforming to the last Census of Population and Housing, in 2010, 112,336,538[2] people inhabited Mexico, 51.2% of which were women and 48.8% were men. In consonance with official data, the rate of natural population growth – in 2010 – was 1.4%, over the official projection of 1.28%, which is above the international average of 1.2% and slightly above the average for

2. *See*: http://www.inegi.org.mx/.

Latin America and the Caribbean of 1.3%. Of course, the Mexican population is not uniformly distributed throughout the country.

11. The States of the north and the peninsulas (excluding Nuevo León and Yucatan) have relatively few inhabitants, especially in terms of their density. Instead, the population density is mainly located in Mexico City and its metropolitan area.

12. In terms of demographic transition, there is a homogenous situation. Whereas in Mexico City, in 2019, the fecundity rate (the number of children that a woman has throughout her life to conserve the present conditions) was 1.47, whereas in the States of Chiapas and Quintana Roo, the fecundity rate was above 2.4.[3]

13. However, during the past several years, a noticeable tendency towards urbanization has been observed. Whereas in 1900, four-fifths of the population of the country inhabited rural areas; by 2019, 80% of Mexicans inhabited urban zones.[4]

14. The annual rate of growth of the rural population has not exceeded 2% per year at any time, whereas in the cities, we have been observing rates above 5%. Mexico is also the country with the greatest indigenous population on the North American Continent.

15. Throughout Mexican territory, around eighty-nine[5] indigenous languages are spoken. For the twenty-first century, 6,044,547 indigenous speakers in the country were reported, most of whom also spoke Spanish. It is estimated that there are about 4 million indigenous people who speak only Spanish, although they retain other distinctive cultural elements.

16. The indigenous languages with the most number of speakers are Nahuatl, Maya, Mixteco and Zapoteca, which comprise 52.1% of the total. Some indigenous languages are spoken by few children, such as Cucapá, Kikapú, Kiliwa and Kumiai; this is important, considering that, by their disuse, these languages are at risk of becoming extinct soon.[6]

II. Legal and Political Structure

17. In accordance with Article 40 of the *Constitution of the United Mexican States* (hereinafter, 'the Mexican Constitution', as amended in 2012), 'It is the will

3. *See*: https://www.gob.mx/segob/prensa/2-1-promedio-de-hijas-e-hijos-por-mujer-en-mexico-en-2019-conapo.
4. *See*: https://datos.bancomundial.org/indicador/SP.URB.TOTL.IN.ZS?locations=MX.
5. Instituto Nacional de Estadística y Geografía, 'Conociendo México' (2012). Available at www.inegi.org.mx.
6. *See*: https://www.milenio.com/cultura/mayoria-lenguas-indigenas-mexico-riesgo-desaparecer.

of the Mexican people to constitute a representative, democratic, laic, and federal Republic composed by States, free and sovereign in all matters concerning their internal affairs; but united in a federation established in consonance to the principles of this fundamental law.'[7]

18. In addition, Article 49 of the Mexican Constitution points out that:

> The Supreme Power of the Federation is divided for its exercise into Executive, Legislative and Judicial branches.

and adds that:

> Two or more of these powers may not be united in one single person or corporation, nor shall the legislative Power be vested in one single person, except for the case where extraordinary powers are granted to the President of the Republic as provided in Article 29. In no other case, except as provided under the second paragraph of Article 131 shall extraordinary powers be granted to legislate.

19. In accordance with constitutional provisions, in Mexico, the Executive Branch rests with a single individual, popularly elected, who holds his or her post for six years without the possibility of re-election (Articles 80, 81 and 83 of the Mexican Constitution).

20. However, the Legislative Branch is composed of the Congress of the Union, divided into two cameras: one of Deputies, with 500 members, elected in full every three years and the other a Chamber of Senators, with 128 representatives, four from each State and from Mexico City, which is renewed every six years (Articles 50, 51, 52 and 56 of the Mexican Constitution).

21. The exercise of the Judicial Power of the Federation is vested in the Nation's Supreme Court of Justice, composed of eleven Justices in an Electoral Court, Collegiate and Unitary Circuit Courts, and District Courts (Article 94 of the Mexican Constitution).

22. In addition, Article 94 of the Constitution establishes that 'Management, supervision and discipline of the Judicial Power of the Federation, except for the Nation's Supreme Court of Justice, shall be entrusted to the Council of the Federal Judiciary.'

---

7. By constitutional reform this article was added with the word *laic*. Diario Oficial de la Federacion (DOF) 30 Nov. 2012.

III. Economic Characteristics

23. Among the developing countries, Mexico is the second-most important destination for foreign direct investment and third in accumulated growth. It is second in tourism, which represents the second-greatest source of income for the country. In addition, Mexico is a world leader in silver, celestine honey, fruit, citrus, fabrics and cement production.

24. In this context, the main source of income in Mexico is remittances sent by workers residing legally or illegally in the US. In 2021 Mexico received 37 billion dollars in remittances.

25. Mexico has gone from being an exporter to an importer of crude oil and refined fuels.

IV. Social and Cultural Characteristics

26. The benefits of all the economic wealth that Mexico gets from its natural resources and the productivity of Mexicans are not equitably distributed. As reported by the World Bank, in 2004, while 10% of Mexico's population received 40% of the nation's income, 40% of the poorest population received only 12%, with some people surviving on just USD 1 per day.

27. Thus, Mexico ranks among the twelve most unequal societies in the world, not only by the disproportionate distribution of wealth but also by the inequalities in access to education, health, water, electricity, etc., not to mention that gender inequalities remain very marked as well.

28. In recent decades, this situation has generated a greater migratory flow to the US, as well as illegal trafficking of natural resources.

V. Main Environmental Problems

29. Among the main environmental problems that Mexico faces are a loss of biological diversity; soil, water and air pollution; and inadequate management of municipal, industrial and hazardous wastes.

30. Undoubtedly, biodiversity loss in both terrestrial ecosystems and coastal and marine ecosystems represents a serious problem. In fact, in consonance with official data, Mexico has one of the most critically threatened areas in the world; this area is located in the south of the country, in the Gulf of Tehuantepec, where two of the largest biogeographical regions of the planet – the neo-arctic and the neo-tropical – merge. Illegal trafficking of species, alteration of habitats and commercial exploitation of flora and fauna species are the major threats to the conservation of biological diversity in Mexico.

31. However, air pollution is an almost generalized problem in the major metropolitan zones of the country, particularly in the Metropolitan Zone of the Valley of Mexico, where it has assumed critical levels. For this reason, the government is obtaining better-documented information in this area and has been trying to establish more rigorous public policies. Nevertheless, the legislative and administrative measures taken until now have far from succeeded in reducing levels of certain pollutants, such as lead, sulphur dioxide and total suspended particles.

32. The problems of water management are very serious as well. Even though, in general, availability is greater than extraction, there are regions in the country where the extraction rate surpasses the recharge rate by far, as, for instance, in the north of the country and the Valley of Mexico.

33. Data show that there are eighty aquifers with more than 20% of overexploitation, which has resulted in problems of marine intrusion in the aquifers of Baja California, Baja California Sur, Sonora and Veracruz, as well as salinity problems in Durango, Aguascalientes and Coahuila.

34. In addition, discharges of municipal and industrial residual waters, residues of pesticides from agricultural activities and the waste generated in the process of the extraction of minerals are the main sources of pollution of inland and marine waters.

35. In Mexico, industries annually generate about 8 million tons of hazardous waste, without considering the mining wastes that can be regarded as such and that occur in quantities of between 300,000 and 500,000 tons per day.

36. By contrast, the existing infrastructure for the management, supervision and control of such waste is precarious: currently, there are only two authorized disposal sites for hazardous waste in the country. Therefore, clandestine deposits of hazardous wastes are frequently discovered in municipal dumps, ravines, municipal sewers, water bodies and, in general, fields and other land areas of public and private ownership.

37. This situation is particularly worrisome given that almost 90% of hazardous waste is in liquid, gaseous or semi-liquid states, or they are mixed in with waste water discharges.

§2. Basic Principles of Environmental Law

I. Definitions and Notions

38. In accordance with Article 1 of the Ecological Equilibrium and Environmental Protection General Act (hereinafter, 'the Environmental Act'), this law regulates the provisions of the Mexican Constitution that refer to conservation and preservation of the ecological balance as well as environmental protection, and it pursues as a general objective the establishment of the basis for promoting sustainable development in the country. In addition, to achieve that general mission, the Environmental Act sets up the following specific objectives:

(1) to guarantee the right of all persons to live in a suitable environment for their development, health and well-being;
(2) to define the principles of environmental policy and the instruments for its application;
(3) the preservation, restoration and improvement of the environment;
(4) the preservation and protection of biodiversity, as well as the establishment and management of protected natural areas;
(5) the viable use, preservation and, when appropriate, natural restoration of soil, water and other resources, so that they make compatible the generation of economic benefits and the activities of society with the preservation of ecosystems;
(6) the prevention and control of water, air and soil pollution;
(7) to guarantee co-responsible participation of the people, in individual or collective form, the preservation and restoration of ecological balance and the protection of the environment;
(8) the exercise of powers that in environmental matters correspond to the Federation, the States, Mexico City and the Municipalities, under the principle of concurrence established by Article 73, section XXIX-G of the Mexican Constitution;
(9) the establishment of coordination mechanisms, induction and agreement between and among authorities and the social and private sectors, as well as between people and groups, in environmental matters; and
(10) the establishment of measures of control and security to guarantee the fulfilment and application of this Law and the provisions that are derived from it, as well as the imposition of the administrative and criminal sanctions that correspond.

39. Nevertheless, to meet such objectives, the Environmental Act should clearly define the objects that it protects. In this regard, it is important to consider that the Environmental Act is intended to protect different objects, such as the environment, biodiversity and sustainable development. In the same way, it is intended to prevent pollution, conserve natural resources and preserve and restore them. Thus, it is fundamental to understand these concepts.

A. *Environment*

40. The environment is defined by the Environmental Act as 'the set of natural and artificial elements introduced by humans who make possible the existence and development of human beings and other living organisms that interact in a specific space and time' (Article 3, section I).

41. However, both previous legislation and the subsequent entry into force of the Environmental Act use the terms *environment, natural resources, biodiversity* and *wildlife* to refer either to the environment as a whole or one or many of the natural elements that comprise it (Article 1).

42. For example, the General Act of Wildlife (hereinafter, 'the Wildlife Act') refers to the conservation and sustainable use of wildlife and its habitat in the territory of the Mexican Republic and the zones where it exerts its sovereignty and jurisdiction.

43. In the same way, the objective of enforcing the General Act for Sustainable Forest Development (hereinafter, 'Forest Act') is to 'regulate and promote conservation, protection, restoration, production, management, cultivation, and use of forest ecosystems of the country and its resources', and the General Act for the Comprehensive Prevention and Management of Waste (hereinafter, 'Waste Act') is aimed at regulating only this form of pollution.

44. Despite the aforementioned issues, the Environmental Act incorporates the concept of ecological balance, which is defined as 'the relation of interdependence among the elements that compose the environment and makes possible the existence, transformation, and development of human beings and other ways of life' (Article 3, section XIV).

45. Nevertheless, incorporating the concept of the environment into the Environmental Act has not brought any consequences, neither in its regulatory structure nor in the legal institutions regulated by it, which still refer separately to the various elements of the environment, but not to the environment in and of itself.

B. Pollution

46. Fighting against pollution is, without any doubt, one of the central objectives of the Environmental Law, but its effectiveness can fail if the legislation is constructed based on a concept of pollution that is not sufficiently precise. For example, the Environmental Act defines pollution in general terms as 'the presence in the environment of one or more pollutants or any combination of them that may cause an ecological imbalance' (Article 3, section VI). However, it does not establish any criteria to determine the emission level of pollutant agents that can cause such an imbalance.

47. Moreover, normally, the administrative measures that aim to reduce and eliminate pollution are characterized by their individual application, while the environmental imbalances tend to be the result of synergies produced by several pollutant discharges combined with the action of other factors, including those not of an anthropogenic origin. Accordingly, the concept of pollution is far from being accurate.

C. Conservation

48. Conservation is an important area of environmental protection and, therefore, tends to be one of the objectives of environmental and natural resources legislation in Mexico. Mexican law has opted to use as synonyms for the term *conservation* the concepts of preservation, protection, and sustainable use of natural resources.

49. Thus, according to Environmental Act, *preservation* means 'the set of policies and measures to maintain the conditions conducive to the evolution and continuity of ecosystems and natural habitats, as well as to conserve viable populations of species in their natural environments and the components of biodiversity outside their natural habitats' (Article 3, section XXV), while *protection* includes 'the set of policies and measures to improve the environment and control its deterioration' (Article 3, section XXVII). However, sustainable use is 'the use of natural resources in a form that respects the operational integrity and the capabilities of the burden of systems that are part of these resources for indefinite periods' (Article 3, section III).[8]

D. Ecosystems and Sustainability

50. In accordance with the Environmental Act, an *ecosystem* is 'the basic functional unit of interaction of living organisms among themselves and with the environment, in a certain space and time' (Article 3, section XIII). Moreover, this Law is the only legal instrument that refers to the concept of *sustainable development,* defining it as:

> the measurable process through criteria and indicators of environmental, economic, and social trends to improve the quality of life and the productivity of persons, which is based on appropriate measures for the preservation of the ecological balance, environmental protection, and use of natural resources, so that the satisfaction of the future generations needs is not compromised. (Article 3, section XI)

However, such a definition is very vague.

E. Biodiversity and Ecological Integrity

51. *Biodiversity* is defined by the Environmental Act as 'the variability of living organisms from any source, including, among others, terrestrial ecosystems, maritime and other aquatic ecosystems, and complex ecological systems of which such organisms are a part; comprising diversity within each species, and among species

8. By reform of the Environmental Act published into the DOF 28 Jan. 2011, sections of Art. 3 were reorganized and the definition of 'sustainable use' was eliminated.

and ecosystems' (Article 3, section IV). However, biodiversity is just a part of the subject protected under the Environmental Act. As its name indicates, this Law protects the ecological balance as a whole and not the natural elements in separate ways. This means that the Environmental Act integrates in a comprehensive way the legal protection of the environment. Nevertheless, this approach is contradicted by the existence of other environmental laws that protect natural elements in separate ways.

II. Constitutional Provisions

52. At the national level, the first source of environmental law is the Constitution, particularly Articles 4, 25, 27 and 73, section XXIX-G. Due to the concurrent compentences system established by the Constitution, general environmental laws passed by the Federal Congress, on such Constitutional basis, are the foundation for local laws in the areas of environmental protection, waters, waste and forests, as well as for municipal regulations in these areas.

§3. Role of Government Institutions in the Shaping and Administration of Environmental Law and Policy

I. Background

53. In 1972, the Undersecretary for the Improvement of the Environment was established within the structure of the Ministry of Public Health with the objective of enforcing the Federal Law to Prevent and Control Environmental Pollution of 1971.

54. Nevertheless, given that the Environmental Act of 1972 did not regulate all aspects related to environmental protection but only those regarding environmental pollution, and given that protection of natural elements such as terrestrial and aquatic flora and fauna were the subjects of other legal instruments whose application was also entrusted to the federal governmental level, other administrative agencies participated in environmental management as well.

55. For example, the Ministry of Hydraulic Resources was responsible for the matters of prevention and control of water pollution, the Ministry of Agriculture was responsible for the matters of prevention and control of soil pollution and the Ministry of Industry and Trade was responsible for the matters of prevention and control of industrial and commercial pollutant activities.

56. In 1982, the Ministry of Urban Development and Ecology was created to enforce both urban and environmental laws. Thus, the Ministry of Urban Development and Ecology concentrated on the faculties that had previously rested with the Ministries of the Environment, Agriculture and Hydraulic Resources, Public Health, and Fishing.

57. The Ministry of the Urban Development and Ecology was eliminated in 1992 when the Ministry of Social Development was created and it was vested with the authority to enforce the law in some areas of environmental protection, whereas other areas were reassigned to the Ministries of Agriculture and Hydraulic Resources and the Ministry of Fishing and the Ministry of Maritime Affairs.

58. The new Ministry was vested with few of the responsibilities that had previously corresponded to the Ministry of Urban Development and Ecology. Within the new Ministry, two administrative bodies were created: the National Institute of Ecology (NIE) and the Federal Attorney General's Office for Environmental Protection (the Office of Environmental Prosecutor).

59. The NIE was constituted as the body in charge of regulating different aspects that fall under the aegis of environmental matters. However, the Office of Environmental Prosecutor oversaw exercising authority in the matters of inspection and monitoring compliance with environmental legislation within the sphere of responsibility of the Ministry of Social Development.

60. Nevertheless, other offices of the federal government, such as the Ministries of Agriculture and Hydraulic Resources, the Ministry of Fishing and the Ministry of Maritime Affairs, were entrusted with the enforcement of specific environmental laws.

61. In 1994, the Ministry of the Environment, Natural Resources and Fishing was created. As had happened in the case of the Ministry of Urban Development and Ecology, all the functions in the field of compliance with and enforcement of environmental legislation were assigned to the new Ministry.

62. The Environmental Prosecutor, the NIE and other agencies, such as the National Waters Commission (NWC) and the National Institute of Fishing, which previously had been separate entities, were grouped into the new Ministry of the Environment.

63. Finally, in the year 2000, enforcement of fishing law was transferred to the Ministry of Agriculture, and the Ministry of the Environment, Natural Resources and Fishing was transformed into the Ministry of the Environment and Natural Resources (Ministry of the Environment).

II. The Governmental Institutions and Their Competencies

64. In Mexico, environmental management is distributed among federal, local, and municipal authorities in accordance with provisions of the Environmental Act, the Wildlife Act, the Forest Act, the Waste Act, the Climate Change Act, and the Urban Act.

65. Currently, the Ministry of the Environment and Natural Resources leads environmental management in Mexico at the federal level, whereas in some cases, local governments have created specialized institutions or have entrusted previously existing institutions to enforce the local legislation.

66. Conforming to Article 32*bis* of the Organic Law of the Federal Public Administration, it falls to the Ministry of the Environment to formulate and conduct national policy in the matters of natural resources, ecology, environmental cleaning, water, and environmental regulation of urban development and fishing activities.

67. The Ministry of the Environment exerts its authority through three Undersecretary's offices and several semi-autonomous agencies. The Undersecretary's offices are:

(a) the Undersecretary of Planning and Environmental Policy;
(b) the Undersecretary of Promotion and Environmental Standardization; and
(c) the Undersecretary of Management for Environmental Protection.

68. The semi-autonomous agencies are:

(a) NWC;
(b) NIE;
(c) Office of Environmental Prosecutor;
(d) the National Commission of Protected Natural Areas (NCPNA); and
(e) the National Agency for Industrial Safety and Environmental Protection of the Hydrocarbon Sector (Environmental Agency for Energy Sector).

69. The Ministry of the Environment is entrusted with regulatory authority, such as the elaboration and promulgation of environmental standards that establish maximum limits of emission of pollutant agents, the authorization of the evaluation of environmental impact, or the authorization of management of natural resources. The Ministry of the Environment also has the power to enforce environmental legislation through its semi-autonomous agencies: the Office of Environmental Prosecutor, NWC, and the Environmental Agency for Energy Sector.

70. The Office of Environmental Prosecutor, the NWC, and the Environmental Agency for Energy Sector are vested with authoritative functions. In general terms, the Office of Environmental Prosecutor oversees the enforcement of environmental legislation, excepting the Waters Act, whose enforcement is entrusted to the NWC and excepting the enforcement of environmental legislation in the case of hydrocarbons activities that is vested in the Environmental Agency for Energy Sector.

71. Nevertheless, in concordance with the mentioned Law, the Ministry of the Environment has limited jurisdiction. It can take care of matters of natural resources only when they do not correspond to another governmental agency, as in the case of waters and marine zones, which are under the jurisdiction of the Ministry of Marine Affairs, or in the case of urban lands, whose regulation is governed by the Ministry of Agrarian and Urban Affairs.

72. However, in relation to the formulation and conduction of policy in the matters of ecology, environmental cleaning, water, environmental regulation of urban development and fishing activities, the jurisdiction of the Ministry of the Environment is not absolute, but other agencies take part as well, as in the case of environmental pollution when it becomes a matter of public health and moves to the scope of competence of the Ministry of Health; or in the promotion of forest plantations, in which case the Ministry of the Environment must allow the participation of the Ministry of Agriculture. The situation is different regarding the formulation and conduction of policy in the matters of climatic change and the protection of the ozone layer, since, in both cases, authority is designated exclusively to the Ministry of the Environment.

73. At the local level, States and municipalities have created institutions in charge of environmental management as well. In some of the States that are part of the Mexican Federation, as in the States of Guanajuato and Guerrero, the Attorney General's Offices enforce local environmental laws; whereas, in other States, such task has been entrusted to the Ministries of the Environment.

§4. Sources of Environmental Law

I. International Sources

74. International environmental treaties are the fundamental source of environmental law in Mexico. The first international convention for the protection of wild species at the global level was the Convention for the Protection of Birds Useful to Agriculture, signed in Paris on 19 March 1902;[9] while the first treaty relating to the protection of wildlife in a particular region was the Convention to ensure the Conservation of the Diverse Species of Animals Living in the Wild in Africa that are Useful and Harmless to Man.[10] The 1902 Convention, cited above, was replaced by the Convention Relative to the Preservation of Fauna and Flora in the Natural State, also known as the London Convention of 1933 and in 1940 the Washington Convention on Nature Protection and Wild Life Preservation in the Western Hemisphere was adopted.

9. The background to this Convention dates back to 1872, when Switzerland proposed the adoption of an international regulation to protect birds. This was followed by the International Ornithological Congress and the creation of the International Ornithological Committee in 1884. The Convention for the Protection of Birds Useful to Agriculture focused on the protection of birds, their nests and their young.
10. Philippe Sands, *Principles of International Environmental Law. Frameworks, Standards and Implementation*, vol. 1. Manchester, Manchester University Press, 1995, p. 27.

75. In terms of water protection under international law, the first precedent is the Boundary Waters Treaty signed in 1909 between the US and Canada to prevent pollution. In the 1950s, the first attempts were made to combat marine pollution. One of the most important conventions in this field was the International Convention for the Prevention of Pollution of the Sea by Oil, adopted in London on 12 May 1954, which was later replaced by the International Convention for the Prevention of Pollution from Ships (MARPOL) of 1973. However, international environmental law really began to be organized until the 1970s. Since that decade, international conventions have multiplied as a result of the United Nations General Assembly Resolution of 3 December 1968, which convened the United Nations Conference on the Human Environment (Stockholm Conference) in 1972.

76. In the following years, agreements were adopted such as: Convention on Wetlands of International Importance, Ramsar, 1971; Convention Concerning the Protection of the World Cultural and Natural Heritage, Washington, 1972; Convention on the Prevention of Marine Pollution by Dumping of Wastes and Other Matter, London, Mexico, Moscow and Washington, 1972; Convention on International Trade in Endangered Species of Wild Fauna and Flora, Washington, 1973; International Convention for the Prevention of Pollution from Ships, London, 1973; United Nations Convention on the Law of the Sea, Montego Bay, Jamaica, 1982; Convention on the Control of Transboundary Movements of Hazardous Wastes and Their Disposal, 1989, Basel, Switzerland; Convention for the Protection of the Ozone Layer, Vienna, Austria, 1985; Convention on Biological Diversity (CBD), Rio, Brazil, 1992; United Nations Framework Convention on Climate Change, New York, USA, 1992; and United Nations Convention to Combat Desertification, Paris, France, 1994, among others.[11]

77. Currently, Mexico has adopted dozens of multilateral treaties[12] that establish the rules for the protection of the global environment.[13]

78. Similarly, Mexico has signed many international declarations in the field of environmental protection, such as the Declaration of the United Nations Conference on the Human Environment (1972), the Rio Declaration on Environment and Development (1992), the Johannesburg Declaration on Sustainable Development

---

11. UNEP, *Register of International Treaties and Other Agreements in the Field of the Environment.* Nairobi, UNEP, 1997, p. 474.
12. Here, the term 'Treaty' is used in the sense given to it by the Vienna Convention on the Law of Treaties in its Art. 2, para. 1(a), which states: 'treaty means an international agreement concluded between States in written form and governed by international law, whether embodied in a single instrument or in two or more related instruments and whatever its particular designation'.
13. Mexico ratified sixty-eight treaties between 1940 and 1993, which address issues related to the conservation and protection of the environment. Most of these agreements signify for Mexico the commitment with the international community to incorporate into its internal legislation certain mechanisms for the protection of the environment and its elements, in order to collaborate with the global effort in favour of the conservation of the planet.

(2002), and the Río+20 Declaration: The future we want of 2012; and the 2030 Agenda for Sustainable Development and its 17 Sustainable Development Goals (SGD) in 2015.

II. The United Nations Declarations

A. *The United Nations Conference on the Human Environment (Stockholm Conference)*

79. On 5 June 1972, the United Nations Conference on the Human Environment opened in Stockholm, Sweden, attended by 1,500 delegates representing 113 countries from all regions of the world, forty intergovernmental bodies, and 600 observers from 250 non-governmental organizations.

80. From the beginning of the Conference, the General Secretariat of the Conference stressed that the main theme of the Conference should be environment and development.[14]

81. Several documents were adopted as a result of the Conference:

(a) The Declaration on the Environment.
(b) Plan of action for the environment.
(c) The Resolution on institutional and financial arrangements.
(d) The Resolution on World Environment Day.
(e) The Resolution on Nuclear Weapons Tests.
(f) The Resolution on the Second Conference on the Environment.

82. Without a doubt, together with the creation of the United Nations Environment Programme (UNEP), the most important of these instruments is the Stockholm Declaration, whose twenty-six principles substantially influenced the legislative agendas of the member countries of the international community in subsequent years. These principles refer to the following issues:

(a) Natural resources.
(b) Management of the natural patrimony by the man.
(c) Exploitation of non-renewable resources.
(d) Discharges in the environment.
(e) Contamination of food by contamination of the marine environment.
(f) Protection of the environment.
(g) International cooperation.
(h) Nuclear weapons.

14. Catherine Roche, *Droit de l'environnement*. París, Gualino éditeur, 2001, p. 19.

83. Most authors agree that, although these principles are not binding, since they are only guidelines and declarations of intentions, they do constitute sources of international environmental law and national environmental law.

84. In particular, the Stockholm Declaration established a series of principles that proposed the adoption of new environmental policy instruments that would later be incorporated into the environmental legislations of several countries of the world. Among these principles, the following stand out: right to an adequate environment and non-discrimination (Principle 1); intergenerational responsibility (Principle 2); environmentally feasible development (Principles 3, 4, 5, 8 and 13); prevention of environmental damage (Principles 6 and 7); obligation to cooperate (Principles 9, 10, 11, 12 and 24); development planning (Principles 14, 15 and 17); planning for population growth (Principles 15 and 16); duty to put science at the service of society (Principle 18); duty to use education and research as instruments of environmental policy (Principles 19 and 20); right to information (Principle 19, part two); sovereign right of States to exploit their own resources (Principles 21 and 23); reparation of damage (Principle 22); duty to prevent the proliferation of nuclear weapons (Principle 26); and duty to conserve the environment (Principle 25).

85. It is not insignificant that after the Stockholm Conference, or prior to it, environmental laws were passed in several countries, for example, the National Environmental Policy Act in the US (1970), the Federal Act to Prevent and Control Pollution in Mexico (1971), the National Code of Renewable Natural Resources and Environmental Protection in Colombia (1974), Ontario's Environmental Assessment Act in Canada (1975), the Law for the Prevention and Control of Environmental Pollution in Ecuador (1976), the Law on the Protection of Nature in France (1976), the Organic Law on the Environment in Venezuela (1976), the Law on the Protection of the Environment and the Rational Use of Natural Resources in Cuba (1981) and the Law Providing for the National Policy on the Environment, its Purposes and Mechanisms of Formulation and Application and Other Provisions, in Brazil (1981), among others.

86. The Stockholm Declaration is definitely one of the most relevant sources for the development of environmental law at the global level.

B. Rio Declaration on Environment and Development

87. The analysis of environmental problems, presented at the 1972 Stockholm Conference, was deepened at the 1992 Rio Summit. The main result of this new conference was to reach an agreement on the need to promote the idea of sustainable development as one that meets the needs of the present generation without jeopardizing the ability of future generations to meet theirs.

88. In addition, during the Rio Conference, five documents were approved:

(a) Agenda 21, which is not a Convention in terms of the Treaty of Vienna, but a plan of action at the global level of the 179 countries that participated in it.[15]
(b) The Rio Declaration on Environment and Development, which contains twenty-seven principles, most of which represent a commitment for the signatory States to introduce certain environmental policy instruments into their internal law.
(c) The Declaration of principles for a global consensus on the management, conservation and ecologically viable exploitation of all types of forests.
(d) The United Nations Framework Convention on Climate Change,[16] which implies commitments by States to achieve stabilization of greenhouse gas concentrations in the atmosphere at a level that prevents dangerous anthropogenic interference with the climate system, which also means the incorporation of legal instruments for that purpose into national and international law.
(e) The CBD, which pursues the multiple purposes of: the conservation of biological diversity, the sustainable use of its components, as well as the fair and equitable sharing of the benefits arising from the utilization of genetic resources.

89. As in the case of the Stockholm Declaration, the principles contained in the Rio Declaration mean for the signatory countries the commitment to adapt their legislation on the subject, as Principle 11 points out:

> States shall enact effective environmental legislation. Environmental standards, management objectives and priorities should reflect the environmental and developmental context to which they apply. Standards applied by some countries may be inappropriate and of unwarranted economic and social cost to other countries, in particular developing countries.

90. Among the principles ratified or added by the Rio Declaration are: the right to a healthy environment (Principle 1); the right to information and public participation (Principle 10); national implementation of sustainable development (Principles 3, 4, 8, 20 and 21); the obligation to cooperate (Principles 5 and 7); the obligation to avoid environmental damage by recognizing the principle of prevention, regulation and control of hazardous activities and substances and the introduction of a system of environmental impact assessment (EIA) of certain projects or activities (Principles 2, 14 and 17); obligation to repair environmental damage, legislating on environmental damage but also granting appropriate legal legitimacy in court (Principle 13); the polluter must pay, introducing the use of economic instruments in environmental management (Principle 16); recognition of the rights of minorities (Principle 22) and the precautionary principle (Principle 15).

91. The Rio Summit was the second element in the evolution of global environmental law, as a new wave of environmental laws was generated in the years following the Summit. For example, Chile's General Environmental Bases Law

15. According to Guillermo J. Cano, Agenda XXI constitutes what Peter Sands calls soft law but which in some cases has been adopted by internal legislation. *See*: Peter Sands, *The Effectiveness of International Environmental Agreements*. Cambridge, UNCED, 1992, p. 18.
16. This Convention had previously been signed in New York on 9 May 1992.

(1994); Colombia's Law 99 (1993); Honduras' General Environmental Law (1994); Paraguay's Environmental Impact Law (1994); and Uruguay's Law 16,466 (1993), among many others.

92. In Mexico, the Environmental Act was almost completely reformed in 1996 to incorporate into its text provisions relating to access to information and economic instruments of environmental policy, as well as to add to the provisions of the same rule relating to the protection of biological diversity in the light of the CBD.

C. The Johannesburg Declaration on Sustainable Development

93. The Johannesburg summit held in 2002 approved a Political Declaration and a Plan of Implementation of the Decisions of the World Summit on Sustainable Development,[17] which, unlike the Rio and Stockholm declarations, does not contain specific principles for them to be considered as sources of environmental law, but has certain importance because, as José Juste says: 'commits itself to building a humanitarian, equitable and generous global society, aware of the need to respect the dignity of all human beings'.[18]

94. In that sense, in the Declaration of Johannesburg, the signatory countries:

(1) express the collective responsibility to promote and strengthen, at the local, national, regional and global levels, the economic and social development as well as environmental protection; independent and synergistic pillars of sustainable development;
(2) affirm that poverty eradication, unsustainable patterns of protection and consumption, and protection and management of the natural resource base for social and economic development are primary objectives and fundamental requirements of sustainable development;
(3) recognize that the global environment continues to deteriorate and say they are determined to rapidly increase access to basic services such as safe drinking water, sanitation, adequate shelter, energy, health care, food security and the protection of biodiversity (the so-called Wahab initiative);
(4) commit themselves to work together to help each other in several areas, such as accessing financial resources, opening markets, promoting capacity building, using modern technology to achieve development and ensuring that technology transfer, human resource upgrading, education and training are encouraged to eradicate underdevelopment forever; and

---

17. United Nations. Report of the World Summit on Sustainable Development. Johannesburg, South Africa, 26 Aug. 2002 to 4 Sep. 2002.
18. José Juste Ruiz, *Protección del Medio Ambiente y Comercio Internacional*. Valencia, Mimeo, 2004, p. 10.

(5) they affirm that multilateralism is the future and must be configured as an inclusive process in which all the major groups and governments that participated in the historic Johannesburg summit must intervene.

95. The effects of the Johannesburg Declaration on national law have not been as evident as in the case of the 1972 and 1992 Declarations, in the sense that it did not provoke national legislative movements such as those that those had.

D. The Río+20 Declaration: The Future We Want

96. The last United Nations Conference on Sustainable Development was held in Rio de Janeiro, Brazil, from 20 to 22 June 2012, twenty years after the 1992 Rio Summit. The main objective of the Conference was to renew political commitment to sustainable development, for which two essential issues were discussed: on the one hand, the issue of the green economy in the context of sustainable development and, on the other, that of poverty eradication and the institutional framework for sustainable development.[19]

97. The Rio+20 Summit concluded with the approval of an Action Plan called 'The Future We Want', which reaffirms: the principles established by the 1992 Rio Conference; the provisions of the other documents approved at the Conference; the commitments acquired at the United Nations Conferences and Summits in economic, social and environmental matters, such as the United Nations Millennium Declaration, the United Nations Framework Convention on Climate Change, the CBD, and others. These reaffirmations gave ground for the adoption of the principle of non-regression. In addition, for the fulfilment of the main objective of the Conference, the document, 'The Future We Want', sets out the commitments to which the parties are submitted in areas such as: work, energy, sustainable cities, food security and sustainable agriculture, water, oceans and disaster management.

98. Finally, the document establishes the rules to be followed for the elaboration of the 'SGD' that are intended to replace the Millennium Development Goals.

E. The Sustainable Development Goals

99. As mentioned, solutions to the most complex environmental problems are first raised at the level of international law through international environmental treaties, bilateral, regional or multilateral treaties, but then they must be implemented at the national level. On many occasions, this process of adapting the obligations undertaken by nation-states within the international community is complex and it often happens that national law itself prevents the adequate incorporation of international commitments into internal law; on other occasions, especially in those

19. *See*: http://www.un.org/.

States whose legal system has adopted the monist thesis of international law, the process is simpler. The SGD is an initiative promoted by the United Nations to give continuity to the development agenda after the Millennium Development Goals, which were eight aims of human development set in 2000, which sought to solve different problems of daily life. The SDG are 17 goals that include new spheres such as climate change, economic inequality, innovation, sustainable consumption and peace, and justice, among other priorities. In September 2015, the Sustainable Development Summit took place in New York. During this summit, the Agenda 2030 was approved by more than 150 heads of state and government. This Agenda contains the seventeen universally applicable goals that, from 1 January 2016, guide countries' efforts to achieve a sustainable world by 2030.

III. The Hierarchy of Environmental Treatises

100. The Mexican Constitution recognizes the supremacy of international treaties in Article 133, which holds that:

> This Constitution, the laws of the Congress of the Union which shall be enacted in pursuance thereof and all treaties in accordance therewith, celebrated or which shall be celebrated by the President of the Republic with the approval of the Senate, shall be a supreme law of the Union. The judges of each federative entity shall comply with the Constitution, laws and treaties, notwithstanding any provisions to the contrary in the Constitutions or laws of the federative entities.

101. Although for many years, the National Supreme Court of Justice (SCJN) held that international treaties were hierarchically at the same level as the federal laws, in 1999 and 2007; it issued a new ruling which states that international treaties are held hierarchically above federal laws and in a second level regarding the Federal Constitution. Finally, in 2013, the Supreme Court of Justice ruled that International Treatises regarding human rights are hierarchically at the same level as the Constitution. The ruling reads as follows:

> INTERNATIONAL TREATIES. WHEN CONFLICTS ARISE IN RELATION TO HUMAN RIGHTS, THEY SHOULD BE PLACED AT THE SAME LEVEL OF THE CONSTITUTION.
> The treaties or conventions signed by the Mexican State relating to human rights must be placed at the same level as the Political Constitution of the United Mexican States, because these international instruments are conceived as an extension of the provisions of that Fundamental Law with respect to human rights, as they constitute the reason and purpose of the institutions. Therefore, the principles that make up public subjective law must be adapted to the various purposes of the mechanisms of defense provided for in the Constitution itself, and in accordance with article 133 of the Constitution, the

Mexican authorities must respect them, so that under no circumstances can they be ignored by the authorities when acting within their sphere of competence.

(PRIMER TRIBUNAL COLEGIADO EN MATERIAS ADMINISTRATIVA Y DE TRABAJO DEL DECIMO PRIMER CIRCUITO AMPARO DIRECTO 1060/2008. 2 de julio de 2009. Mayoría de votos. Disidente: Hugo Sahuer Hernández. Ponente: Juan García Orozco. Secretario: Víctor Ruiz Contreras Localización: Novena Época, Instancia: Tribunales Colegiados de Circuito, Fuente: Semanario Judicial de la Federación, Página: 2079, Tesis: XI.1o.A.T.45 K Tesis Aislada, Materia(s): Común).

Regarding the ruling above, the Supreme Court of Justice has emitted another two rulings. First, in 2011 the Court determined in an isolated thesis that the condemnatory sentences of the International Court of Human Rights are binding on the Judiciary in their terms. This decision reads as follows:

JUDGMENTS ISSUED BY THE INTER-AMERICAN COURT OF HUMAN RIGHTS IN CASES WHERE THE MEXICAN STATE WAS A PARTY. IN ORDER FOR ITS CRITERIA TO BE BINDING, THEY DO NOT NEED TO BE REITERATED.

Also in 2011, in another isolated thesis, the Court determined that the interpretative criteria contained in the jurisprudence of the International Court of Human Rights are guiding for the Federal Judiciary when Mexico is not a party to the cases in which such jurisprudence was generated. This thesis stated:

From paragraphs 339 and 347 of the judgment issued by the Inter-American Court of Human Rights in the case of Radilla Pacheco v. United Mexican States, it is clear that domestic judges and courts, in addition to ensuring compliance with international provisions, must take into account the interpretation made by the Court, as well as the State's obligation to ensure that the conduct that gave rise to its responsibility is not repeated. From the foregoing, it follows that the interpretation of human rights made by the International Court, when resolving a case in which the Mexican State was a party, even when it is an isolated judgment, acquires the character and binding force of jurisprudential precedent, especially since this High Court, in the isolated thesis P. LXV/2011 (9th.), under the heading: 'SENTENCES ISSUED BY THE INTER-AMERICAN COURT OF HUMAN RIGHTS. THEY ARE BINDING IN THEIR TERMS WHEN THE MEXICAN STATE WAS PARTICIPANT IN THE LITIGATION', derived from the resolution of the file several 912/2010, held that the resolutions pronounced by the Inter-American Court are binding for all the organs of the Mexican State, having been part of a specific litigation, being binding for the Judiciary. Therefore, in order for the criteria of the judgments issued by the Inter-American Court of Human Rights in matters where the Mexican State was a party to acquire the character of binding, they do not need to be reiterated, especially since the rules for the formation of jurisprudence set forth in Article 192 of the Amparo Law do not apply to these judgments.

Amparo in review 133/2012. August 21, 2012. Majority of eight votes; voting with qualifications: José Ramón Cossío Díaz, Jorge Mario Pardo Rebolledo and Luis María Aguilar Morales; voting against: Sergio Salvador Aguirre

Anguiano and Margarita Beatriz Luna Ramos. Absent: José Fernando Franco González Salas. Speaker: Olga Sánchez Cordero de García Villegas. Secretary: Rosalía Argumosa López.

The second relevant ruling occurred in 2013 when, in resolving contradiction of thesis 293/2011, the Supreme Court of Justice of the Nation held that:

HUMAN RIGHTS CONTAINED IN THE CONSTITUTION AND IN INTERNATIONAL TREATIES. THE FIRST PARAGRAPH OF ARTICLE 1 OF THE CONSTITUTION RECOGNIZES A SET OF HUMAN RIGHTS WHOSE SOURCES ARE THE CONSTITUTION AND THE INTERNATIONAL TREATIES TO WHICH THE MEXICAN STATE IS A PARTY.

The first paragraph of Article 1 of the Constitution recognizes a set of human rights whose sources are the Constitution and the international treaties to which the Mexican State is a party. From the literal, systematic and originalist interpretation of the content of the constitutional reforms of June sixth and tenth, two thousand eleven, it is clear that the norms of human rights, regardless of their source, are not related in hierarchical terms, understanding that, derived from the final part of the first paragraph of said article 1, when in the Constitution there is an express restriction to the exercise of human rights, The principle that gives supremacy to the Constitution implies that the Constitution is the fundamental norm of the Mexican legal order, which in turn implies that the rest of the legal norms must be in accordance with it, both in a formal and material sense, a circumstance that has not changed; What has evolved as a result of the constitutional reforms in question is the configuration of the set of legal norms with respect to which such supremacy can be predicted in the Mexican legal order. This transformation is explained by the expansion of the catalog of human rights provided for in the Political Constitution of the United Mexican States, which evidently can be qualified as part of the set of norms that enjoy such constitutional supremacy. In this sense, human rights, as a whole, constitute the parameter of control of constitutional regularity, according to which the validity of the norms and acts that form part of the Mexican legal order must be analyzed. Contradiction of thesis 293/2011. Between those sustained by the First Collegiate Court in Administrative and Labor Matters of the Eleventh Circuit and the Seventh Collegiate Court in Civil Matters of the First Circuit. September 3, 2013.

A. *Mexican Sources*

1. The Constitution and National Laws

102. Since it was approved in 1917, the Mexican Constitution included many references to the subject of natural resources protection but not to the protection of the environment in itself.

103. However, during the period 1970–2012, the Constitution was amended six times to incorporate environmental concerns, and in 2010, 2011, and 2012, several Constitutional provisions were also modified to strengthen the foundations for access to environmental justice.

104. Currently, the Mexican Constitution includes rules regarding the following:

(a) The original text of the Political Constitution of the United Mexican States, as approved in 1917, referred to the subject discussed in Article 27, third paragraph, stating that the nation shall at all times have the power to impose on private property the modalities dictated by the public interest, as well as to regulate the use of natural resources susceptible of appropriation. In this way, the constitution provided enough basis for passing laws on the use of natural resources and their conservation from a public law perspective.

(b) In 1971, Article 73, section XVI of the Constitution was added with the fourth base that empowered the General Health Council to adopt the necessary measures to prevent and combat environmental pollution.[20]

(c) In 1983, Article 25 of the Constitution was amended to include a reference to the relationship between the environment and economic development in the following terms: 'Social and private sector enterprises shall be supported and fostered under criteria of social equity, productivity and sustainability, subject to the public interest and the use of the productive resources for the general welfare, preserving them and the environment.' For some authors, this reform established the basis for sustainable development in Mexico.[21] However, it is with the 1999 constitutional reform when the principle of sustainability was expressly included in the mentioned provision by establishing: 'it corresponds to the State the rectory of national development to guarantee that this is integral and sustainable, that strengthens the sovereignty of the nation and its democratic regime and that through the promotion of economic growth and employment and a fairer distribution of income and wealth, allows the full exercise of freedom and dignity of individuals, groups and social classes, whose security is protected by this constitution'.

(d) In 1987, an amendment to Article 27 of the Constitution specified that the exercise of the nation's powers to impose on private property the modalities dictated by the public interest or regulate for social benefit the use of natural elements susceptible of appropriation should have, among other objectives, the preservation and restoration of the ecological balance. The incorporation into

---

20. With respect to this reform, Marisol Angñés points out that from this modification, both the prevention and control of pollution became a federal matter. Marisol Anglés Hernández, *Instrumentos de política ambiental sobre residuor peligrosos*. México, Porrúa, 2004, p. 18 (Colección Breviarios Jurídicos).

21. Among them is Raúl Brañes, who points out that this reform consolidates the principle of sustainable development proposed by the Stockholm Declaration; however, sustainability is not fulfilled by its mere mention in a legal text, but it requires a series of fundamental transformations of the legal framework.

the constitutional text of the concept of 'ecological balance' opened the possibility of protecting the environment as a whole, and not only the natural resources.

(e) In 1987, Article 73 of the Constitution was modified in order to add a section XXIX-G empowering the Federal Congress to 'issue laws establishing the concurrence of the federal, local and municipal governments, within the scope of their respective competences, in matters of environmental protection, preservation and restoration of the ecological balance'.[22] As a result of this reform, for the first time, it became possible for local governments to legislate on some aspects related to environmental protection and for municipalities to issue regulations in this area.

(f) In 1999, an important step forward was taken by incorporating the right to an adequate environment as a public subjective right into Article 4 of the constitutional text. The added text states: 'All persons have the right to an environment adequate for their development and well-being.' However, that incorporation of the right to an adequate environment into the constitutional order represented at that time only a mention whose implementation depended on secondary legislation development. Nevertheless, in 2011,[23] the right to an adequate environment was grounded in a human rights approach by virtue of a new constitutional reform.[24]

(g) It was not until the 2012 constitutional reform of the fifth paragraph of Article 4 of the Constitution when the basis for the enforcement of that right was established. This reform introduced, besides the right to an adequate environment, the principle of liability for environmental damage, by stating: 'Environmental damage and deterioration will generate liability for whoever causes it in terms of what the secondary law provides.' It is important to note that, in accordance with the second transitory article of this constitutional reform, the Federal Congress was obliged to pass a new law in this matter.[25]

(h) In 2012, the fourth article of the Constitution was again amended to incorporate the sixth paragraph, thereby incorporating the so-called right of access to water. The added text reads as follows: 'All persons have the right to access, disposal and sanitation of water for personal domestic consumption in a sufficient, healthy, acceptable and affordable manner. The state will guarantee this right and the law will define the basis, supports and modalities for the equitable and sustainable access and use of water resources, establishing the participation of the federal, local and municipal governments, as well as the participation of the population for the achievement of these aims.' According to the constitutional amendment, the Federal Congress was obliged to enact a new General Waters Act, but until now, such a law has not been approved:

22. Diario Oficial de la Federación 10-08-1987.
23. Diario Oficial de la Federación 10-06-2011.
24. In October of the same year, a third paragraph was added to the fourth article, moving the following paragraphs, so that the recognition of the right to an adequate environment went from the fourth paragraph to the fifth paragraph.
25. The Federal Act of Environmental Liability was published 7 Jun. 2013.

(i) In 2010, Article 17 of the Constitution was amended granting legal standing to file collective actions in environmental matters.[26]
(j) In 2011, Article 107, section I of the Constitution was amended in order to recognize the collective legal interest of filing injunction actions to combat unconstitutional resolutions issued by environmental authorities.[27]

The following sections will explain all these constitutional reforms.

a. Article 27 of the Mexican Constitution of 1917 and Natural Resources Protection

105. For many years, Article 27 of the Mexican Constitution provided enough basis for legislation on natural resources protection. First, the first paragraph of Article 27, as it was passed in 1917, recognized that the original property of the lands and waters of the Mexican territory was vested in the Nation and it had the power of transferring their domain to private persons to create a private property on land and waters. Second, conforming to paragraph two of Article 27, the State can use its power of eminent domain to compel a private property owner to relinquish ownership and dominion of any property to the state, but it only may be taken for reasons of public use and subject to payment compensation.

106. Third, paragraph 3 of Article 27 empowered the Nation to impose on private property such restrictions as the public interest may demand, as well as to regulate, for social benefit, the use and exploitation of those natural resources, which are susceptible of appropriation.

107. Finally, paragraphs 4 and 5 of Article 27 provided the basis for the rectory of the state on the use, exploitation, and conservation of certain natural resources considered as strategic. In consonance with them, waters and natural resources of the subsoil are considered as exclusive property of the Nation and, therefore, can only be exploited by individuals through the granting of concessions and contracts in the case of hydrocarbons, but the domain of the Nation on the mentioned resources is inalienable and imprescriptible.

108. Based on such constitutional provisions, the Federal Congress passed the Federal Law to Prevent and Combat Pollution of 1972 and the Federal Environmental Protection Act of 1981.

---

26. DOF, 29 Jul. 2010.
27. DOF, 06 Jun. 2011.

b. Article 73, Section XVI of the Mexican Constitution of 1917 and the Faculties of the General Council of Health to Adopt Measures to Prevent and to Deal with Environmental Pollution

109. The ideas of preventing and combating environmental pollution, as an important part of environmental law, were expressly included into the Constitutional text with the Reform of 1971, which added a fourth paragraph to section XVI of Article 73 of the Constitution.[28] That Reform empowered the General Health Council to adopt measures aimed at preventing and combating environmental pollution. In addition, the constitutional reform empowered the Federal Congress to review the measures made by the Council by saying:

> 4° The measures that the Council has put into effect in the campaign against alcoholism and the sale of substances that poison individuals or degenerate the human species, as well as those measures adopted to prevent and fight against environmental pollution, shall thereafter be examined by the Congress of the Union in the cases under its jurisdiction.

c. Article 25 of the Mexican Constitution of 1917 and the Relationship Between Environment and Social and Economic Development (Article 25)

110. Article 25 of the Mexican Constitution has been also modified twice regarding the ideas of sustainability and social and economic development, as explained below.

111. In 1983, Article 25 of the Mexican Constitution was amended to include a reference to the relationship between the environment and economic development as follows:

> Under criteria of social equity and productivity, enterprises of the social and private sectors of the economy will be supported and encouraged, holding them to the modalities issued by the public interest and to the use, in general benefit, of productive resources, taking care of their conservation and the environment.

112. For some authors, that reform established the principles that give substance to the model of sustainable development in Mexico. However, the constitutional basis of sustainable development in Mexico was not introduced with the 1983 amendment to Article 25, but with two other constitutional amendments. First, the reform of 1987 to Article 27 not only establishes the exclusive property of the Nation over certain natural resources but also empowers it to impose modalities on private property in cases where the elements of the environment form part of this patrimonial regime or to regulate their use when considered as *res nullius*.

---

28. DOF, 6 Jul. 1971.

113. Second, the reform of 1999 to Article 25 expressly included the concept of sustainability into the constitutional text. The new article wording is as follows:

> The State has the responsibility for the direction of national development; to ensure that this is integrated and sustainable; to strengthen the sovereignty of the nation and its democratic system, and that through the promotion of economic growth and employment and a fairer distribution of income and wealth, there will occur the full exercise of freedom and dignity of individuals, groups, and social classes, whose security protects this Constitution.

d. The Amendment of 1987 to Articles 25 and 73, Section XXIX-G

114. In 1987, an important reform to Articles 27 and 73 of the Constitution was passed.[29] The amendment to Article 27 ruled that the exercise of the powers of the Nation to impose on private property those modalities dictated by the public interest or to regulate the use of natural elements susceptible of appropriation, should have as an objective – among others – the preservation and restoration of the ecological balance.

115. Thus, the mentioned provision was worded as follows:

> The Nation will have at any time the right to impose on private property those modalities dictated by the public interest, as well as to regulate, for social benefit, the development of the natural elements susceptible to appropriation, to make possible an equitable distribution of public wealth, taking care for their conservation, to achieve a balanced development of the country and to improve the life of the rural and urban population. Thus, the Nation will take the necessary steps for managing human settlements and establishing adequate provisions, uses, reservations, and destinations of land, water, and forests to execute public works and plan and regulate the foundation, conservation, improvement, and growth of the population centres; *to preserve and restore the ecological balance* … .

116. With this reform, for the first time, the possibility of expanding the range of legal mechanisms to protect the environment, and not only natural resources as foreseen by the pristine text of Article 27 of the Constitution, was opened.

e. The Distribution of Powers Between the States and the Federation in Environmental Matters (Article 73, Section XXIX-G)

117. The constitutional reform passed in 1987 also introduced the system of concurrent competences on the matters of environmental protection and restoration of

29. DOF, 10 Aug. 1987.

ecological balance, under the premise that in environmental issues it is not convenient to centralize functions, but it requires the participation of all levels of authority.

118. This amendment allowed the thirty-two entities comprising the Federal pact – including Mexico's City – to issue their own local environmental laws and allowed the municipalities to dictate ordinances and regulations on environmental matters. Thus, based on this amendment, the protection of the environment had to be regarded as a case in which the three levels of government are competent to issue laws and regulations.

119. The Federal Congress, for the first time, interpreted the Constitutional reform of 1987 when it passed the Environmental Act.[30] Article 1, section VII established as one of its objectives to set up the bases for the concurrence of the federal government, local governments, and the municipalities in this matter, and Second Chapter of the First Title established the rules that govern concurrent jurisdictions system.

120. The Constitutional reform of 1987 is particularly relevant, as it, for the first time, gave the Constitution a clear basis for the enactment of specific laws in the field of environmental protection, and not just regarding natural resources protection.

121. In 2001, the National Supreme Court of Justice, in ruling on a constitutional controversy filed by the federal government against the Government of Mexico City in relation to local education, resolved, that section XXIX-G of Article 73 of the Constitution must be interpreted as meaning that the Congress of the Union is empowered to issue general environmental laws. These general laws should have two different aims. On the one hand, to distribute powers among the federation, the states, Mexico City, and the municipalities; and on the other hand, to establish the federal system regulating the performance of the central powers in the matter in question. Since this is a decision on a constitutional controversy, it constitutes binding jurisprudence.[31] The National Supreme Court of Justice ruling is as follows:

---

30. This Law was passed by the Federal Congress in 1987 but it was published into the DOF on 28 Jan. 1988.
31. In Mexico, jurisprudence is generated by three means: the first one is through five uninterrupted resolutions that resolve a dispute in the same sense, which must be issued by the Judicial Power of the Federation, that is, either in Plenary or Chambers of the Supreme Court of Justice of the Nation and/or by the Collegiate Circuit Courts; the second is through the contradiction of thesis, which is that the Plenary or the Chambers of the SCJN meet the criteria that must be sustained on a particular issue where there are opposing positions either by the Chambers of the SCJN or by the Collegiate Circuit Courts; and the third are the resolutions issued by the SCJN in resolving cases of constitutional controversy or actions of unconstitutionality.

CONCURRING FACULTIES IN THE MEXICAN LEGAL SYSTEM. GENERAL CHARACTERISTICS. Although article 124 of the Political Constitution of the United States of Mexico establishes that: 'Powers not expressly granted by this Constitution to federal officials are understood to be reserved to States.' The Reforming organ of the Constitution determined, in various precepts, the possibility that the Congress of the Union would establish a division of powers, called 'concurrent faculties', between the Federation, the federal entities and the municipalities, and even the Federal District, in some areas, such as education (Article 3, section VIII and 73, section XXV), health (articles 4, paragraph 3 and 73, section XVI), human settlements (articles 27, third paragraph And Article 73, section XXIX-C), public security (article 73, section XXIII), environmental protection (article 73, section XXIX-G), civil protection (article 73, section XXIX-I) and sports Article 73, section XXIX-J). That is, in the Mexican legal system the concurrent faculties imply that the federal entities, including the Federal District, the Municipalities and the Federation, can act on the same matter, but it will be the Congress of the Union that determines the form and the terms of participation of the entities through a general law.
Constitutional controversy 29/2000. Federal Executive Power. November 15, 2001. Eleven votes. Speaker: Sergio Salvador Aguirre Anguiano. Secretary: Pedro Alberto Nava Malagón.
The Plenum Tribunal, at its private meeting held in December 6, approved, with number 142/2001, the jurisprudential thesis above. Mexico, Federal District, on December 6, two thousand and one. After this ruling the Mexican Supreme Court of Justice has issued other rulings that confirms this criterion.

122. In fact, as already mentioned, the enactment of the Environmental Act has been followed by the entry into force of other general laws approved based on the same constitutional provision already mentioned, which also distributes powers among the three levels of government in regard to different natural resources protection, such as the General Law of Wildlife, the General Law of Sustainable Development of Forests, etc.

f. Article 4 of the Mexican Constitution of 1917 and the Right to a Healthy Environment

123. The right to a healthy environment as a fundamental right set forth in the Mexican Constitution was incorporated in the amendment of 1999 to Article 4. That amendment added a fourth paragraph to the mentioned provision, which states: 'Every person has the right to a suitable environment for his or her development and welfare.' By Constitutional reform passed in 2011, this fourth paragraph was moved to fifth paragraph.[32]

---

32. DOF, 13 Oct. 2011.

124. By Constitutional reform of June 2011, the right to a healthy environment, as well as other fundamental rights were considered human rights instead of individual warranties.

g. Article 4 of the Mexican Constitution of 1917 and the Right of Access to Water

125. The background to the incorporation of the right of access to water and sanitation can be found in various documents of an international nature, including:

- *Observation number 15* of the Committee on Economic, Social, and Cultural Rights 2002.
- Resolution 64/292, the United Nations General Assembly of 28 July 2010.

Council's *observation number 15*, Article I.1, stated that 'the human right to water is indispensable for a dignified human life'. The same document defines the right to water as the right of everyone to have enough, healthy, acceptable, physically accessible, and affordable water for their personal and domestic use.

126. The United Nations Resolution recognizes that '*the* right to safe drinking water and sanitation is an essential human right to the full enjoyment of life and all human rights' and 'urges States and international organizations to provide financial resources and to enhance capacity and technology, transfer through international assistance and cooperation, particularly to developing countries, in order to intensify efforts to the entire population an economic access to drinking water and sanitation'.

127. With this background, a constitutional reform of 2012 adds to Article 4 of the Mexican Constitution a sixth paragraph that provides:

> Everyone has the right to adequate, safe, acceptable and affordable access, disposal and sanitation of water for personal and domestic consumption. The State will guarantee this right and the law will define the basis, supports and modalities for the access and equitable and sustainable use of water resources, establishing the participation of the federation, the federal entities and the municipalities, as well as the participation of citizenship for the attainment of these purposes.

128. The new precept adopted the same formula that at this moment was used when recognizing the right to a healthy environment, it gives the State the responsibility to guarantee this right and it transfers to the secondary legislation the obligation to define its content and scope. The constitutional precept indicates that this right must guarantee enough, healthy, acceptable, and affordable access but it does not clarify what is meant by each one of these concepts. Secondary legislation is expected to address the issue.

129. In fact, the Decree that promulgated the mentioned reform contains a third transitory article that obliges the Congress of the Union to issue a General Waters Act for a term of 360 days. Although the new law has not yet been approved, the General Law initiative that has been submitted to the consideration of the Congress of the Union contains a Title II called 'Human Right to Water' that is integrated by Articles 40–53. Article 46 of the initiative states that 'norms relating to the human right to water shall be interpreted in accordance with the Political Constitution of the United Mexican States and international treaties of the subject, always favouring persons the widest protection'.

h. Article 4 of the Mexican Constitution of 1917 and the Principle of Liability for Environmental Damage

130. In 2012, the fifth paragraph of Article 4 of the Constitution was added with a second part which states: 'Those generated environmental damage are liable in the terms set forth by the law.' A transitory provision of this last amended obliged the Federal Congress to pass a law regulating liability for environmental damages in a term of six months from the day the constitutional amendment came into force. Based on this constitutional reform, in 2013, the Federal Congress passed the Federal Environmental Liability Act.[33]

i. Article 17 of the Mexican Constitution of 1917 and the Legal Standing to File Collective Actions in Environmental Matters

131. As mentioned before, during the twenty-first century, several constitutional reforms have been passed with the aim of making possible access to environmental justice. The first constitutional reform was passed in July 2010.[34]

132. The new provision obliged the Federal Congress to pass a law regulating collective actions, including judicial procedures and a mechanism for the restoration of environmental damage. In consonance with this Constitutional reform, jurisdiction to decide on these matters is vested in federal judges. Thus, in 2012 the Federal Code of Civil Procedure was added with a fifth book that regulates collective actions.[35]

33. DOF, 7 Jun. 2013.
34. DOF, 29 Jul. 2010.
35. DOF, 9 Apr. 2012.

j. Article 107 of the Mexican Constitution of 1917 and the Recognition of Collective Legal Interest to File Injunction Actions to Combat Unconstitutional Resolutions Issue by Environmental Authorities

133. A second constitutional reform, which modified Articles 94, 103, 104, and 107 of the Federal Constitution, was passed in 2011.[36] These articles regulate one of the most important instruments for human rights protection in Mexico: the Amparo Trial (injunction). However, these provisions were crafted to protect only individual interests. The reform to Article 107 means that for the first time an *amparo* action may be filed not only to protect individual and direct interests, as the original text of the Constitution provided, but also in defence of the indirect and collective legal interests, such as the collective interest in protecting the environment. Article 107, as amended, reads as follows:

> Article 107. All dispute considered under article 103 shall be subject of the proceeding and formalities established by the law, in accordance with the following bases:
>
> > 'The Amparo trial must always be initiated at instance of injury party, having this character those who argument to have a right or individual or collective legitimate interest, under the condition that the act claimed violets a right recognized by this Constitution and with that it its juridical interest directly or because its especial legal situation'.

Based on this constitutional reform, in 2013, the Federal Congress passed a new Law ruling the *Amparo* Trial.[37]

2. The New General Laws

134. Given that section XXIX-G of Article 73 of the Mexican Constitution allows the enactment of several general laws, so far during the twenty-first century, the Federal Congress has enacted: (a) the General Act of Wildlife of 2000 (Wildlife Act as amended in 2010);[38] (b) the General Act for Sustainable Forest Development of 2018;[39] (c) the General Act for Prevention and Integral Management of Waste of 2003[40] (Waste Act as amended in 2006 and 2007); (d) the General Act of Sustainable Fisheries and Aquaculture of 2007[41] (amended in 2012); (e) the General Act of climate change of 2012;[42] (f) the Federal Environmental Liability Act of 2013;[43] the

36. DOF, 6 Jun. 2011.
37. DOF, 2 Apr. 2013.
38. DOF, 3 Jul. 2010.
39. DOF, June 2018.
40. DOF, 8 Oct. 2003.
41. DOF, 24 Jul. 2007.
42. DOF, 6 Jun. 2012.
43. DOF, 7 Jun. 2013.

General Act of Human Settlements, Territorial Ordinance and Urban Development of 2016;[44] while the National Waters Act (Water Act of 1992) was substantially modified in 2004.

3. Doctrine

135. Whereas in many countries, law treatises, particularly those written from the perspective of public law, have contributed not only to the best interpretation of environmental legal regimes but also, in some cases, to its development. In Mexico, the role of scholars in the field of environmental law is still precarious.

136. By 1988, when the Environmental Act went into force, just one book on environmental law had been written in Mexico, and although by 2019, a dozen texts on the subject had been published, most of them are not well documented or are only partially developed.

137. However, one must recognize the influence of the pioneering work of Ramon Ojeda Mestre, founder of the Mexican Academy of Environmental Law more than twenty-five years ago, in teaching and research on environmental law, as well as the work of Carmen Carmona, whose bachelor's degree thesis in the 1980s focused on that subject.

138. On the same plane, the work written by Raul Brañes in 1988 and re-edited in 1994 and 2000 by the *Fondo de Cultura Económica* (Fund of Economic Culture), entitled *Manual de Derecho Ambiental Mexicano* (Manual of Mexican Environmental Law), is – although a descriptive work – a systematic handbook that refers to all areas of Mexican environmental law.

139. At the present time, one of the most proactive institutions in promoting the study of Mexican environmental law is the Metropolitan Autonomous University, Campus Azcapotzalco, whose Department of Law offers an Environmental Law Master's Degree.

140. Currently, that institution has opened a Master's Degree in Environmental law.

141. At the same time, the *Revista Mexicana de Legislación Ambiental (Mexican Journal of Environmental Legislation)*, founded in 1999, is one of the main sources of the generation of new and serious knowledge in the legal discipline of environmental law.

44. DOF, 29 Nov. 2016.

4. Jurisprudence (Judicial Decisions)

142. In Mexico, Judiciary power has played different roles in the field of environmental protection. It has acted:

(a) as the controller of administrative enforcement;
(b) as the protector of the right to a healthy environment; and
(c) as the interpreter of the environmental rules established by the Constitution.

a. The Judiciary as Controller of Administrative Enforcement

143. The first role of the courts in the field of environmental protection was as a reviser of the administrative authorities' enforcement activities. The SCJN has adopted nearly a hundred of judicial rulings revising acts of the administrative authorities during the administrative procedure of environmental law enforcement.

b. The Judiciary and the Right to a Healthy Environment

144. By the 1990s, the role of the Judiciary started to focus more on issues related to the rights to information and public participation in the decision-making process as a way of protecting the right to a healthy environment.

145. In 1996, a non-governmental organization called *Grupo de los cien internacional* (The hundred international) – filed an injunction action (*amparo*) to combat an administrative resolution issued by the General Director of Legal Affairs of the Ministry of the Environment. This resolution rejected the petition formulated by 'The hundred international' requesting the Ministry of the Environment to revise a decision through which that Ministry exempted from environmental impact authorization several industrial activities. The petitioners believed that the ministerial decision was contrary to the right to a healthy environment recognized by the Environmental Act and many international agreements adopted by the Mexican government.

146. The Fifth District Court of Mexico City decided that the case held by the petitioners had no legal standing to file the injunction action because the ministerial decision did not directly affect them.

147. However, the Court of Appeals (*Primer Tribunal Colegiado en Materia Administrativa*) that revised the judicial ruling made by the District Court reversed the first judicial ruling based on the argument that the recognition of the right to information by Article 33 of the Environmental Act meant that the petitioners had legal standing to participate in protecting the environment, and consequently it asserted that all people have legal standing to intervene and participate in enforcing environmental laws and regulations.

148. In a similar case filed in 1997 by the union of environmentalist groups, the Council for the Defence of the Pacific Coast, Green Peace Mexico, and the Mexican Centre of Environmental Law against the same Ministerial Decision analysed in the previously mentioned case, a District Court decided that the petitioners had no legal standing to file the injunction action. Different from what happened in the case of 1996, the new judicial ruling was confirmed by the Court of Appeals.

149. In another injunction case filed in 1997 by the Foundation to Environmental Education, the SCJN held that the community had the legal standing to file an injunction action because of the collective character of environmental rights.

150. Currently, legal standing to combat administrative decisions issued by environmental authorities is widely recognized by the Constitution as well as by the Environmental Act.[45]

c. The Judiciary as Interpreter of the Environmental Principles Recognized by the Constitution

151. The role of the Judiciary as interpreter of environmental rules recognized by the Constitution can be seen in *Convimar v. Federal Government*. In 1994, the company Convimar, S.A. de C.V filed an injunction action against the environmental standard '*Norma Oficial Mexicana de Emergencia (NOM-EM-136-ECOL-2002, protección ambiental-especificaciones para la conservación de mamíferos marinos en cautiverio)*', arguing that paragraphs 5.8.7 and 5.8.7.1 prohibited temporal or itinerant exhibition of cetaceans. The Fourth Administrative Appeals Court rejected the petition, considering that, in accordance with Article 40, paragraph 4, Article 25, paragraph 6, and Article 73, section XXIX-G of the Federal Constitution, the protection of a healthy environment, natural resources, and environmental restoration are fundamental principles protected by the Constitution, so that even when it does not establish the way to protect such principles, by definition, its content is a matter of a systematic and comprehensive interpretation of the different laws and statutes that address this objective.

152. In the same vein, in 2000, the SCJN adopted an important decision interpreting Article 73, section XXIX-G of the Federal Constitution that established a rule stating that the power to enact laws regarding environmental protection is shared among the federal and local governments. The National Supreme Court holds that it corresponds to the Federal Congress enacting of general laws aimed at distributing jurisdictions among the three levels of government to legislate on environmental matters.

---

45. Legitimate interest is recognized by the Arts 17 and 107 of Federal Constitution, and by Art. 180 of the Environmental Law.

Part I. Pollution Control

Chapter 1. General Law

§1. The Environmental Impact Assessment

153. The EIA is an administrative procedure aimed at preventing environmental degradation and protecting natural resources. Hence, this section will begin with an analysis of the legal frame that governs this legal procedure.

I. Concept

154. Article 28 of the Environmental Act defines the EIA as 'the procedure through which the Ministry of the Environment establishes the conditions that will govern the conduction of projects or activities that may cause ecological imbalance or may surpass the limits and conditions set up by the applicable provisions to protect the environment and to preserve and restore the ecosystems, in order to avoid or reduce to the minimum their negative effects on the environment'.

155. Consequently, it is possible to assert that the EIA is an instrument of environmental policy of a preventive nature and that assumes the form of a sui generis administrative procedure.

156. The EIA is of a preventive nature because, in line with the first paragraph of Article 28 of the Environmental Act, only those activities that would cause an ecological imbalance or would surpass the limits and conditions established by the applicable legal provisions aimed at protecting the environment and preserving and restoring ecosystems should be evaluated.

157. However, the evaluation of the environmental impact is a sui generis procedure because, first, different from what happens in other administrative procedures, during the process of evaluation, public participation of communities that could be affected by the final resolution is allowed. Second, the administrative decision issued by the Ministry of the Environment at the end of the procedure have a regulatory character.

II. Legal Framework

158. At the federal level, the EIA procedure is governed by:

(1) the Environmental Act;
(2) the Regulations under the Environmental Act regarding to EIA of 2000;
(3) the Federal Act of Administrative Procedure (FAAP); and
(4) the ten Official Mexican Norms. which are:

NOM-002-SAG-BIO/SEMARNAT-2017 Establishing the characteristics and requirements to be contained in the evaluation studies of the possible risks that the experimental release of genetically modified organisms may cause to the environment and biological diversity, as well as animal, plant and aquaculture health (30-10-2018).

NOM-115-SEMARNAT-2003, which establishes the environmental protection specifications that must be observed in the drilling and maintenance activities of land-based oil wells for exploration and production in agricultural, livestock and wasteland areas, outside protected natural areas or forest land.

NOM-116-SEMARNAT-2005, which establishes the environmental protection specifications for land seismological surveys carried out in agricultural, livestock and wasteland areas.

NOM-117-SEMARNAT-2006, which establishes the specifications for environmental protection during installation, major maintenance and abandonment of liquid and gaseous hydrocarbon and petrochemical pipeline systems that are carried out in existing rights of way located in agricultural, livestock and wasteland areas.

NOM-120-SEMARNAT-2020, which establishes the environmental protection specifications for direct mining exploration activities in agricultural, livestock or wasteland areas and in areas with dry and temperate climates where xerophytic scrub, tropical deciduous forest, coniferous forests and oak forests develop. (11-11-2020).

NOM-129-SEMARNAT-2006, Natural gas distribution networks – Establishes environmental protection specifications for site preparation, construction, operation, maintenance and abandonment of natural gas distribution networks intended to be located in urban, suburban and industrial areas, urban equipment or services.

NOM-130-SEMARNAT-2000 Environmental protection-Fibre optic telecommunications systems-Specifications for planning, design, site preparation, construction, operation and maintenance (23-03-2001).

NOM-141-SEMARNAT-2003 Establishing the procedure to characterize tailings, as well as the specifications and criteria for the characterization and preparation of tailings, design, construction, operation and post-operation of tailings dams (13-09-2004).

NOM-143-SEMARNAT-2003, which establishes the environmental specifications for the management of congenital water associated with hydrocarbons.

NOM-150-SEMARNAT-2017, which establishes the technical specifications for environmental protection that must be observed in the construction activities and preliminary evaluation of geometric wells for exploration, located in agricultural, livestock and wasteland areas, outside protected natural areas and forest land (22-11-2017).

159. However, because of the concurrent jurisdictions system in environmental matters established by the Mexican Constitution, local environmental laws regulate the procedure of EIA as well

160. Conforming to Articles 5, section X and 28 of the Environmental Act, the federal environmental authorities evaluate the environmental impact of projects or activities listed in Article 28, while in agreement with section XVI of Article 7, as well as to Article 32*bis* 2 of the Environmental Act, local governments are empowered to evaluate the environmental impact that could be caused by works or activities not included in those listed in Article 28.

III. Projects and Activities Requiring EIA Granted by the Federal Government

161. As mentioned above, Article 28 of the Environmental Act lists in twelve sections the projects and activities subject to the previous evaluation of their environmental impact by the Federal Ministry of the Environment. The list includes the following projects and activities:[46]

I. Hydraulic facilities, general ways of communication, pipelines, gas lines, carbon ducts, and poly ducts;
II. The petroleum, petro chemistry, chemistry, steel, wastebasket, sugar bowl, cement-production industries and electricity generation;
III. Exploration, exploitation, and benefit of minerals and substances reserved to the Federation in the terms of the Mining Laws and Regulations of Article 27 of the Mexican Constitution in nuclear matters;
IV. Treatment facilities, disposition, or elimination of hazardous wastes, as well as radioactive residuals;
V. Forest uses in tropical forests and species of difficult regeneration;
VI. (repealed);
VII. Changes of uses of the Land of forest areas, as well as in forests and arid areas;
VIII. Industrial parks where the occurrence of highly risky activities is foreseen;
IX. Urban developments that affect the coastal ecosystems;
X. Works and activities in wetlands, swamps, lagoons, rivers, lakes, and connected tidelands as well as on their coasts or Federal areas;

46. Original Text of Art. 28 had thirteen sections, but s. VI was repealed.

XI. Works and activities in natural Federally protected areas;
XII. Fishing or agricultural activities that could endanger the preservation of species or lives, or cause damage to ecosystems, and
XIII. Works or activities that relate to matters of Federal competition that could cause serious and irreparable ecological imbalances, damage to public health or ecosystems, or that surpass the limits and conditions set forth in the legal provisions relative to preservation of the ecological balance and protection of the environment.

162. This list is general in nature; there are several situations that may modify its content.

163. First, the Environmental Act points out that the Regulations in this field shall specify their scope. In this sense, the final part of Article 28, paragraph 1 of the Environmental Act mandates that the Regulations shall determine in detail the works and activities that must be evaluated, as follows:

> In the cases determined by the Regulations that will be issued, those who seek to carry out some ... projects or activities will require the previous authorization of environmental impact granted by the Ministry (Ministry of Environment).

164. Second, in its penultimate paragraph, Article 28 of the Environmental Act establishes that the Regulations for the EIA shall define the projects or activities that, despite being included in the list, are exempted from evaluation in the following terms:

> The Regulation under the present Law shall determine the projects or activities that, because of their location, dimensions, characteristics, or scope, do not produce significant environmental impacts, do not cause or may not cause ecological imbalances, nor surpass the limits and conditions established by legal provisions regarding the preservation of ecological balance and environmental protection, should not be submitted to the procedure of environmental impact assessment.

165. Third, section XIII of Article 28 of the Environmental Act allows the Ministry of the Environment to demand the evaluation of the environmental impact of certain projects or activities not included in the list. This section points out that the Ministry of Environment shall require EIA in cases of 'projects or activities that relate to matters under federal jurisdiction that could cause serious and irreparable ecological imbalances, damage to public health or ecosystems, or surpass the limits and conditions established by the legal provisions regarding the preservation of ecological balance and environmental protection'.

166. Finally, the Environmental Act also establishes a series of cases in which projects or activities included in sections I–XII of Article 28 do not require evaluation of the environmental impact, and therefore, those interested in its execution shall instead simply present a preventive report to the environmental authority for evaluating their environmental impact.

167. In this sense, Article 31 of the Environmental Act points out that the works and activities referred to in sections I–XII of Article 28 require the preparation of a preventive report instead of an EIA in the following cases:

(a) When there are Official Mexican Norms or other provisions that regulate emissions, discharges, uses of natural resources, and, in general, all environmental impacts that could be produced by such projects or activities.
(b) When the projects or activities are included in a partial plan of urban development or in an ecological zoning programme which environmental impact has been previously evaluated by the Ministry.
(c) When facilities are located in industrial parks which environmental impact has been previously authorized by the Ministry.

IV. Projects and Activities Requiring EIA Granted by the Local Governments

168. Per the Environmental Act, the works and activities listed in Article 28 are not the only ones that must undergo a prior environmental impact assessment. Article 35*bis* 2 of the law mentioned above states that the environmental impact that may be caused by works or activities not included in Article 28 will be evaluated by the authorities of the federal entities with the participation of the municipalities and territorial districts of Mexico City where such projects and activities are located. Local legislations must indicate those works or activities that produce significant environmental impacts due to their location, dimensions or characteristics and are subject to environmental impact authorization. The 2018 amendment established in the Environmental Act that in the case of works or activities under federal jurisdiction that intend to obtain the corresponding environmental impact authorization, such authorization may be processed jointly with the authorizations regarding land use, construction, *subdivisions* or any other procedure established by local law.

V. The Environmental Impact Statement and Its Content

169. In accordance with Article 30 of the Environmental Act, those interested in obtaining the environmental impact authorization must submit to the Ministry of the Environment an environmental impact statement (EIS), which should contain at least:

(a) a description of the possible effects on the ecosystems that could be affected by the project or activity concerned, taking integrally into account all the elements of such ecosystems;
(b) the actions to prevent, mitigate or avoid and reduce the negative effects on the environment; and
(c) a study of risk in the case of activities considered highly risky conforming to the Environmental Act.

170. However, the Regulations for the EIA points out that the EIS may have either a 'particular' or a 'regional' modality (Article 10). In accordance with Article 11, the EIS must be elaborated upon from a regional modality only in the cases of:

(a) Industrial and aquaculture parks, aquaculture farms bigger than 500 hectares, roads and railways, projects of nuclear energy generation, dams, and, in general, projects that alter the watersheds.
(b) A set of works or activities that are included in a plan or partial programme of urban development or environmental management.
(c) A set of works, projects, and activities carried out in an ecological region.
(d) Projects to be conducted in areas where possible residual, synergic, or accumulative impacts could cause destruction, isolation, or fragmentation of ecosystems.

171. In any other cases, the EIS could be submitted upon from a modality. According to Article 12 of the Regulations for the EIA, the EIS must contain, in a particular modality, the following:

(a) general data about the project, promoter, and responsible person for the EIS;
(b) a description of the project;
(c) linkage of the project with the legal systems applicable in environmental matters and with land-use regulations;
(d) a description of the environmental system and identification of the environmental problems detected in the area of influence of the project;
(e) identification, description, and evaluation of environmental impacts;
(f) environmental impacts preventive and mitigation measures;
(g) environmental forecasts and evaluation of alternatives; and
(h) identification of the methodological and technical elements that underpin the information indicated in the previous sections.

172. In consonance with Article 13 of the Regulations for the EIA, the regional EIS shall contain the following information:

(a) general data about the project, promoter, and responsible person for the environmental impact study;
(b) a description of the projects or activities and the programmes or partial plans of development;

(c) linkage of the project with the instruments of planning and legal systems applicable;
(d) a description of the regional environmental system and trends of development and deterioration of the region;
(e) identification, description, and evaluation of the cumulative and residual environmental impacts on the regional environmental system;
(f) strategies for prevention and mitigation of cumulative and residual environmental impacts on the regional environmental system;
(g) regional environmental forecasts and valuation of alternatives; and
(h) identification of the methodological and technical elements that underpin the results of the statement of the environmental impact.

173. In addition, in line with Article 30 of the Environmental Act, in the case of activities considered highly risky, the EIS must include the study of risk. This provision is complemented by Articles 17 and 18 of the Regulations for the EIA, which establish the following:

> Article 17: The developer must submit to the Ministry of the Environment the application for approval in the field of environmental impact, attaching
>
> I. The environmental impact statement;
> II. A summary of the content of the environmental impact statement, presented in electronic format; and
> III. A copy of the record of the payment of rights.
>
> In the case of activities highly risky in terms of the law, it should include a study of risk.
> Article 18: The study of risk referenced by the previous article will incorporate into the environmental impact statement the following information:
>
> I. Scenarios and preventive measures resulting from the analysis of the environmental risks related to the project;
> II. A description of the protection zones around the facilities; and
> III. Identification of the security measures to be taken in environmental matters.
>
> The Ministry of the Environment has published, in the DOF and in the Ecological Gazette, guides to facilitate the presentation and delivery of the study of risk.

VI. The Procedure for the EIA

174. The procedure for the EIA is divided into three phases: (1) integration of the administrative *dossier*, (2) technical evaluation of the project or activity by the Ministry of Environment, and (3) the issuance of the resolution.

A. The Dossier *Integration*

175. The procedure for the EIA starts with the submission of an application from those interested in carrying out projects or activities subject to the EIA by the Environmental Act (Article 17 of the Regulations for the EIA), but this application must be accompanied by a technical document called 'environmental impact statement' (EIS) (Article 30 of the Environmental Act).[47] In accordance with the Regulations for the EIA, the application for approval in the field of environmental impact, its annexes, and any additional information must be submitted in electronic form and accompanied by four hard copies of its content (Article 19).

176. In line with Article 20 of the Regulations for the EIA, the Ministry of the Environment, when receiving the request and its annexes, can communicate to the applicant the existence of formal deficiencies that can be corrected at that time. However, it may not reject any request in terms of Article 43 of the Federal Law on Administrative Procedure. This provision holds:

> In no case administrative offices in charge of receipting documents are allowed to reject any petition.

177. So, once the request for evaluation of EIS has been received by the environmental authority, it is obliged to integrate the dossier within the following ten days (Article 35 of the Environmental Act and Article 21 of the Regulations on EIA).

178. Within that period, the authority carries out a documentary revision process merely for verifying that the application conforms to the formalities of the law, regulations, and applicable Official Mexican Norms.

179. Neither the laws nor the Regulations for the EIA mention the consequences of a request lacking any of the requirements specified in Article 17 of the same Regulations – in other words, if the request is not accompanied by: (a) the EIS, (b) a summary of the content of the EIS, submitted electronically, (c) a stamped copy of the payment of fees, and (d) the study of risk; or if the information is not submitted according to the terms of Article 19; if the EIS does not satisfy the provisions of Articles 12 and 13 of the Regulation for EIA; or if the study of risk is not

---

47. In some cases, the EIA procedure starts with a request from the authority. An example of such a case is when the interested party submits to the authority a preventive report with the objective of obtaining a resolution exempting the project or activity from the procedure for the EIA and the authority decides that the project or activity in question is not within the scope of Art. 31 of the Environmental Act and, therefore, it must be submitted through the EIS procedure (Art. 31, para. 2 of the Environmental Act). Another example is the case envisaged in the last paragraph of Art. 28 of the Environmental Act, conforming to which, in the cases described in s. XIII of that article, the Ministry of the Environment shall notify the interested party of its intent to subject the project to the procedure of the EIA, explaining the reasons that justify such decision.

produced according to the terms of Article 18 of the Regulations. However, the authority may decide not to process the *dossier* and, thus, not to continue with the procedure of the EIA.

180. Legislation has failed to indicate whether the authority should or should not communicate this last fact to the petitioner, which is certainly an important legal gap, given that the petitioner likely considers that because he or she has initiated an administrative procedure, he or she should not remain ignorant of the fact that the *dossier* has not been processed.

181. However, a case of non-compliance with the necessary requirements, which can lead to the *dossier's* not being processed, should not be confused with a case of a request for additional information. This last scenario occurs when the authority requires additional elements for evaluation and not when the *dossier* triggers some legal requirement.

182. Once the *dossier* is integrated, the procedure of evaluation continues through three avenues that operate in parallel: the technical and scientific evaluation, the notification to local governments, and the public consultation.

B. Evaluation of the Dossier

1. Technical Evaluation

183. Articles 1 and 35 of the Environmental Act establish the rules governing the assessment of the EIA by the authority, as follows:

(a) The Ministry of the Environment shall evaluate the EIA in consonance with the Environmental Act, the Regulations for the EIA, and the Official Mexican Norms, as well as the urban development programmes and ecological zoning plans of the territory, the declarations of protected natural areas, and other applicable legal provisions.
(b) The Ministry of the Environment should assess the potential effects of such projects or activities on the ecosystems concerned.

184. In addition, the Regulations for the EIA set forth the following rules:

(a) The Ministry of the Environment may request, in the terms laid down in the Federal Act on Administrative Procedure, the technical opinion of other agencies of the Federal Public Administration, when required because of the type of project or activity (Article 24).
(b) The Ministry of the Environment may consult with groups of experts when, because of the complexity or the singular circumstances of the project, it considers that their opinions can provide better elements for the decision-making (Article 24).

(c) The Ministry of the Environment must include in the file: (i) the additional information that is generated; (ii) the technical opinions that had been requested; (iii) the comments and opinions made by the interested parties in the process of public consultation, as well as the extract of the project that during that process has been published; (iv) the resolution; (v) the guarantees; and (vi) the amendments to the project that have been made (Article 26).

185. It should be noted that paragraph 2 of Article 22 of the Regulations for the EIA provides in the administrative field the exact observance of the provisions of Article 35 A of the Environmental Act by saying:

> The Ministry of the Environment may request clarification, corrections, or extensions to the content of the environmental impact statement submitted to it, suspending the term to conclude the procedure. In any case, the suspension may not exceed sixty days from the time that it is declared by the Ministry of the Environment, and provided that the required information is submitted.

2. Notification to the States

186. In the case of the projects or activities referred to by sections IV, VIII, IX, and XI of Article 28 of the Environmental Act, the Ministry of the Environment shall notify the State and municipal governments or Mexico's City government,[48] as appropriate, that it has received the EIS, so that they can express their opinions and comments (Article 33 of the Environmental Act)

187. The State's opinions and comments are not mandatory for the process of decision-making.

3. Right to Information and Public Participation

188. In line with Article 34 of the Environmental Act, once the Ministry of the Environment has received the EIS and has processed the *dossier*, in accordance with Article 35, it is obliged to make the *dossier* available for the public. In addition, the Ministry of the Environment, upon request of any person of the community involved, may carry out a public consultation. The Regulations for the EIA govern, in Articles 40, 41, and 42, the public consultation procedure.

48. In 2016 the Mexican constitution was amended to modify the political status of the Federal District that used to be not considered as a state member of the Mexican Federation. In concordance with this amendment, the forma name of Federal District changed by Mexico City. However, word wide Federal District was known as Mexico City. DOF 29 Jan. 2016.

C. The Decision by the Ministry of the Environment

189. The procedure for the EIA concludes with the issuance of an administrative decision by the authority. The following subsections describe the process of the decision-making.

1. The Deadline for Issuing the Decision

190. Article 35*bis*[49] of the Environmental Act stipulates that a decision must be made within sixty days after an application has been filed. However, there are two cases in which this term can be modified:

(a) when there is a suspension of the procedure under which the Ministry of the Environment requests clarification or extensions of information; and
(b) when necessary because of the complexity and the dimensions of a project or activity.

191. In the first case, in terms of Article 22 of the Regulations for the EIA, the suspension of the procedure can be decreed only once and within forty days after the application has been filed when the EIS has inadequacies that make impossible the evaluation of the project until more detailed information is provided by the applicant. In this case, the term of the resolution is suspended until the petition for information is fulfilled. Article 22 stipulates:

> In cases in which the environmental impact statement has inadequacies that make impossible the evaluation of the project, the Ministry of the Environment may request the developer, for one time and within forty days from the integration of the dossier, clarifications, corrections, or extensions to the content of it and, in that case, it can suspend the term of sixty days referred to in article 35A of the Law.

192. The suspension of the procedure may not exceed sixty days from the day on which it was declared. After this period, if the developer does not submit the requested information, the Ministry of the Environment may declare the expiration of the procedure pursuant to Article 60 of the Federal Law of Administrative Procedure.

193. The second scenario, in which the modification of the deadline to issue the final decision operates, is when – conforming to the terms of Article 46 of the Regulations for the EIA – because of the magnitude and complexity of the projects or activity, it is justifiable for the authority to take a longer period to make a decision; this period will be 120 days.

---

49. By constitutional reform this article was added. DOF, 13 Dec. 1996.

2. The Content of the Decision

194. Article 35 of the Environmental Act notes that the authority may decide on a petition in three different ways:

(i) By authorizing the realization of the work or activity in question, in the requested terms;
(ii) By authorizing with conditions, the work or activity in question; or
(iii) By denying the requested authorization.

195. In the last case, the Environmental Act establishes only three cases for which the authority can decide in the negative (Article 35, section III):

(1) when the work or activity is contrary to established by-laws, regulations, the Official Mexican Norms, or any other applicable provisions;
(2) when the work or activity in question can result in one or more species being declared as endangered or threatened with extinction or when it affects one of these species; or
(3) when false information has been provided by the applicants with respect to the environmental impacts of the work or activity in question.

196. Given that in line with Article 28 of the Environmental Act, the objective of EIA is to establish the conditions that will govern the realization of works or activities that may cause ecological imbalance or may surpass the limits and conditions set up by the applicable provisions to protect the environment and preserve and restore the ecosystems; usually, the authority's decision is issued in the sense of authorizing the work or activity but under certain environmental conditions.

3. The Guarantees for Compliance with the Conditions

197. Article 35 of the Environmental Act stipulates that 'the Ministry of the Environment may require the granting of insurance or guarantees regarding the fulfilment of the conditions set forth by the authorization, in the cases expressed in the Regulations for the EIA, when, during the realization of the works, serious damage to ecosystems may be caused'.

§2. Official Mexican Norms

198. Official Mexican Norms (OMNs) have played a very important role in environmental law and policy in Mexico since 1988, when the Environmental Act went into force, given that many themes of environmental regulation have been developed through OMNs.

199. This regulatory method was introduced almost simultaneously in the Mexican legal system by the Federal Act of Metrology and Standardization (the Standardization Act), and by the Environmental Act, both passed in 1988. However, the Environmental Act referred to OMNs as being specifically related to environmental protection using the term *technical ecological norms* (TENs), while the Standardization Act referred to OMNs in a broader sense, embracing the regulation of almost all the areas of economic activity and using the term Normas Oficiales Mexicanas (OMNs).

200. While the OMNs had a compulsory character, the TENs did not. This meant that while the OMNs were mandatory in other areas of economic activity, in the field of environmental protection, they were voluntary. However, this characteristic was not unusual because environmental legislation did not have real applications during the period 1988–1992. However, neither the Environmental Act nor the Standardization Act regulated the process of the elaboration of OMNs.

201. In 1992, a new Standardization Act was passed by the Federal Congress. It introduced two changes. First, this Law established a procedure for the elaboration and approval of OMNs and second, it introduced a new category of regulation: the Mexican Norms (MNs) which were not mandatory.

202. According to the Act of 1992, both OMNs and MNs are considered standards that establish rules, specifications, attributes, test methods, guides, characteristics, or prescriptions related to products, processes, facilities, systems, activities, services, or production methods or operations, as well as rules regarding labelling, marking, terminology, symbols, and packaging. However, their approval processes are different.

203. On July 1, 2020, the new Quality Infrastructure Act came into force, which aims to:

> set and develop the bases of industrial policy within the scope of the National Quality Infrastructure System, through the activities of normalization, standardization, accreditation, Conformity Assessment and metrology, promoting economic development and quality in the production of goods and services, in order to expand production capacity and continuous improvement in value chains, promote international trade and protect the legitimate objectives of public interest provided for in this Law.

This new Act repealed the 1992 Act. Therefore, all matters related to the process of elaboration, publication and enforcement of the OMNs are now governed by the provisions of this Act.

Among the relevant changes introduced by the new Act, it can be noted that Standards replace Mexican Norms. According to Article 4 section X of the law, Standards are technical documents that provide for everyday and repeated use of rules, specifications, attributes or test methods applicable to a good, product, process or service, as well as those related to terminology, symbology, packaging, marking, labelling or concordance. Per section XVI of the provision mentioned above, a OMNs is a mandatory technical regulation issued by the competent Standardization Authorities whose essential purpose is the promotion of quality for economic development and the protection of the legitimate objectives of public interest outlined in this ordinance, through the establishment of rules, denomination, specifications or characteristics applicable to a good, product, process or service, as well as those related to terminology, marking or labelling and information. The OMNs shall be considered as Technical Regulations or Sanitary or Phytosanitary Measures, according to the corresponding definitions outlined in the international treaties to which the Mexican State is a Party.

In essence, the new law maintains the difference that the 1992 law established between OMNs and Standards.

204. However, OMNs are projected by Standardizing Authority which is the Ministry responsible for the control or regulation of the products, methods, processes or activities or areas that will be regulated by the norm; however, they should be approved by the National Advisory Committees of Standardisation, which are integrated by technical 'personnel competent in the matter that corresponds to the committee and to industrial organizations; lenders of services; merchants; agricultural, forest, or fishing producers; centres of scientific or technological research; professional schools; and consumers'. Therefore, OMNs have to be published in the DOF as a condition of validity.

205. In both cases, participation of regulated subjects in the elaboration process plays an important role because they are part of the Normalization Organizations as well as the National Advisory Committees that approve the standards. Besides, the projects of Official Mexican Norms should be submitted to public consultation by the government. Thus, in a way, standards are mechanisms of self-regulation.

206. Although the Standards are not mandatory, there are ways to enforce compliance. For example, an OMN may refer to a Standard to comply with the requirements established by that OMN, or sometimes an environmental authorization issued by the Ministry of Environment may require compliance with the Standard provisions or requirements.

§3. Environmental Licences

207. Polluting activities are subject to different permits. Air pollutant emissions from fixed sources subject to federal jurisdiction require an operation licence in agreement with Articles 111*bis* of Environment Act and 18 of the Regulation for

Prevention and Control of Air Pollution,[50] whereas in most cities, air pollutant emissions from vehicles are required to pass the certification of emissions tests granted by local governments.

208. In accordance with Article 88 of the National Waters Act, water pollutant discharge to national water bodies requires a discharge permit.[51] Finally, as stated by Articles 46, 47, and 48 of the General Waste Act and 152 of the Environmental Act, great hazardous waste generators[52] need to report to the environmental authority the type and amount of hazardous waste generated by them.

209. Since the middle of the 1990s, the Ministry of the Environment has been trying to integrate all such permits – including the environmental impact authorization – into a unique environmental licence.

210. Aimed at such an objective, in 1996, the Federal Congress approved an amendment to the Environmental Act to include Articles 35*bis* 3, 109*bis*, and 109*bis* 1.

211. As stated by Article 35*bis* 3, the Ministry of the Environment, upon request by the promoter, will integrate with the environmental impact authorization the other permissions, licences, and authorizations under its jurisdiction. In addition, Article 109*bis* holds that the Ministry of the Environment shall integrate an inventory of waste, air, and water emissions under Federal jurisdiction, as well as a comprehensive system of environmental information based on the permits and licences granted by it.

---

50. According to Art. 111*bis* of Environmental Law, the following are considered fixed sources of federal jurisdiction: chemical, petroleum, and petrochemical industries, paints and inks, automotive, pulp and paper, metallurgy, glass, electric power generation, industry of asbestos, cement and lime, and treatment of hazardous waste.
51. Fifth paragraph of Art. 27 of the Mexican Federal Constitution listed those water bodies that are considered as national property. The list includes: waters of territorial sea in the extension and under the terms set forth by international law; over internal waters; waters of lagoons and estuaries permanently or intermittently connecting with the sea; those of natural inland lakes which are directly connected with streams constantly flowing; river waters and their direct and indirect tributaries, from the site of the riverbed where the first permanent, intermittent, or torrential waters start to flow, to their mouth in the sea, lakes, lagoons, or estuaries owned by the nation; those of constant or intermittent streams and their direct or indirect tributaries, whenever their beds along all the length of its way or in a portion thereof serve as a boundary line of national land territory or between two States, or when they flow from one State to another or cross the Republic's boundary line; those of lakes, lagoons, or estuaries whose beds, zones, or streams are crossed by boundary lines dividing one or more States or between the Republic and a neighbouring country, or when the stream shoreline serves as a boundary between two States or between the Republic and a neighbouring country; those of springs flowing from beaches, maritime areas, streams, basins, river beds, banks of lakes, lagoons, or estuaries owned by the Nation, and the ones extracted from mines; and the streams, beds, or banks of lakes and interior streams in the extensions established by the Law.
52. According to Art. 5, s. XII of the Waste Act, Great Generator: A person or company that generates an amount equal to or greater than 10 tons. In total gross weight of waste per year or its equivalent in another unit of measurement.

212. Finally, Article 109*bis* 1 establishes that the Secretariat shall set up the necessary mechanisms and procedures for the interested parties to obtain, through a single procedure, all permits, licences, or authorizations that must be granted by the Ministry of the Environment.

213. In the same vein, in 2004, the Regulation under the Environmental Act regarding the Register of emissions and transference of pollutants was published in the DOF. In line with the new Regulation, all sources of pollution subjected to federal jurisdiction are obliged to report to the Ministry of the Environment their emission and transference of pollutant to air, water, soil, subsoil, hazardous materials, and waste on an annual basis.

§4. Environmental Audits

214. In 1996, the Environmental Act was amended to introduce a section focused on self-regulation and the environmental audits integrated by Articles 38, 38*bis*, 38*bis* 1, and 38*bis* 2, and on 29 April 2010, the new Regulation under the Environmental Act regarding self-regulation and environmental audits was published in the DOF.[53] Environmental audits may be a more effective method to improve the environmental performance of companies than inspection and monitoring, but a scenario where the environmental authority waives its obligation to apply the Law and becomes a mere promoter of its fulfilment is not possible according to the provisions of the Political Constitution of the United Mexican States.

215. In accordance with Article 38*bis* of the Environmental Act, the environmental audit allows those in charge of the operation of a company to voluntarily carry out a methodological examination of their operations with respect to the pollution and the risk that they generate, as well as of the level of compliance with environmental regulations and the international parameters and good practices of applicable operation and engineering, with the intention of defining the necessary preventive and corrective measures to protect the environment.

216. The Ministry of Environment plays an essential role in environmental audits. Paragraph 2 of Article 38*bis* establishes that the Ministry of the Environment will develop programmes to stimulate the accomplishment of environmental audits and mentions that the Ministry shall supervise their realization. According to Article 38 *bis* 2, the local governments may establish systems of self-regulation and environmental audits within the scope of their respective competences.

53. However, the origins of the environmental audit in Mexico go back to 1992 when Attorney General Office for environmental Protection was created and within this a Deputy Attorney General in charge of this function. *See* the Agreement that regulates the organization and internal functioning of INE and PROFEPA published in the DOF on 13 Dec. 1996.

217. Those conducting environmental audits are legible to obtain the certificate of clean industry. The clean industry certificate is a document granted by the Attorney General's Office for Environmental Protection to those industries that have satisfactorily implemented the plan of action derived from an environmental audit. Nevertheless, this certificate does not grant any type of legal advantage over other companies that have not conducted an environmental audit, but simply a greater social acceptance and a better position in the market. Article 28 of the Environmental Act Regulations on Self-Regulation and Environmental Audits states:

> Article 28. In consideration of the activity carried out by the Companies, the Certificate issued by the Attorney General's Office shall have the following modalities:
>
> I. Clean industry: for works and activities of the industrial sector;
> II. Tourism environmental quality: for tourism sector activities and services, and
> III. Environmental quality: for those activities not contemplated in the two previous fractions.
>
> Each of these modalities will have different levels of Environmental Performance, according to the established in the Terms of Reference and based on this will be granted the corresponding Certificate.
>
> The Certificates will have a validity of two years counted from its notification.

218. Despite the voluntary nature of the environmental audit, the administrative authority plays an important role in the regulatory process derived from environmental auditing for a variety of reasons.

219. First, the second paragraph of Article 38*bis* states that the Ministry of the Environment will develop a programme aimed at stimulating the performance of environmental audits and mentions that, in its case, the aforementioned unit will supervise its execution with that purpose:

> I. Will elaborate the terms of reference that establish the methodology for the accomplishment of the environmental audits;
> II. Establish a system of approval and accreditation of environmental experts and auditors, determining the procedures and requirements that must be met by interested parties to join the system, and, if applicable, comply with the provisions of the Law on Metrology and Standardization.
>
> To this end, a technical committee composed of representatives of research institutions, colleges and professional associations and organizations of the industrial sector will be integrated;
>
> III. Develop training programs in the area of expertise and environmental audits;

IV. It will implement a recognition and stimulus system that allows to identify the industries that fulfil in a timely manner the commitments acquired in the environmental audits;
V. Promote the creation of regional centres to support the medium and small industry, in order to facilitate the performance of audits in these sectors, and
VI. It will be agreed or with physical or moral persons, public or private, to carry out environmental audits.

220. Second, in accordance with Articles 2, section I and 33 of the Regulations under the Environmental Act on Self-Regulation and Environmental Audit, the entities responsible for conducting the environmental audit have the character of *verification units*, that is, to say, bodies whose power of verification is granted by the authority in terms of Articles 68 of the Law on Metrology and Standardization and 87 of its Regulations.

221. Third, in accordance with Articles 15 and 16 of the Environmental Act Regulations, the environmental authority is aware of the outcome of the environmental audit.

222. Finally, based on the audit report, the environmental authority decides whether to grant the corresponding certificate.

223. Because of this hybrid character, conducting environmental audits frequently leads to a conflict between the authority's obligation to apply the law through the inspection and monitoring procedure and the voluntary commitment assumed by the polluting sources to carry out the action plan derived from an environmental audit.

224. Therefore, environmental audits involve a certain level of secret agreement between regulated subjects and the authority to break the law without facing the consequences.

225. To avoid this irregular appearance, environmental audits should focus on those areas of environmental protection where the government does not have sufficient information to issue regulations and where private actors have sufficient information, capacity, and experience to self-regulate.

226. Finally, although the Environmental Act chapter subject to analysis refers to both environmental audits and self-regulation, this last aspect is not developed in the law or its regulations, since it is exclusively identified with environmental auditing, which, as we have seen, does not have that character of self-regulation, but it is a process of certification.

Chapter 2. Air Pollution

227. Air pollution is a widespread problem in the country's large metropolitan areas, although it has assumed critical levels in the Megalopolis of Mexico City. For this reason, this geographic space has the best-documented information and where they have also tried to establish more rigorous public policies. Thus, with the legislative and administrative measures adopted, it has been possible to reduce the emission of certain pollutants such as lead, sulphur dioxide, or total suspended particles. However, in the same Megalopolis, it is observed that certain pollutants have reached unacceptable levels whose effects are serious for both human health and ecosystems.

228. This is the case of photochemical oxidants, and in particular ozone, whose levels are above the standards on more than 85% of the days of the year. Another case would be that of suspended particles smaller than 10 μm in aerodynamic diameter (μm10) whose concentrations are cause for morbidity and mortality in the population. Together with the above, Mexico has assumed concrete commitments with the international community to reduce certain pollutants, such as those that affect the ozone layer or contribute to climate change.

229. Mexican legislation in this area has advanced substantially in recent years, supporting better environmental management, but it is undeniable that much remains to be done about these problems.

230. Since the 1970s, concern about the consumption of fossil fuels has increased throughout the world, not only because they are not renewable but also because during their production and consumption process, there are negative impacts on the environment and human health. In fact, the consumption of fossil fuels by industries and vehicles is the most important cause of the so-called global warming, which has been considered one of the most important problems facing humanity.

231. According to David G. Victor, more than three-quarters of today's net carbon dioxide emissions are the result of burning fossil fuels, while the remaining quarter of net CO2 emissions are the result of human-induced landscape alterations.[54]

232. Similarly, a report by the UNEP shows that CO2 concentrations are responsible for more than 60% of the increase in greenhouse gas emissions,[55] while many other gases such as methane (CH4) and nitrogen oxide (N2O) contribute less to this effect.

54. Víctor David G. *The Collapse of Kyoto Protocol and the Struggle to Show the Global Warming*. Princeton, New Jersey, Princeton University Press, 2001, p. 119.
55. *See*: *The Greenhouse Effect and the Carbon Cycle*. Available at: http://unfcc.int/ess.

233. Although greenhouse gases have long been present in small amounts in the atmosphere,[56] it was not until 1970 that scientists discovered a dangerous increase in such emissions attributable to human activities that were accelerating the natural 'greenhouse effect' and were having a noticeable impact on 'climate change'.[57]

234. In fact, over the past ten years, CO2 emissions have increased faster than the ability of natural sinks to capture that CO2 through the process of photosynthesis. As a result of this imbalance, the average global temperature has increased by 0.6°C over the last century.[58]

235. In general, industrialized countries are responsible for most of the historical and current CO2 emissions. For example, the US, the countries of the European Union, and the members of the former Soviet Union, as well as some emerging economies in Asia, produce 60% of the 'greenhouse gases'. This explains why the Kyoto Protocol, which is aimed at reducing CO2 emissions by the most polluting countries, required the consent of those countries rather than the participation of most developing countries to enter into force.

236. Mexico is responsible for no more than 1.5% of the world's carbon emissions from fossil fuel combustion, making it the 15th largest in the world. However, its CO2 emissions are concentrated in major metropolitan areas such as Mexico City, Guadalajara, Monterrey, Ciudad Juarez, Toluca, and Mexicali, where 266,738 tons of CO2 are generated each year, causing significant damage to the environment and human health. In fact, Mexico City is considered one of the most polluted cities in the world.

237. Thus, CO2 emissions from fossil fuel consumption rose from 83.96 million metric tons in 1990 to 101.9 million metric tons by 2000. Although in 2001, they decreased to 96.05, in general terms, during the last ten years, the per capita emissions of CO2 in our country have grown more than 20% due to the increase in the use of natural gas and oil. Transport, especially private cars, is the main cause of CO2 emissions. It contributes 70% of total emissions.

238. According to available data, Mexico's fossil fuel consumption increased from 40,000,000 metric tons of oil equivalent in 1970 to 130,612,000 in 1999, including coal and coal products (6,489), crude oil and liquid natural gas (84,928), and natural gas (30,952); these figures represent almost the same amount consumed by all Central American and Caribbean countries. Again, industry (33,461) and vehicles (36,353) are the main causes of this increase.

---

56. Lakshman D. Guruswamy et al., *International Environmental Law and the World Order. A Problem-Oriented Course Book.* St. Paul Minnesota, West Publishing Co., 1994, p. 1001.
57. *See*: Patricia D. Park, *Energy Law and the Environment.* EUA y Canada, Taylor and Francis Inc., 2002, p. 173.
58. *See*: The World Bank, *Fuel for Thought. An Environmental Strategy for Energy Sector.* Washington, The World Bank, 2000, p. 31.

§1. INTERNATIONAL TREATIES ON AIR POLLUTION

I. The Vienna Convention for the Protection of the Ozone Layer and the Montreal Protocol

239. The Vienna Convention was signed in Vienna on 22 March 1985 and ratified by Mexico on 22 December 1987; its basic objective is to protect human health and the environment from adverse effects derived from human activities that modify or may modify the stratospheric ozone layer that provides protection against the sun's ultraviolet rays.

240. The document sets out the general obligation of contracting parties to adopt appropriate measures aimed at preventing the exhaustion of the ozone layer, as well as to achieve the control and reduction of the emissions levels of specific substances known to exhaust it. Accordingly, the Convention provides that signatory parties shall cooperate with each other in the field of research and systematic observations, as well as in the legal, scientific, and technical fields, with the relevant information being transmitted.

241. The Vienna Convention is complemented by the following international instruments:

(a) Protocol on Substances that Deplete the Ozone Layer, adopted in Montreal on 16 September 1987, which concerns chlorofluorocarbons. This protocol is known as the Montreal Protocol.
(b) Adjustments to the Montreal Protocol on Substances that Deplete the Ozone Layer, adopted in London on 29 June 1990.
(c) Amendment to the Montreal Protocol, which, among other things, established the Multilateral Ozone Fund to carry out activities to fulfil the purposes of the Convention, adopted on 29 June 1990.

242. Forty-six countries signed the Montreal Protocol, including Mexico, which approved it on 25 January 1988.

243. The Montreal Protocol establishes some rules in order to implement the provisions of the Vienna Convention, mainly through control measures that consist of the commitment of the parties to progressively reduce the level of consumption of the substances listed in Annex A of the Protocol and which are called ozone-depleting substances.

244. The goal of the Montreal Protocol is that from 1 July 1998 to 30 June 1999, in each twelve-month period thereafter, the calculated level of consumption of each part of the controlled substances listed in Group I of Annex A should not exceed 50% of their calculated level of consumption for 1986. In addition, the protocol sets out measures to control trade with non-parties to the protocol by committing each contracting party to prohibit the import of controlled substances from those states and not to export them to those states.

245. However, developing countries are considered in a special way by the protocol, since it establishes rules that allow in certain cases a postponement of compliance with control measures that seek to facilitate the use of alternative technologies and substitute products by those countries.

246. In 1990, the Amendment to the Montreal Protocol was adopted in London, which was accepted by Mexico and entered into force on 10 August 1992. This amendment sets higher targets for the disappearance of ozone-depleting substances.

II. The United Nations Framework Convention on Climate Change and its Protocols

247. The United Nations Framework Convention on Climate Change was adopted in New York on 9 May 1992. This Convention has, according to its Article 2, the objective of achieving 'stabilization of greenhouse gas concentrations in the atmosphere at a level that prevents dangerous anthropocentric interference with the climate system', and, according to the same article, that level must be achieved within a period sufficient to allow ecosystems to adapt naturally to climate change, ensure that food production is not threatened and allow economic development to continue in a sustainable manner.

248. This Convention contains two types of commitments, those assumed by all parties and those to be assumed by developed countries.

249. Article 4, paragraph 1 provides that all parties, considering their common but differentiated responsibilities and the specificity of their national and regional development priorities, objectives, and circumstances, undertake a commitment to develop, update, and publish their national inventories of artificial emissions of all greenhouse gases not controlled by the Montreal Protocol. In addition, the parties commit themselves to formulate national and regional programmes that contain measures to mitigate and adapt to climate change and its effects; to promote and cooperate in the development of practices and processes for the control, reduction or prevention of artificial emissions from all relevant sectors of the economy; to promote cooperation in the conservation and improvement of greenhouse gas sinks and reservoirs; to take climate change considerations into account when formulating social, economic and environmental policies; to promote and cooperate in scientific and technological research; and to exchange all relevant information.

250. However, paragraph 2 of Article 4 of the Convention establishes that the parties that are developed countries and the other parties included in Annex I, among which are the largest generators of greenhouse gases, assume some specific commitments, which mainly consist of the obligation of adopting national policies and taking the corresponding measures to mitigate climate change, limiting their anthropogenic emissions of such gases and protecting and improving their sinks and deposits.

251. These policies, according to the Convention, should demonstrate that developed countries are taking the lead in modifying longer-term trends in anthropogenic emissions of carbon dioxide and other greenhouse gases, recognizing that a return, before the end of the 1990s, to previous levels of such emissions would contribute to modifying these trends. In addition, these parties undertake to submit, within six months of the entry into force of the convention for each of them and periodically, detailed information to the Conference of the Parties concerning policies and measures adopted, as well as the resulting projections of anthropogenic greenhouse gas emissions by sources and sink absorption for that period, with a view to either individually or jointly returning to 1990 emission levels.

252. However, Article 4 paragraph 3 states that developed country parties and other developed parties listed in Annex II shall provide new and additional financial resources to cover the agreed full costs that developing country parties incur in meeting their obligations.

253. Signatory parties of this Agreement are divided into three categories. Annex I includes developed countries as well as emerging economies. Annex II lists the countries that must give economic and technological support to the signatory parties with fewer resources to face the effects of climate change. Finally, there is a group called 'non-Annex I countries' which includes developing countries (e.g., Mexico) that are not part of either Annex I or Annex II.

254. Under this international agreement, all signatory countries, taking into account their common but differentiated responsibilities and their priorities, objectives, and circumstances, have general obligations such as to: (1) develop national inventories of anthropogenic emissions by sources and removals by sinks of greenhouse gases not controlled by the Montreal Protocol; (2) formulate and implement national and, where appropriate, regional programmes containing measures to mitigate climate change taking into account emissions and removals as well as facilitating adequate adaptation to climate change; (3) promote and cooperate in the diffusion of technologies, practices, and processes that reduce or prevent anthropogenic emissions of greenhouse gases not controlled by the Montreal Protocol; (4) promote the proper management, conservation, and enhancement of sinks and reservoirs of these greenhouse gases; and (5) cooperate in preparing for and adapting to the impacts of climate change.

255. As a Framework Treaty, this Convention contains only non-binding recommendations for industrialized countries to return to 1990 emission levels of CO2 and other gases (not controlled by the Montreal Protocol) by the year 2000.

256. By the mid-1990s, however, most of these countries had not returned anthropogenic greenhouse gas emissions to 1990 levels. On the contrary, overall global anthropogenic emissions of almost all greenhouse gases, particularly CO2, continued to increase.

257. To stop this trend, the Kyoto Protocol to the Framework Convention on Climate Change was adopted at the Third Conference of the Parties in December 1997.

258. In 1997, the Kyoto Protocol was approved, establishing binding targets for reducing greenhouse gas emissions in thirty-seven industrialized countries and the European Union, which are primarily responsible for the high levels of these gases caused by the burning of fossil fuels for more than one hundred and fifty years. This Protocol obliged several countries to establish laws and policies to meet their commitments and thus strengthen the strategy to combat climate change problems at the local level. The Kyoto Protocol targets range from an obligation to reduce emissions by 8% (for the European Union and many Central European countries) to an authorization to increase emissions by 10% (Iceland) and 8% (Australia).

259. The Kyoto Protocol's reduction targets only apply to thirty-eight industrialized countries and countries with emerging economies. The basic obligation accepted by Annex I countries is to ensure that their aggregate anthropogenic carbon dioxide emissions of the gases listed in the Annex do not exceed their assigned amounts, with a view to reducing their excess emissions of such gases by at least 5% below 1990 levels within the commitment period 2008–2012 (Article 3).

260. However, as Yamin Farhana explains:

> countries bound by the Kyoto Protocol can meet their reduction obligations through domestic efforts to reduce greenhouse gases (GHG) in other countries at a lower cost than it would be to do so locally through the three flexible mechanisms established by the Protocol: joint implementation, the clean development mechanism and international emissions trading.[59]

261. Emissions trading is only applicable to Annex I (cc) parties with commitments in Annex B (of the Protocol), i.e., countries that have mandatory targets under the Protocol. According to Article 17 of the Protocol:

> The Conference of the Parties shall define the relevant principles, modalities, rules and guidelines, in particular for verification, reporting and accountability for emissions trading. The Parties included in Annex B may participate in emissions trading for the purposes of fulfilling their commitments under Article 3. Any such trading shall be supplemental to domestic actions for the purpose of meeting quantified emission limitation and reduction commitments under that Article.

262. These modalities were added in Marrakech, after four years of negotiations.

---

59. Yamin Farhana, *Climate Change in Carbón Markets. A Handbook of Emissions Reduction Mechanisms.* RU, Earthscan, 2005, p. XXXIX.

263. According to the Marrakesh Accords, explains Yamin Farhana, Annex B parties 'shall have access to units of the assigned quantity and, subject to the modalities agreed at Marrakesh, and not otherwise, may transfer and acquire those units and the wide range of Kyoto units from one to another to meet their commitments under Article 3.1'.[60]

264. This means that Annex B parties can meet their commitments under the Kyoto Protocol by buying or acquiring credits that represent greenhouse gas reductions in other countries. This mechanism allows an Annex I country to purchase emission reduction credits from another Annex I country where they could be more cost-efficient than generating a domestic reduction (Article 17).

265. As Kirby mentioned, emissions trading can occur at three levels: (1) state-state trading; (2) state-private entity trading; and (3) private entity trading.[61]

266. Joint implementation allows industrialized countries to obtain credits when they implement specific projects that reduce emissions together. Article 6 states that for the purpose of meeting its commitments under Article 3, any Party included in Annex I may transfer to or acquire from any other of these Parties, emission reduction units resulting from projects aimed at reducing anthropogenic emissions by sources or increasing anthropogenic removals by sinks of greenhouse gases in any sector of the economy. However, the acquisition of emission reduction units must be complementary to domestic actions taken to meet the commitments under Article 3. As already mentioned, this mechanism is only applicable to Annex I countries, but this does not prevent a subsidiary company of a non-Annex I country located in a country that is a party to the Kyoto Protocol from participating in a joint implementation project.

267. Finally, the Clean Development Mechanism allows industrialized nations to obtain credits by implementing projects in developing nations. According to the second paragraph of Article 12, the purpose of the clean development mechanism is to assist non-Annex I Parties to achieve sustainable development and contribute to the ultimate objective of the Convention, as well as to assist Annex I Parties to meet their quantified emission limitation and reduction commitments under Article 3.

268. The objective of this mechanism is to provide geographic flexibility and reduce the cost of meeting the Kyoto targets. The Kyoto Protocol did not introduce new obligations for developing countries, at least for the initial phase. However, as explained above, developing countries can participate in the Clean Development Mechanism.

---

60. Yamin Farhana, *The International Rules of the Kioto Protocol and Carbon Markets. A Handbook of Emissions Reduction Mechanism.* UK, Earthscan, 2015, p. 27.
61. Peter Kirbi, 'Emissions Trading in the International Context: Kioto Implementation and International Trade Agreements', in Mar Campins Eritja (coord.), *Los retos de la aplicación del Protocolo de Kioto en España y Canadá* Barcelona, Atelier, 2005, p. 96.

269. This is the case of Mexico, which is a party to the Kyoto Protocol but has no obligation to reduce its CO2 emissions because it is considered a 'non-Annex' country of the Convention and is not included in Annex B of the Protocol.

270. In 2015, during the twenty-first Conference of the Contracting Parties to the United Nations Framework Convention on Climate Change, the Paris Agreement was adopted in which the signatory countries committed themselves to reduce their carbon emissions as soon as possible in order to maintain global warming 'well below 2°C'. However, as with the Kyoto Protocol, this agreement would enter into force when fifty-five countries representing at least 55% of global emissions have deposited their instruments of ratification.

III. Treaty on Principles Governing the Activities of States in the Exploration and Use of Outer Space, Including the Moon and Other Celestial Bodies

271. In 1967, the Treaty on Principles Governing the Activities of States in the Exploration and Use of Outer Space, including the Moon and Other Celestial Bodies, was adopted. For Mexico, this treaty entered into force on 31 January 1968. Fundamentally, the treaty refers to the fact that the exploration and use of outer space are open to all mankind and will not lead to the appropriation of that space by any country, as well as establishing a ban on placing objects carrying nuclear weapons and other weapons of mass destruction in outer space, obliging contracting countries to use the moon and other celestial bodies for exclusively peaceful purposes. The Treaty also provides that contracting countries shall avoid harmful pollution of outer space and adverse changes to the Earth's environment resulting from the introduction of extra-terrestrial material into outer space.

IV. Convention on Cooperation for the Protection and Improvement of the Environment in the Border Area (Peace Convention)

272. This Convention, signed in La Paz (Baja California, Mexico) on 14 August 1983, entered into force on 16 February 1984 and established the agreement between Mexico and the US to coordinate their efforts in accordance with their own national legislation and bilateral agreements in force to address air, land, and water pollution in the border area (Article 5). In this sense, this convention has two annexes relating to air pollution. 'Annex IV on cooperation between Mexico and the US on transboundary air pollution caused by copper smelters' and 'Annex V on international transport and urban air pollution'.

273. The first seeks to reduce air pollution produced by copper smelters in the border area.

274. The second annex seeks to ensure the reduction of air pollution concentrations for the benefit of citizens living in urban areas along the US-Mexico border and, to that end, Article II establishes general obligations for each of the parties, highlighting the obligation to conduct air quality monitoring.

V. Agreement on the Protection and Improvement of the Environment in the Border Zone (Mexico-Guatemala)

275. This agreement was signed between Mexico and Guatemala (in Guatemala City, Guatemala) on 10 April 1987 and entered into force on 22 March 1988, establishing as objectives: cooperation between both countries in the tasks of environmental protection and improvement and conservation of natural resources in the border area, on the basis of equality, reciprocity, and mutual benefit, in accordance with their respective laws, regulations, and national policies in the field.

276. To achieve these objectives, the parties commit themselves, as far as possible, to adopt measures to prevent, reduce, and eliminate in their territory the sources of pollution affecting the border area.

VI. The Convention Between the United Mexican States and Belize on the Protection and Improvement of the Environment and the Conservation of Natural Resources in the Border Zone

277. This Convention was signed in the city of Belmopan, Belize, on 20 September 1991 and was ratified by the Mexican Senate on 20 December of the same year. Article 1 of the Convention establishes the agreement between the countries to cooperate among themselves in the tasks of environmental protection and improvement and the conservation of natural resources in the border area, on the basis of equality, reciprocity, and mutual benefit and in accordance with their respective laws, regulations, and national policies on the matter.

278. Likewise, both countries commit themselves, to the extent possible, to adopt appropriate measures to prevent, reduce and eliminate in their respective territories, the sources of contamination that affect the border zone, as well as the sources of deterioration and degradation of the habitats and wild populations found in the border zone.

VII. The Paris Agreement

279. The Paris Agreement was adopted on 12 December 2015, during the 21st Conference of the Parties (COP 21) to the United Nations Framework Convention on Climate Change.[62] This instrument has already been ratified by more than fifty-five countries that account for 55% of global emissions of greenhouse gases, so it entered into force on 4 November 2016, but its implementation began in 2020.

280. Confirming Article 2, the Paris Agreement aims to 'strengthen the global response to the threat of climate change, in the context of sustainable development and efforts to eradicate poverty'. To achieve this objective, the Agreement proposes the following actions:

(a) holding the increase in the global average temperature to well below 2°C above pre-industrial levels and pursuing efforts to limit the temperature increase to 1.5°C above pre-industrial levels, recognizing that this would significantly reduce the risks and impacts of climate change.
(b) increasing the ability to adapt to the adverse impacts of climate change and foster climate resilience and low greenhouse gas emissions development, in a manner that does not threaten food production; and
(c) making finance flows consistent with a pathway towards low greenhouse gas emissions and climate-resilient development.

281. Pursuant to Article 6 of the Agreement, Mexico has published its nine voluntary commitments:

(1) 50% reduction in pollutant emissions, compared to those generated in 2000. However, the ministry warned that before 2020 there will be a peak in emissions after the implementation of the energy reform 'due to a greater supply of natural gas and the introduction of clean energy', said a presentation of the ministry.
(2) There will be 25% less greenhouse compound emissions. According to the ministry, greenhouse gases will be reduced by 22% and black carbon by 51% to reach the target.
(3) 43 out of 100 energy sources will be clean. That is to say, they will come from renewable sources, in cogeneration with natural gas and thermoelectric plants with carbon dioxide capture. An advance of 35% is expected by 2024. In addition, the country pledged to promote the domestic use of solar heaters and cells.
(4) Eliminate 25 of every 100 controlled methane leaks and burns.
(5) Achieve zero deforestation through commercial forest plantations and restoration of natural ecosystems.
(6) Guarantee and monitor the treatment of urban and industrial waste water in human settlements with more than 500,000 inhabitants.
(7) To homologate environmental regulations for vehicles and to have ultra-low sulfur gasoline and diesel.
(8) Recovery and use of methane in municipal sanitary landfills and waste water treatment plants.

62. The Agreement was opened for signature on 22 Apr. 2016, the date on which Earth Day is celebrated.

(9) Installation of biodigesters in agricultural farms and recovery of pastures, as well as technification of the Mexican countryside.

§2. National Legislation on Air Pollution

I. Background

282. The Civil Code for the Federal District in Matters of Common Jurisdiction and the entire Republic in Matter of Federal Jurisdiction passed in 1928 dealt with the prevention and control of air pollution, although not from an environmental perspective, but as part of the regulations relating to so-called neighbourhood relations.

283. Thus, Article 845 of the Civil Code prohibited the construction of chimneys near another's wall or for the installation of establishments intended for dangerous or harmful uses, without keeping the distances prescribed in the applicable regulations.

284. The Sanitary Code of the United Mexican States of 1934 included within the chapters denominated 'Of the Health of the workers' and 'Sanitary Engineering', precepts that must be observed in the industrial or commercial activities where emissions to the atmosphere are generated. Within the first of these chapters, when regulating the conditions that 'workplaces' must cover, it is foreseen that the establishments are classified as industrial and commercial, and in both cases, they could be 'harmless, annoying, unhealthy and dangerous' (Article 230).

285. The Health Code also stated that the conditions for its operation and the necessary measures to protect neighbours from nuisance, unhealthy and dangerous establishments would be determined in the regulations issued (Article 231).

286. The chapter on 'Sanitary Engineering' provided that constructions intended for 'factories, workshops or industries' and other buildings, must meet the conditions of sanitary engineering provided for in the law itself, as well as others determined in the relevant regulation (Articles 262, 264, 273, 275 and 282).

287. Based on the aforementioned precepts, on 25 October 1940, the Regulation for Industrial or Commercial Establishments, Nuisance, Unhealthy or Dangerous was issued, published in DOF of the same year.

288. Air pollution went from being a sanitary concern to becoming an environmental concern both in the Federal Law for the Prevention and Control of Environmental Pollution, as well as its Regulations for the Prevention and Control of Pollution Originating from the Emission of Smokes and Dusts, published in the DOF on 23 March 1971 and 17 September 1971, respectively.

289. In addition, based on the aforementioned Law and Regulations, various technical standards on the prevention and control of air pollution were issued.

290. On 11 February 1982, the Federal Law on Environmental Protection was published in the DOF, which in matters of air pollution practically does not modify the provisions established by the previous Law. Under this Law, several Official Mexican Norms were also issued to complement those issued under the 1971 law. The 1982 law was repealed in 1988 by the Environmental Act which includes a chapter on air pollution, but specifically, the phenomenon of climate change as an associated matter of air pollution is the subject of the 2012 Climate Change Act.

II. Currently in Force Legislation

291. In Mexico, as mentioned above, air pollution is regulated at the federal level by the Environmental Act, its Regulations on Prevention and Control of Air Pollution and Registration of Emissions and Transfer of Pollutants, and the Climate Change Act and Regulations on National Registry of Emissions, as well as the Official Mexican Norms in this area. At the local level, in accordance with Article 73, section XXIX-G of the Constitution and the above-mentioned general laws, local legislatures have also issued laws on ecological balance and environmental protection and laws on climate change. Both legislative categories will be analysed in this chapter.

A. The Environmental Act

292. The Environmental Act refers to the prevention and control of air pollution in the second chapter of its Title IV, 'Prevention and Control of Atmospheric Pollution'. This chapter is composed of only six articles that refer to the aspects discussed below.

293. First, in Article 110 of the Environmental Act indicates the criteria that have to be taken into account for air protection. These criteria are as follows:

(a) Air quality must be satisfactory in all human settlements and regions of the country.
(b) To ensure air quality is satisfactory for the well-being of the population and for ecological balance, pollutant emissions, whether from fixed or mobile, artificial or natural sources, should be reduced and controlled.

294. Now, in accordance with section X of Article 3 of the Environmental Act, the criteria are defined as 'the mandatory guidelines contained in this law, to guide the actions of preservation and restoration of ecological balance, sustainable use of natural resources and protection of the environment, which will have the character of instruments of environmental policy'.

295. However, Article 113 of the Environmental Act establishes that pollutants that cause or could cause ecological imbalances or damage to the environment must not be emitted into the atmosphere, so that all emissions into the atmosphere must comply with the provisions of the Environmental Act, its regulations, and the respective Official Mexican Norms. Now, according to our legislation, pollution that affects the atmosphere provides two types of sources: fixed and mobile.

296. The Environmental Act does not define these concepts, but Article 6 section IV of its 1988 Regulations on the Prevention and Control of Air Pollution establishes that a fixed source is any installation established in a single place, the purpose of which is to develop industrial, commercial or service operations or processes or activities which generate or may generate polluting emissions into the atmosphere.

297. However, this same article in its section V considers as mobile sources aeroplanes, helicopters, railways, trams, tractors, integral buses, trucks, automobiles, motorcycles, boats, non-fixed equipment, and machinery with combustion engines and similar that generate or could generate polluting emissions to the atmosphere.

298. The Environmental Act established as one of its objectives prevention and control of air pollution (Article 1, section VI), indicating in Articles 5, 7, 8 and 9 that it corresponds to the Federal government regulation of air pollution from all types of emitting sources, while the prevention and control of air pollution correspond to the federal authorities only when it is a matter of fixed and mobile sources of federal jurisdiction. Article 111 establishes the powers of the Ministry of the Environment to control, reduce or prevent atmospheric pollution, among these powers are those of:

- To issue the official Mexican Norms in matters of environmental quality of the different areas, zones or regions of the national territory; maximum permissible levels of emission of odours, gases as well as solid and liquid particles into the atmosphere; for the establishment and operation of air quality monitoring systems; for the certification by the competent authority, of the levels of emission of pollutants into the atmosphere from determined sources, among others.
- To integrate and maintain the updated inventory of the sources emitting pollutants to the atmosphere of federal jurisdiction, and to coordinate with the local governments for the integration of the national and regional inventory.
- To formulate and apply programmes for the reduction of the emission of pollutants to the atmosphere.
- To promote and technically support local governments in the formulation and application of air quality management programmes.
- To require the responsible parties to comply with the maximum permissible pollutant emission limits.
- To define maximum permissible levels of emission of pollutants into the atmosphere by sources, areas, zones or regions, in such a way that the assimilation capacities of the atmospheric basins are not exceeded and official Mexican air quality standards are complied with.

- To promote, in coordination with the competent authorities, systems of transferable rights for the emission of pollutants into the atmosphere.
- To approve air quality management programmes prepared by local governments.
- To promote the application of new technologies with the purpose of reducing their emissions to the atmosphere.
- To promote, in coordination with the Secretariat of Energy, local governments in the formulation and application of programmes to prevent, reduce and control light pollution.

299. In its Article 111*bis*, the Environmental Act states that the chemical, petroleum and petrochemical, paint and inks, automotive, cellulose and paper, metallurgy, glass, electric power generation, cement and lime, and hazardous waste treatment industries are fixed sources of federal jurisdiction. Consequently, any other fixed source of air pollution does not fall within the scope of the provision invoked and it is considered to be of local jurisdiction and, therefore, subject to the provisions of state law.

300. However, the law does not specify which are the mobile sources of local jurisdiction, but in the light of the Environmental Act Regulations on the Prevention and Control of Atmospheric Pollution, it can be concluded that, as a general rule, mobile sources of air pollution are of local jurisdiction unless they are motor vehicles that require a concession granted by the federal authority to circulate, as may be the case of passenger or cargo motor transport, railways, or aeroplanes, as well as motor vehicles until they leave the production plant (Article 11 fraction II, f and g, Articles 31 and 32).

301. Prevention and control of air pollution generated by fixed or mobile sources of local jurisdiction is under the jurisdiction of both local and municipal governments, according to the following rules:

(1) The States and the Federal District are responsible for the prevention and control of atmospheric pollution generated by fixed sources that function as industrial establishments, as well as by mobile sources, which according to the provisions of the Law do not fall under federal jurisdiction.
(2) The application of legal provisions concerning the prevention and control of air pollution generated by fixed sources operating as commercial or service establishments, as well as the emission of pollutants into the atmosphere from mobile sources that are not considered to fall under federal jurisdiction.

1. Pollutant Emissions from Fixed Sources

302. The Environmental Act and its regulations attempt to rule out air pollution by imposing both technical and administrative obligations on fixed sources.

a. Administrative Obligations

303. Among the administrative obligations are to: obtain the Single Environmental License, integrate the inventory of emissions, submit the certificate of operation before the authority, and keep the corresponding logs.

i. The Operating License and the Integrated Environmental License

304. Article 111*bis* of the Environmental Act states that for the operation and functioning of fixed sources of federal jurisdiction that emit or may emit odours, gases or solid or liquid particles into the atmosphere, the authorization of the Ministry shall be required. This authorization, in accordance with Article 18 of the Environmental Act Regulations on the Prevention and Control of Air Pollution, is referred to as an 'operating license'.

305. However, Article 109*bis* 1 of the Environmental Act obliges the Ministry of the Environment to establish the necessary mechanisms and procedures, with the purpose that the interested parties carry out only one process, in those cases in which for the operation and functioning of industrial, commercial or service establishments, it is required to obtain various permits, licences, or authorizations that must be granted by the Ministry itself. Based on this provision, the Integrated Environmental License has been established as an administrative simplification mechanism, merging in a single document the operating licence, the authorization for the generation of hazardous waste, and the waste-water discharge permit, but which in no way has a regulatory character different from that of the different permits or authorizations that it integrates.

ii. The Inventory of Emissions

306. According to Article 17, fraction II of the Environmental Act Regulations on the Prevention and Control of Air Pollution, those responsible for fixed sources must integrate an inventory of their air pollutant, as well as measure and record their results in the format determined by the Ministry of the Environment and submit the records to Ministry upon request.

307. Measurements of air pollutant emissions shall be carried out in accordance with the sampling and quantification procedures established in the corresponding Official Mexican Norms. In order to evaluate the total emission of atmospheric pollutants from multiple sources, the individual emissions from existing chimneys must be added together (Article 26 of the Environmental Act Regulations on the Prevention and Control of Air Pollution).

iii. The Annual Certificate for Operation

308. The operation certificate is, in accordance with section II of the Environmental Act Regulation on the Registration of Emissions and Transfer of Pollutants, the instrument for reporting and compiling information on emissions and transfer of pollutants to the air, water, soil and subsoil, hazardous materials, and waste, used to update the registry's database. This database is defined in *section Iter* of the same provision as the set of information stored in an orderly and logical way in a computer system.

309. However, Article 21 of the Environmental Act Regulation on the Prevention and Control of Air Pollution states that the certificate of operation must be presented annually by those responsible for the fixed sources, who have previously obtained their operating licence. This certificate contains the update of the information that was included when the latter was requested and must be sent to the authority within the period between 1 March and 30 June of each year.

310. Article 11 of the Environmental Act Regulations on Registration of Emissions and Transfer of Pollutants also states that the certificate of operation must be presented between 1 March and 30 June of each year but does not subject this obligation to the condition that the Single Environmental License has been previously obtained. These Regulations state that regulated entities must report on the annual certificate of operation the period of operations carried out by the establishment subject to report from 1 January to 31 December of the immediately preceding year.

311. The Environmental Act Regulations on Registration of Emissions and Transfer of Pollutants indicates in its Article 9 that the following subjects are obliged to present the annual certificate of operation:

(1) those indicated in the second paragraph of Article 111*bis* of the Law, including those who carry out activities in the Hydrocarbons Sector;
(2) the generators of hazardous waste in terms of the applicable provisions, and
(3) those that discharge waste water into receiving bodies that are national waters.

312. Finally, it should be noted that according to Article 10 of the Environmental Act Regulations on Registration of Emissions and Transfer of Pollutants, the annual certificate of operation must contain the following information:

(1) Identification data and signature of the promoter, name of the individual, or name or corporate name of the company, Federal Taxpayer Registry, and address or other means to hear and receive notifications.
(2) Identification data of the establishment subject to federal jurisdiction report, which will include its domicile and geographic location, expressed in geographical coordinates or Universal Transverse of Mercator.

(3) Administrative data, in which will be expressed: date of the beginning of operations, capital participation, Chamber to which it is affiliated, if applicable, data of the Headquarter or Corporate to which it belongs, number of personnel employed, and work periods.

(4) The general technical information of the establishment, which will include the diagram of operation and functioning that will describe the productive process from the input and its transformation, until the emission, discharge, generation of hazardous waste or total or partial transfer of pollutants is produced, as well as data on inputs, products, by-products and energy consumption used.

(5) That relating to emissions of pollutants into the atmosphere, which shall include the characteristics of the machinery, equipment or activity that generates them, describing the point of generation and the type of emission, as well as the characteristics of the chimneys and ducts that discharge these emissions. In the case of atmospheric pollutants whose emission is regulated in Official Mexican Norms, the results of sampling and analysis carried out in accordance with such standards must also be reported. The information referred to in this fraction shall also be reported per contaminant.

(6) The information regarding the use of water, record of discharges and transfer of pollutants and substances to water, which will report the sources of extraction of water, general data on discharges, including those made to receiving bodies and sewerage, as well as the characteristics of such discharges.

(7) That inherent to the generation and transfer of hazardous waste, which will contain the generator's registration number, the generation and transfer data of hazardous waste, including their storage within the establishment, as well as their treatment and final disposal.

(8) Information concerning the release and transfer of those substances determined by the Ministry to be subject to reporting in the corresponding Official Mexican Standard, as well as data related to their production, manufacture or use.

(9) The information referring to those emissions or transfers derived from accidents, contingencies, leaks or spills, start of operations and scheduled shutdowns, which must be reported for each event that has taken place, including open-pit combustion.

(10) That relating to the prevention and management of pollution, in which the prevention activities are carried out at the source and their area of application, as well as those of reuse, recycling, energy generation, treatment, control or final disposal of the substances referred to in section VIII of this article shall be described.

iv. The Obligation to Keep Logs

313. According to Article 17 section VI of the Environmental Act Regulation on the Prevention and Control of Air Pollution, those responsible for fixed sources are obliged to keep a log of the operation and maintenance of their process and control equipment.

b. Technical Obligations

314. The technical obligations of those responsible for fixed sources of air pollution are contained in Articles 17, 23, 24, 26, and 27 of the Environmental Act Regulation on the Prevention and Control of Air Pollution, these obligations are to:

(1) use equipment and systems that control emissions into the atmosphere, so that they do not exceed the maximum permissible levels established in the corresponding Official Mexican Norms (Article 17 section II);
(2) install sampling platforms and ports (Article 17 section III);
(3) carry out perimeter monitoring of their polluting emissions into the atmosphere when the source in question is located in urban or suburban areas when its borders protected natural areas, and when, in the opinion of the Ministry, their operating characteristics or their raw materials, products and by-products may cause serious deterioration to ecosystems (Article 17 section IV);
(4) send advance notice to the Ministry of the start of operation of its processes, in the case of programmed shutdowns, and immediately in the case of circumstantial shutdowns, if they may cause pollution (Article 17 section VII);
(5) immediately notify the Ministry in the event of failure of the control equipment, so that the Ministry may determine whether the failure may cause contamination (Article 17 section VIII);
(6) channel emissions of atmospheric pollutants generated by fixed sources of federal jurisdiction through pipelines or discharge chimneys, which must have the necessary effective height, according to the corresponding Official Mexican Standard to disperse pollutant emissions (Articles 23 and 24). In addition, Article 27 prohibits open-air combustion and states that it is only permitted in areas of federal jurisdiction when it is carried out with the permission of the Ministry to train and capacitate personnel in charge of firefighting;
(7) keep the sampling platforms and ports safe and maintain calibrated measuring equipment, in accordance with the procedure laid down in the corresponding Official Mexican Standard (Article 26).

2. Contamination from Mobile Sources

315. Federal legislation hardly deals with the prevention and control of air pollution from mobile sources. Although in 1988, the Environmental Act Regulations for the Prevention and Control of Pollution Generated by Motor Vehicles Circulating in the Federal District and the Municipalities of its Suburban area were promulgated, their provisions have been left without subject matter because, in 1993, a reform to the Constitution granted the Federal District Legislative Assembly the power to issue its own local environmental law that in fact takes up the content of said Regulations. Likewise, in accordance with the reforms made in 1996 to the Environmental Act, the local Congresses have dictated local environmental laws that incorporate the content of this regulation.

316. The main instrument for controlling air pollution from fixed sources is the verification of pollutant emissions from vehicles in several states of the country, as well as the traffic restriction that applies exclusively in the metropolitan area of Mexico City.

317. For these purposes, several Official Mexican Norms are currently in force that establish maximum levels of pollutant emissions as well as the procedures to be followed in order to verify such emissions.

3. The Climate Change Act

318. This Law, published in the DOF on 6 June 2012, is regulatory Articles 4, 27, 25 and 73, section XXIX-G of the Constitution that refer to:

- The right to an adequate environment.
- Liability for environmental damage.
- The regulation of the use of natural resources and the environment.
- Sustainable development.
- Preservation and restoration of the ecological balance.
- The power of the Congress of the Union to distribute competences in the field of climate change.

319. Like all environmental laws, this Law establishes the concurrence of the three orders of government in the application of the measures they are responsible for mitigating, adapting and reducing vulnerability in a balanced manner. Among the main environmental policy instruments established by the Law, the following stand out:

- The National Climate Change System is constituted as a permanent mechanism for concurrence, communication, collaboration, coordination and agreement among the three levels of government, as well as the private sector and the social sector.
- As part of the National Climate Change System, the Inter-Ministerial Commission on Climate Change is created.
- The Climate Change Council is created.
- The National Institute of Ecology and Climate Change was created as a decentralized public organism of the Federal Public Administration. Consequently, the current National Institute of Ecology disappears.
- The Evaluation Coordination is constituted and has the faculty to issue recommendations to the National Climate Change System. In addition, it will periodically and systematically evaluate the national climate change policy.

320. Nevertheless, it is a merely programmatic law that doubles the content of the Environmental Act on air pollution and does not establish specific regulations on mitigation and adaptation to climate change, always referring to other laws such as those relating to renewable energies and energy transition, as well as to the Special Climate Change Programme and the National Climate Change Strategy.

321. In 2014 was published in the DOF, the Regulation of the Climate Change Act in matters of National Registry of Emissions, which regulates the provisions on the Registry of Emissions created in the Climate Change Act. This Regulation indicates which activities must report greenhouse gas emissions to the Ministry of the Environment.[63]

322. The Act does not create any direct regulatory mechanism, so, in the area of air pollution, the Environmental Act and its regulations continue to apply.

4. OMNs

323. In the case of the use of fossil fuels in fixed sources under federal jurisdiction, the same rules will apply, i.e., they will have to obtain their integrated environmental licence and comply with the other associated obligations.

324. However, this use of fossil fuels also occurs in the case of mobile sources. At the federal level, there are few plans to deal with this issue, as it is a matter for the state or municipal authorities. The main instrument for controlling air pollution from mobile sources is the verification of pollutant emissions from vehicles in several states of the country, as well as the traffic restriction that applies exclusively in the metropolitan area of Mexico City.

325. For these purposes, several Official Mexican Norms are currently in force that establish maximum levels of pollutant emissions, as well as the procedures to be followed to carry out the verification of such emissions.

§3. Carbon Tax and Carbon Credits

326. As mentioned above, there is no emissions market in Mexico, despite the fact that the Environmental Act refers to it as a market-based instrument of environmental policy. However, recently the so-called carbon tax was incorporated into the Special Tax on Production and Services Act. In fact, this tax taxes the consumption of fossil fuels in three different ways. In the first place, Article 2° of the mentioned Law, in its section I, indicates that the Special Tax on Production and Services will be caused in the sale and importation of automotive fuels, at the rate of the following quotas:

(a) Gasoline less than 91 octanes MXN 5.4917 per litre.
(b) Gasoline greater than or equal to 91 octanes MXN 4.6375 per litre.

63. DOF, 3 Jun. 2004.

(c) Diesel MXN 6.0354 per litre.

327. In the second place, paragraph (h) of the cited precept charges, for the second time, the sale and import of fossil fuels in accordance with the following quotas:

> Fossil Fuels: Quota Unit of Measurement
> Propane: 8.2987 cents per litre
> Butane: 8.42 cents per litre
> Gasoline and Airplane gasoline: 11.41 cents per litre
> Turbosin: 17.3851cents per litre
> Diesel: 17.6624cents per litre
> Fuel oil: 18.8496 cents per litre
> Petroleum coke: 21.8784Pesos per tonne
> Coke of coal: 51.2901Pesos per tonne
> Coal: 38.6201Pesos per tonne
> Other fossil fuels: 55.8277Pesos per tonne of carbon contained in the fuel.

328. Finally, in 2016, the above-mentioned Law was amended to include Article 2-A, according to which:

> without prejudice to the provisions of article 2, section I, paragraphs d) and h), in the sale of gasoline and diesel within the national territory, the following quotas shall apply:
>
> VI. Gasoline less than 91: octane 48.4720 cents per liter;
> VII. Gasoline greater than or equal to 91 octanes: 59.1449cents per liter;
> VIII. Diesel: 40.2288cents per liter.

329. All these tax provisions are aimed at reducing the consumption of fossil fuels and, therefore, the reduction of greenhouse gas emissions because they can be considered as the Mexican carbon tax. However, in addition to the foregoing, Article 5 of the aforementioned Law states that: 'In the case of the tax referred to in paragraph (h) of section II of this Law, taxpayers may choose to pay the tax through the delivery of carbon credits referred to in section XXIX of Article 3.' This means that, although the tax punishes the consumption of fossil fuels, this punishment can be cushioned by obtaining carbon credits that, according to the precept itself, must be the result of projects approved by the United Nations in accordance with the Convention on Climate Change.

Chapter 3. Water Pollution

§1. Regulation of Water Use

330. Paragraph 1 of Article 27 of the Mexican Constitution prescribes that ownership of lands and waters within the boundaries of the national territory is vested originally in the Nation, which has had and still has the right to transmit the title thereof to private persons, thereby constituting private property. Consequently, the Mexican Constitution allows private property of water with some limitations. In this regard, Article 27 points out that:

(a) only Mexicans by birth or naturalization and Mexican companies have the right to acquire domain over lands, waters, and their appurtenances or to obtain water exploitation concessions;
(b) the State may grant the same right to foreigners, if they agree before the Ministry of Foreign Relations to consider themselves as nationals in respect to such property and not to invoke the protection of their governments about said property, under penalty, in case of defaulting on the agreement, of forfeiting in benefit of the Nation, the property acquired by virtue thereof; and
(c) in no case may foreigners acquire direct domain over lands and waters in a zone of 100 km along the international borders and 50 km along the shore.

331. Private property of waters is not an absolute right. In agreement with paragraph 3 of Article 27, the Nation shall at all times have the right to impose on private property of waters such restrictions as the public interest may demand, as well as to regulate, for social benefit, the utilization of those waters so as to make an equitable distribution of public wealth, conserve them, achieve a balanced development of the country, and improve the living conditions of rural and urban populations.

332. Consequently, Article 27 of the Mexican Constitution empowers the Nation to issue measures aimed at establishing adequate provisions, uses, reserves, and allocations of waters to carry out public works and plan and regulate the creation, maintenance, improvement, and growth of population centres; to preserve and restore environmental balance; to provide, under the terms set forth by the Law, collective exploitation and prevent the destruction of natural resources and damages that property may suffer to the detriment of society.

333. However, in consonance with paragraph 5 of Article 27 of the Mexican Constitution, the property of certain specific waters is vested in the Nation. This provision points out that:

> The Nation has full ownership over the waters of territorial sea in the extension and under the terms set forth by international law; internal waters; waters of lagoons and estuaries permanently or intermittently connecting with the sea; those of natural inland lakes that are directly connected with streams constantly flowing; river waters and their direct and indirect tributaries, from the

site of the riverbed where the first permanent, intermittent, or torrential waters start to flow, to their mouth in the sea; lakes, lagoons, or estuaries owned by the Nation; those of constant or intermittent streams and their direct or indirect tributaries, whenever their beds along all the length of their way or in a portion thereof serve as a boundary line of national land territory or between two States, or when they flow from one State to another or cross the Republic's boundary line; those of lakes, lagoons, or estuaries whose beds, zones, or streams are crossed by boundary lines dividing one or more States or between the Republic and a neighboring country, or when the stream shoreline serves as a boundary between two States or between the Republic and a neighboring country; those of springs flowing from beaches, maritime areas, streams, basins, riverbeds, banks of lakes, lagoons, or estuaries owned by the Nation, and the ones extracted from mines; and the streams, beds, or banks of lakes and interior streams in the extensions established by the Law.

334. In addition, paragraph 6 of Article 27 of the Mexican Constitution holds that the Nation's dominion of the aforementioned waters is inalienable and not subject to the statute of limitations, and consequently, the use or enjoyment of such waters by private persons or by companies incorporated in accordance with Mexican laws may not be undertaken except by means of concessions granted by the President of the Republic and in accordance with the rules and conditions set forth by the Laws.

335. By contrast, according to paragraph 5 of Article 27, underground waters are not considered to be national property. Thus, using and enjoining underground waters do not require a concession. That provision recognizes that such waters may be freely extracted by artificial works and may be appropriated by the owner of the land where such waters are located.

336. However, the final part of paragraph 5 of Article 27 establishes that whenever the public interest should so require it, or whenever other uses are affected, the President of the Republic may regulate the extraction and use of underground waters and may even establish banned zones, and the same may be done regarding other waters of national property. In these cases, using or enjoying underground waters by individuals or Corporations shall require a concession, as in the case of national waters.

337. Based on the above listings of the Constitution, the National Waters Act regulates the establishment of reserves of waters, regulated areas of extraction, and banned zones. The Act also regulates the administrative procedure through which the Nation grants concessions to use and enjoy national waters or underground waters in regulated or banned zones. Marine waters are regulated by the Federal Act of the Sea (FAS).

338. However, paragraph 5 of Article 27 prescribes that any other waters not included in the list above shall be considered as an integral part of the land through which they flow or where their deposits are located, but should they be located in two or more lots, the use of such waters shall be considered of public convenience and subject to provisions issued by the States. Consequently, local governments have jurisdiction to legislate on waters not included in the list of paragraph 5 of Article 27.

I. Reserves, Regulations, and Banned Zones

339. The Waters Act defines the meaning of reserved areas, regulated areas, and banned areas in the following terms:

- Reserved areas: those specific areas of aquifers, watersheds, or hydrological regions in which there have been established limitations for exploitation, use of a portion or all of the water available, with the aim of providing a public service, introducing a restoration or preservation programme, or when the State has decided to exploit these waters for public utility reasons (National Waters Act, Article 3, section LXIV).
- Regulated areas: those specific areas of aquifers, hydrological basins, or hydrological regions that, because of their characteristics of deterioration, hydrological unbalance, risk or damage to water or the environment, fragility of ecosystems, over-exploitation, as well as to their reorganization and restoration, require specific hydro management to guarantee hydrological sustainability (National Waters Act, Article 3, section LXIII).
- Banned areas: those specific areas of hydrological regions, watersheds, or aquifers for which water uses are not allowed in addition to those legally established and that are controlled by specific regulations, undergoing deterioration of water in quantity or quality by their allocation to the hydrological, sustainability or by damage to the bodies of water on their surface and underground (National Waters Act, Article 3, section LXV).

340. This means that reserved areas, regulated areas, and banned areas are legal institutions that do not prevent the use or enjoyment of national waters, but their use is regulated. The establishment of a regulated area limits but does not forbid the granting of concessions for the use or enjoyment of national waters.

341. For its part, the establishment of a banned area does not prohibit the granting of licences for using waters, but, in the case of groundwaters, it restricts the right of free access guaranteed by paragraph 5 of Article 27 of the Constitution, cited above, whereas, in the case of surface waters nationalized in paragraph 5 of Article 27, banned areas result in the requirement of concessions for their use or exploitation by individuals.

342. Furthermore, in the case of national surface waters, the requirement of concessions is due not by the shortage of resources, but by the national character of the waters, addressed in paragraph 5 of Article 27, according to which the use of a resource under the public domain of the Nation, which is also inalienable, requires the granting of concessions.

343. In contrast, in the case of groundwater that can be freely extracted and appropriated by the landowner, a grant is required only when a banned area has been declared because otherwise, the concession would be unnecessary.

344. The National Waters Act notes general rules that apply to decrees establishing reserve areas and regulated or banned areas. Finally, it contains specific rules for issuing each one of these legal instruments.

II. Assignments and Concessions

345. The Waters Act points out in Article 1 that the objective of regulating the exploitation, use, or enjoyment of these waters, its distribution and control, as well as the preservation of its quantity and quality, is to achieve its integral sustainable development.

346. National waters are defined in Article 3 of the Waters Act as 'the waters that are the property of the Nation, in terms of paragraph 5 of Article 27 of the Mexican Constitution'. Article 16 of the Waters Act adds to the list contemplated in that Constitutional precept the residual waters coming from the use of national waters.

347. In the same vein, Article 18 of the Waters Act stipulates that the national waters of the subsoil may be freely extracted by artificial works, except when the Federal Executive, for reasons of public interest, regulates its extraction and its use or establishes banned areas.

348. The Waters Act refers in Title VI to different types of uses of national waters: urban public use, agricultural use, use in electric power generation, and use in other productive activities. The Act also states in Article 20 that in all cases, exploitation, use, or enjoyment of the national waters by individuals or Corporations will be through concessions granted by the Federal Executive through the National Water Commission and that, in the case of any department or agency, decentralized public administration, or federal, State, or municipal council, use or exploitation is allowed by assignment. Extension of the rights granted by concession or assignment ranges from five to thirty years (Article 24 of the Waters Act).

349. Concessions and assignments confer an onerous use of the national waters. Pursuant to sections IV and V of Article 29 and Article *29bis* of the Waters Act, concessionaires and allocators have, among others, the obligation 'to pay duties for extraction, consumption, and use of the national waters' and 'to pay duties in accordance with the established Federal Tax Laws in force and in other applicable provisions'.

350. Reiterating this obligation, Article 112 of the Waters Act provides that the exploitation, use, or enjoyment of national waters, including those from the subsoil, will require the payment by the user of the duties established by the Federal Tax Laws.

351. In addition, Article 222 of the Federal Duties Act (FDA) stipulates that:

> Individuals and Corporations that use, exploit or enjoy national waters, either in fact or covered by titles of assignment, concession, authorization, or permission granted by the Federal government, according to the area of availability of water in which it carries out its extraction in accordance with the territorial division contained in Article 231 of this Law, are liable for payment of the duty on water.

352. Pursuant to the transcribed Article, the payment of the duty is calculated on the basis of the volume of water allocated or exploited measured in cubic metres, while the rate is established in Article 223.

§2. WATER POLLUTION

353. At the Federal level, pollution of national waters is regulated by the Waters Act, the Environmental Act, the Federal Sea Act, the Federal Fees Act. These laws establish the following instruments to deal with water pollution: declarations of classification of national bodies of water, the obligation of giving treatment to water prior to its discharge, discharge permits, permits for infiltration of waters, 'particular conditions of discharge', limits of pollutant discharges, and payment for rights for discharge. These are described below.

I. Declaration of Classification of Bodies of Waters

354. The general instrument for regulating water pollution is constituted by the Declaration of Classification of Bodies of National Waters. However, the legislation does not define this instrument, and Article 87 of the Waters Act simply points out that:

> The authority of the water shall determine the parameters that will met by the discharges, the capacity of assimilation, and the dilution that national waters have and the pollutant discharges that these can receive, as well as the parameters of quality and the terms necessary to reach them, by means of the expedition of the Declaration of Classification of Bodies of National Waters, which will be published in the DOF.

355. The declaration shall include the following:

(1) the delimitation of the classified body of water;

(2) the parameters that will complete the discharges pursuant to the classified body of water and the periods foreseen in the regulation of this Law;
(3) the capacity of the classified body of water to dilute and assimilate pollutants; and
(4) the maximum limits of discharge of the analysed pollutants, based on fixing the conditions unique to the discharge.

II. The Obligation of Giving Previous Treatment to Residual Water Discharges

356. Another general obligation regarding water pollution is established by Article 121 of the Environmental Act. As stated in this provision, no one is allowed to discharge or infiltrate into anybody or flow of water or on the ground or underground, residual waters that contain pollutants, without prior treatment and the permission or authorization granted by federal authority or by the local authority in cases of discharges into waters of local jurisdiction or municipal drainage systems and sewer systems of centres of population.

357. In addition, the General Act of Health, in Article 122, reiterates this obligation, pointing out that it is forbidden to discharge residual waters without treatment so that those discharges meet the sanitary standards enacted by the Secretary of Health to avoid risks to public health.

III. Discharge Permits

358. As stated in paragraph (b) of section XL of Article 3 of the Waters Act, the permit for discharge is the 'Title that the Federal Executive grants through "the Commission" or the Organization of Basins, according to their respective competences, for the discharge of residual waters in receiving bodies of national property, to individuals or to public or private Corporations.'

359. Article 88 of the Waters Act establishes that 'individuals and Corporations shall require discharge permission issued by the "authority of the water" to pour residual waters in permanent or intermittent ways into receiving bodies that are national waters or other property, including marine waters, as well as when they infiltrate them into lands that are national property or on other lands when they can contaminate the underground water or aquifers'. Reiterating this obligation, section I of Article 88*bis* of the Waters Act points out that individuals or Corporations that discharge residual waters into receiving bodies that are governed by law should have discharge permission.

360. As an exemption, Article 88*bis* 1 points out that discharges of residual waters from domestic use that are not part of a municipal system or sewer system do not require permission but only have to meet the limits established by the Official Mexican Norms.

361. The Environmental Act also refers to the permit for the discharge of residual waters in Article 121, according to which no one is allowed to discharge into anybody or flow of water or on the ground or underground, residual waters that contain pollutants, without prior treatment and the permission or authorization granted by federal authority or by the local authority in the cases of discharges into waters of local jurisdiction or municipal drainage systems and sewer system of centres of population.

362. Finally, this Law points out that the permission or authorization of discharge of residual waters can be denied or revoked when the Ministry of Environment detects that the residual waters affect or can affect sources of the supply of water (Article 124).

IV. Particular Conditions for Discharge

363. In accordance with section XIV of Article 3 of the Waters Act, particular conditions for discharge are defined as 'the group of physical, chemical, and biological parameters and of their maximum levels allowed in the discharges of residual water, determined by "the Commission" or for the Organization of Basins that corresponds, according to their respective competences, to each user for a certain use or users of a specific receiving body with the purpose of preserving and controlling the quality of the waters according to the present law and the regulations issued under it'.

364. The particular conditions of discharge can be issued for all discharges in the collector nets, rivers, aquifers, basins, beds, glasses, marine waters, and other deposits or currents of water and the spills of residual waters on the ground or their infiltration into lands (Article 123 of Environmental Act).

V. Standards for Discharge (Official Mexican Norms)

365. As stated by Article 123 of the Environmental Act, all the discharges in collector nets, rivers, aquifers, basins, beds glasses, marine waters, and other deposits or currents of water and the spills of residual waters on the ground or their infiltration into lands will satisfy the Official Mexican Norms issued for such effect.

366. Article 119 of the Environmental Act established that the Ministry of Environment will issue Official Mexican Norms that are required to prevent and control pollution of the national waters in line with the Waters Act, the Regulations under this Act, and other applicable provisions.

367. However, the Waters Act states, in section XXXVIII of Article 3, that the Official Mexican Norms are those set forth by the Ministry of the Environment in terms of the Standardization Act related to conservation, security, and quality in the exploitation, use, enjoyment, and administration of the national waters and the national property referred to in Article 113 of Waters Act.

368. These norms appear under the nomenclature 'Ministry of the Environment'. Thus far, three have been enacted: ONM-001-Ministry of the Environment-1996, which establishes the maximum permissible limits of pollutants in discharges of residual waters in national waters and national property, published in the DOF on 6 January 1997; ONM-002-Ministry of the Environment-1996, which establishes the maximum permissible limits of contamination in discharges of residual waters to urban or municipal sewer systems, published in the DOF on 3 June 1996; and ONM-ECOL-003-1997, which establishes the maximum permissible limits of pollutants for residual waters that are reused in services, published in the DOF on 21 September 1998.

VI. Duties for Discharge

369. In consonance with Article 276 of the FDA, those individuals or Corporations that permanently, intermittently, or continuously discharge residual waters in rivers, basins, beds, glasses, marine waters, and other deposits or flows of water, as well as those that discharge residual waters in soils or infiltrate them in lands that are national property or that can contaminate underground water or aquifers, by the terms of this Act, are obliged to pay duties for discharge.

370. Article 278 of FDA states that:

> For the use of property under the public domain of the nation such as receiving bodies for discharges of residual waters, the duty will be assessed according to the volume of discharged water and the pollutants contained therein when the discharge surpass the maximum permissible limits set forth under the particular conditions of discharge or for lack of these, by this Law.

371. That is, the assessment of the duty is determined by two precepts of the FDA. On the one hand, Article 276 establishes the generic obligation of paying the assessment without any condition, while on the other hand, Article 278 states that the assessment is caused only when the maximum permissible limits are surpassed.

372. This idea is confirmed by Articles 278(c) and 282 of the FDA. The first Article points out that 'to calculate the duty to pay for each kind of pollutant that surpasses the maximum permissible limits, the volume of residual waters will be considered', while the second Article exempts from payment those taxpayers whose pollutants do not surpass the maximum permissible limits set forth in the FDA or under the particular conditions of discharge.

373. However, Article 112 of the Waters Act points out that:

> The exploitation, use, or enjoyment of property of the public domain of the Nation such as receiving bodies of discharges of residual waters shall require the payment of the duty established by the FDA. The payment is independent of the fulfillment of provisions established by this Law on prevention and control of the quality of the water, by the Environmental Act; and by the Health Act.

374. In this case, in keeping with the principle of legality of the taxes consecrated by section IV of Article 31 of the Mexican Constitution, the approach that should prevail is the one established by tax law, according to which the duty is paid only when the limits are surpassed.

§3. Local Waters Law

375. As soon as waters are allocated to a State or municipal system of drinkable water or a sewer system, the rule established by Article 45 of the Waters Act is applicable, according to which:

> The competence of the municipal authorities, with the participation of the local governments in the terms of this Law, exploitation, includes the use or enjoyment of the national waters that have been allocated to them, including the residual ones, from the point of their extraction or of their delivery on the part of 'the authority of the water', until the place of their discharge to receiving bodies that are national property.

376. Thus, local governments are deemed competent to legislate on such waters, that is, to regulate the exploitation, use, and even the preservation of the quality and quantity of the waters that have been allocated to them, and, more concretely, legislate the cycle that begins at the time when national waters flow into the conduits of drinkable water and until the time when the residual waters flow out of the sewer system to be deposited or infiltrate national bodies of water or the ground.

377. However, the Environmental Act holds, in Article 119*bis*, that regarding the prevention and control of water pollution, States and municipalities have authority, in accordance with the distribution of competences established by the Act, over the following:

(1) the control of discharges of residual waters to drainage systems and sewer systems;
(2) the enforcement of Official Mexican Norms, as well as requiring those who generate discharges to these systems but do not fulfil the Official Mexican Norms, the installation of treatment systems;
(3) the determination of the amount of the corresponding duties so that the municipality or State can carry out the necessary treatment; and

(4) the upgrading of the registration from the discharges to the drainage systems and sewer systems that administer them to be integrated into the national registration of discharges, which are in charge of the Secretary.

378. In addition, Article 122 of the Environmental Act establishes that residual waters that are discharged into municipal drainage systems and sewer systems or in the basins, rivers, glasses, and other deposits or flows of water, as well as those that infiltrate the ground through any means, and in general, those that spill out onto the ground, coming from public urban uses and industrial or agricultural uses are required to meet the necessary conditions to prevent the following:

(1) pollution of the receiving bodies;
(2) interferences with the processes of purification of waters; and
(3) dysfunctions, impediments, or alterations in the correct uses or the operation of the systems and the hydraulic capacity of the basins, beds, glasses, mantle aquifers, and other deposits of national property, as well as of the sewer systems.

379. Pursuant to Article 120 of the Environmental Act, the following are subject to local regulation:

(1) discharges of industrial origin, those derived from agricultural activities; those coming from the application of pesticides, fertilizers, and toxic substances that are discharged to bodies of water assigned to a State or to a sewer system;
(2) the infiltrations that affect mantle aquifers; and
(3) the dumping of solid residuals coming from the treatment of residual waters into bodies and currents of water.

380. In addition, Article 119*bis* of the Environmental Act establishes the responsibilities that correspond to the governments of the States, the municipalities, and the Federal District regarding the prevention and control of water pollution.

381. States and municipalities have the following responsibilities to:

- control discharges of residual waters to the drainage and sewer systems;
- require those who generate discharges to these systems and do not satisfy the parameters established by Official Mexican Norms, to install treatment systems;
- determine the amount of the corresponding duties so that the municipality or the State can carry out the necessary treatment;
- upgrade the registrations from the discharges to the drainage nets and sewer systems that they administer to integrate them into the national registers of discharges, which is in charge of the Secretary.

382. The above-mentioned responsibilities coincide with paragraph 2 of Article 88 of the Waters Act, which points out that 'the control of residual water discharges to municipal drainage systems or sewer systems of population centres corresponds to municipalities, with the cooperation of the States when necessary or when it is established by the laws'.

§4. Protection of Marine Waters

383. Marine waters are protected under the Environmental Act, the FAS, its Regulations on Marine Waters Pollution, and the Law of Dumping in Mexican Marine Zones.

384. Conforming to Article 130 of the Environmental Act, an authorization granted by the Ministry of the Environment is required to discharge residual waters in marine waters. According to this Provision, in granting the authorization, the Ministry must fulfil the requirements established by the Waters Act, its own Regulations, and the applicable Official Mexican Norms. In addition, Article 130 of the Environmental Act establishes that, in cases of discharges from mobile sources or fixed platforms in the Territorial Sea and the Exclusive Economic Zone, as well as in cases of discharges from facilities on land to the sea, the Ministry of the Environment shall coordinate with the Ministry of Marine Affairs.

385. The Act of the Sea refers to marine water pollution in three ways:

(1) Article 6 states that national sovereignty is exerted regarding the protection and preservation of marine environments, including the prevention of its pollution.
(2) Article 21 states that, in the exercise of powers, rights, jurisdictions, and competences of the Nation into Mexican marine zones, the Environmental Act, the Health Act, and their Regulations, the Waters Act and other laws and regulations, including this Act, its Regulations, and the international treaties to prevent, reduce, and control pollution of marine environments shall be applicable.
(3) Article 46 states that the Nation exerts in an Exclusive Economic Zone located out of the Territorial Sea and adjacent to its jurisdiction regarding protection and preservation of marine environments.

386. Besides, the regulations of the Convention on the Prevention of Marine Pollution by Dumping of Wastes and other matters points out that no person or Corporation can intentionally dump wastes or other matters into the sea without previous authorization granted by the Ministry of Marine Affairs.

387. The Law of Dumping in Mexican Marine Zones was passed in 2014. In consonance with its Article 1, it has the purpose of controlling and preventing pollution or alteration of the sea by dumping in the Mexican marine areas. In that sense, the Law establishes the terms and conditions in which dumping can be carried out, noting that in accordance with the Act a permit granted by the Ministry of Marine affairs is required.

388. Article 3, the Law of Dumping in Mexican Marine Zones, describes the assumptions in which dumping is considered in the Mexican marine areas:

(A) Any deliberate or accidental disposal, introduction or release in Mexican marine areas of wastes or other matter including non-target ballast water from ships, aircraft, platforms, or other constructions.
(B) The deliberate sinking of ships, aircraft, platforms or other constructions, as well as those derived from it;
(C) The storage of wastes or other matter in the seabed or subsoil thereof from ships, aircraft, platforms, or other constructions.
(D) The abandonment of ships, aircraft, platforms or other constructions, or other objects, including fishing gear, for the sole purpose of deliberately disposing of them.
(E) The discharge of any type of organic matter as attractant of biological species, whose aim is not its fishing.
(F) The placing of materials or objects of any nature, in order to create artificial reefs, piers, breakwaters, or any other structure.
(G) The re-suspension of sediment, consisting of the return of deposited sediment, to a suspended state in the body of water, by any method or procedure, which results in its sedimentation.

389. To define what is to be understood as Mexican marine zones, the Law in question refers to the Federal Law of the Sea that in its Article 3 indicates that the Mexican marine areas are the following:

A) The Territorial Sea,
B) The Inland Marine Waters,
C) The Contiguous Zone,
D) The Exclusive Economic Zone,
E) The Continental Shelf and the Insular, and
F) Any other permitted by international law.

390. However, the Law of Dumping in Mexican Marine Zones establishes the procedure for obtaining the permit of dumping. Article 18 indicates the required documentation, and in Third Chapter of the Law, Articles 8–17 establish the evaluation criteria for the authorization of the permit.

391. Finally, the Law states that the Ministry of Marine Affairs is empowered to carry out inspection and monitoring visits on compliance with the Law. In this way, it points out that derived from these activities, the Secretariat may impose preventive measures tending to avoid contamination or alteration of the marine environment or affect human health. It also indicates a list of infractions, sanctions, which may be imposed by the Secretariat. Article 41 establishes infringements of the following conduct:

(a) To omit to inform of dumping made by reasons of *force majeure*.
(b) Failure to fulfil the obligations referred to in Article 27.

(c) Updating any of the cases referred to in Article 54.
(d) The obligations provided for in Article 23 are not fulfilled.
(e) Failure to comply with the Agreements that is pursuant to this Law, issued by the Secretariat.
(f) Failure to comply with the terms specified in the permit of dumping.
(g) To abandon a ship, aircraft, naval device, structure, or platform without informing the Secretariat in a timely manner.
(h) To carry out verifications without the authorization of the Secretariat.
(i) Perform post-suspension discharges.
(j) Make a discharge after a cancellation.
(k) Incur in any other violation of the provisions of this Law and its Regulations.

392. Regarding sanctions, the Law states in Article 42, the following:

The sanctions will consist of:

I. Suspension of the permit from 1 day to 60 days;
II. Cancellation of the permit, and
III. Fine, which will be determined based on the general minimum wage in force in the Federal District at the time of the violation, from two hundred and fifty to fifty thousand days of minimum wage, depending on the infraction and the damage caused.

The infractions provided for in sections II, V and VI of the previous article shall be sanctioned with suspension of the permit for up to 60 days.
The permit is cancelled, when the permit holder incurs the infractions foreseen in fractions III and IV of the previous articles.
The cases provided for in sections I and VII to XI of the preceding articles shall be sanctioned with a fine, according to the infraction and the damage caused.
The sanctions mentioned above may be imposed, in more than one of its modalities.
If the period of suspension has expired, without the offender having remedied the irregularities that gave rise to it, the Secretariat will proceed to the cancellation of the respective permit.

Chapter 4. Wastes

393. Waste can be classified from different perspectives. For instance, due to their physical state, it is possible to distinguish among liquids, solids, pasty, and gaseous waste, whereas because of their chemical composition, they can be monospecific or polyspecific as well as organic and inorganic. Besides, from their characteristics of dangerousness, they can be separated into dangerous and not dangerous. This category of hazardous waste includes those types of waste that are characterized by the risk they represent to health and the environment. Hazardous waste includes infectious waste from hospitals, obsolete pharmaceutical products, waste from products used as solvents, waste containing Poly Chlorinated Biphenyls (PCB) or polychlorinated terphenyls (TPC), metallic particles or powders, batteries and electric batteries, etc.

394. In Mexico, the generation, management, and final disposition of wastes are regulated by:

a) The General Act for Prevention and Integral Management of Wastes (hereinafter, the Waste Act),
b) The Regulation under the Waste Act,[64]
c) The Environmental Act,
d) 37 MONs,
e) Local laws, and
f) A number of municipal ordinances related to public service of management of residuals.

395. Local laws and municipal regulations generally govern issues related to domestic wastes and industrial wastes that are not considered dangerous, whereas the Environmental Act establishes few rules about the generation, management, and final disposal of hazardous wastes. However, the most important legal body in regard to waste is the Waste Act.

396. The Waste Act is a comprehensive Act that broadly governs hazardous wastes, industrial wastes, and domestic wastes. This Law defines these three types of waste as follows:

(1) Hazardous wastes are those presenting some of the following characteristics: corrosiveness, reactivity, explosively, toxicity, flammability, or having infectious agents that confer upon them danger, as well as their containers, recipients, packing, and floors that have been contaminated when they are transferred to another place (Article 5, section XXXII).

---

64. DOF, 30 Nov. 2006.

(2) Wastes of special management are those generated in the productive processes that do not gather the characteristics to be considered as dangerous or solid urban residuals, or that are produced by large generators of solid urban residuals (Article 5, section XXX).
(3) Solid urban wastes are those generated in houses from the elimination of the materials that are used in domestic activities; those from products that have been consumed and their containers or packing; the residuals that come from any other activity inside establishments or on public roads that generate residuals with characteristic domiciliary; and the resultants of the cleaning of the roads and public places, whenever they are not considered by the Waste Act to be residuals of another nature (Article 5, section XXXIII).

397. In addition, this Act asserts that incompatible wastes are those that in contact or mixed with water or other materials or wastes, react producing heat, pressure, fire, particles, gases, or steams (Article 5, section XXXI).

398. The Waste Act distributes jurisdictions on these issues among the three levels of government, leaving the Federation with the powers related to regulation, standardization, planning, inspection, and surveillance in dangerous residues.

399. Among the policy instruments for the comprehensive management of hazardous waste, this Law includes:

- The National Program for the Prevention and Integral Management of Waste.
- Management plan.
- Authorizations and permits.
- Security measures.
- Inspection and surveillance.
- The right to information.
- Social participation.
- The popular complaint.

400. However, although the Waste Act is the specific law of the subject, the Environmental Act retained the regulation of certain aspects, such as the authorization referred to in Article 151*bis* to:

I. Providing services to third parties for the operation of systems for the collection, storage, transportation, reuse, treatment, recycling, incineration and final disposal of hazardous wastes;
II. Installing and operating systems for the treatment or final disposal of hazardous waste, or for their recycling when it is intended to recover energy, by incineration, and
III. Installing and operating, by the generator of hazardous waste, of systems for its reuse, recycling and final disposal, outside the facility where the waste was generated.

401. Similarly, Article 153 of the Environmental Act regulates the import of hazardous waste, establishing the following rules:

(a) The Ministry of the Environment shall be responsible for the ecological control and surveillance of hazardous materials or wastes imported or to be exported, applying the corresponding security measures, without prejudice to what the Customs Law provides for on this matter.
(b) Import of hazardous materials or waste may only be authorized for its treatment, recycling, or reuse, when its use is in accordance with Mexican laws, Official Mexican Norms, and other provisions in force.
(c) Import of hazardous materials or wastes whose only object is their final disposal or simple deposit, storage, or confinement in the national territory or in the zones where the nation exercises its sovereignty and jurisdiction, or when its use or manufacture is not allowed in the country in which it has been drawn up.
(d) Transit through the national territory of hazardous materials that do not meet the specifications of use or consumption according to which they were elaborated, or whose elaboration, use, or consumption are prohibited or restricted in the country to which they are destined, cannot be authorized; nor may the transit of such hazardous materials or waste be authorized, when they come from abroad to be destined for a third country.
(e) Granting of authorizations for the export of hazardous materials or waste shall be subject to the express consent of the recipient country.
(f) Hazardous materials and waste generated in the production, processing, processing or repair processes in which raw materials introduced into the country under the temporary importation regime, including those regulated in Article 85 of the Customs Law, have to be returned to the country of origin within the period determined by the Ministry for such effect.

402. Granting of authorizations by the Ministry for the importation or exportation of hazardous materials or waste shall be subject to duly ensuring compliance with the provisions of this Law and other applicable provisions, as well as the redress of damages that could be caused both in the national territory and abroad; likewise, the export of hazardous waste must be refused when re-importation into the national territory is contemplated: there is no express consent of the recipient country; the country of destination requires reciprocity or implies a breach of the commitments assumed by Mexico in the International Treaties and Conventions in the matter.

403. In addition to other applicable provisions, the authorizations granted for the import or export of hazardous materials and waste may be revoked, without prejudice to the imposition of the corresponding sanctions, in the following cases:

(a) when by supervening causes, it is found that the authorized hazardous materials or waste pose a greater risk to the ecological balance than that considered for the granting of the corresponding authorization;

(b) when the import or export operation does not comply with the requirements established in the ecological guide issued by the Secretariat;
(c) when the hazardous materials or waste no longer have the attributes or characteristics according to which they were authorized.

404. When it is determined that the authorization was transferred to a person other than the one that requested the authorization, or when the corresponding request contains false information or is presented in a way that conceals information necessary for the correct assessment of the request.

405. The Environmental Act also refers to the reuse and recycling of hazardous waste, pointing out in Article 152:

> The Secretariat will promote programs to prevent and reduce the generation of hazardous wastes, as well as to encourage their reuse and recycling.
>
> In those cases where hazardous waste can be used in a process other than the one that generated them, the Regulations of this Law and the Official Mexican Norms that are issued, shall establish the mechanisms and procedures that make possible their efficient management from the point Environmental and economic view.
>
> Hazardous waste that is used, treated or recycled in a process other than the one that generated them, within the same site, will be subject to internal control by the responsible company, in accordance with the formalities established in the Regulations of this Law.
>
> In the event that the waste indicated in the previous paragraph is transported to a site other than that in which it is generated, it will be according to the regulations applicable to transport of hazardous waste.

406. Finally, the Environmental Act also refers to Articles 151 and 152*bis* to the subject of responsibility for the management of hazardous waste.

407. As mentioned above, the Waste Act regulates these four types of residuals, but in Article 9, section II, it allows the States to enact their own local laws so as to enforce the Waste Act according to their particular circumstances; and, in Article 95, holds that 'the regulation of the generation and integral management of solid urban residuals and the residuals of special management shall be carried out, according to established Law, by the applicable dispositions enacted by the local congresses and other legal provisions'.

408. Article 7 of the Waste Act states that the Federal government's regulatory and normative responsibilities regarding hazardous waste include the following:

(a) To issue regulations, MNs, and other official legal provisions to regulate the integral management of the dangerous residuals and their classification, and to prevent the contamination of places or to carry out their restoration when it happens (section II).

(b) To issue regulations, MNs, and other official legal provisions to regulate the integral management of the residuals of the metallurgic mining industry that correspond to their conformity with this Law and the Mining Law (section III).
(c) To issue Official Mexican Norms for the integral management of solid urban waste and wastes of special management (section IV).
(d) To issue Official Mexican Norms for establishing the approaches to determine what residuals will be subject to management plans that include the listings of these, and that they specify the procedures to be continued in the establishment of these plans (section V).
(e) To issue Official Mexican Norms establishing, among others, environmental and technological efficiency criteria to be met by materials used to elaborate products, containers, packaging and plastic packaging, and discarded Styrofoam that become waste. Such standards must consider the principles of reduce, recycle, and reuse in handling them (section VI).
(f) To regulate and control hazardous wastes coming from small generators, large generators, or micro-generators, when these last are not controlled by local governments (section VII).
(g) To regulate the environmental aspects related to the transport of hazardous wastes (section VIII).
(h) To enact the Official Mexican Norms to prevent pollution for residuals whose final disposition can provoke salinization and excessive increments of organic loads on the ground and in bodies of water (section XXVII).

§1. Hazardous Wastes

409. Hazardous wastes are regulated by both the Environmental Act and the Waste Act.

The Environmental Act refers to this regulatory activity from three perspectives:

(1) Articles 150, 151, and 151*bis* focus on regulating the generation and final disposition of hazardous wastes.
(2) Articles 28 and 30 condition the generation, management, and final disposition of hazardous wastes upon the previous granting of authorization of the EIA and the presentation of a study of risk.
(3) Articles 5, 7, 8, and 9 establish the rules related to the system of shared competences among the federation, States, and municipalities regarding hazardous wastes. Pursuant to such provisions, the regulation and control of the operation of sites for the final disposition of hazardous wastes are exclusively the responsibility of the Federal Authorities.

410. In line with Article 150 of the Environmental Act, hazardous wastes should be managed in accordance with:

- the Environmental Act;
- the Regulations under the Environmental Act regarding hazardous wastes; and
- MONs issued on this matter.

411. However, it is important to mention that the Environmental Act only refers to four aspects related to hazardous wastes, which were developed by the Regulations and the MONs, as will be explained further on. These aspects are the following:

(1) authorization to operate gathering systems, storage, transport, reuse, treatment, recycling, incineration, and final disposition of hazardous wastes (Article 151*bis* to, sections I and II);
(2) reuse and recycling of hazardous wastes (Articles 151*bis* III and 152);
(3) import, export, and traffic in the national territory of wastes and materials (Article 153);
(4) liability for the generation, management, and final disposition of hazardous wastes and materials (Articles 151 and 152*bis*).

412. Article 151*bis* of the Environmental Act, section I, points out that 'providing services of operation of systems for the gathering, storage, transport, reuse, treatment, recycling, incineration, and final disposition of hazardous waste' requires previous authorization from the Secretary.

413. Additionally, in Article 150, the Environmental Act points out that Regulations regarding hazardous wastes, as well as the Official Mexican Norms, shall contain the approaches and listings that identify and classify the materials and hazardous wastes based on their level of danger and their characteristics and volumes.

414. The Environmental Act establishes two authorizations as mechanisms to control those who lend the reception and final disposition of hazardous waste services: an environmental impact authorization and authorization that expressly is required to lend these services. Both authorizations are the exclusive responsibility of the Federal Authorities.

415. In addition, the generation, management, and final disposition of hazardous wastes are also regulated by the Waste Act. This Act points out in Article 1, section V that its objectives are, among others, 'to regulate the generation and integral management of dangerous wastes', which is the reason why it dedicates specific titles to regulate the integral management of hazardous wastes (Articles 40–94).

416. The Waste Act focuses more on the requirements that those interested in building and operating hazardous waste disposal sites must fulfil. Article 65 of this Law states that:

> The facilities for the final disposal of hazardous wastes shall have the necessary characteristics to prevent and to reduce the possible migration of the residuals outside of the cells, in accordance with what establishes the Regulations and the applicable MONs.

417. In this regard, the Regulation under the Waste Act sets up in its Article 97 the criteria that must be observed in selecting the site, designing, building, and operating cells for landfills. Such criteria are:

I. Geological, geophysical, hydrological and hydrogeological characteristics of the site;
II. Type, quantity and characteristics of the waste to be confined;
III. Lixiviation that produce hazardous waste to be confined;
IV. Potential migration of contaminants in soil; and
V. Impact and vulnerability associated with the activity.

418. There have been issued two ONMS in regard to hazardous waste disposal facilities. The first of them is the ONM-057-Ministry of the Environment-1993, which, in item 1.5, refers to the design and construction of final disposal cells. The Official Mexican Standard establishes nine requirements for the construction of the disposal cells, which must be properly fulfilled for the project's approval and the evaluation of its environmental impact. However, the Official Mexican Standard establishes six restrictions for the construction of cells, which have to be taken into account during the evaluation of the environmental impact.

419. The second Official Mexican Standard is the NOM-055-SEMARNAT-2003 that establishes the requirements to be met by the site designated for the controlled confining of hazardous waste previously stabilized.

420. Regarding the location of sites for the final disposition of hazardous wastes, the Waste Act requires that they be kept a minimum distance from population centres larger than 1,000 inhabitants. Indeed, paragraph 2 of Article 65 of the Act holds that:

> The minimum distance that facilities for disposal of hazardous wastes must be kept from population centres larger than one thousand inhabitants, according to the last population census, shall not be less than 5 kilometres, and, when their location is planned, it shall be necessary to take into consideration the ecological classification of the territory and the applicable urban development plans.

421. The Waste Act also established mechanisms for the management and final disposition of hazardous wastes with several authorizations. In this regard, Article 50 requires that authorization be granted by the Ministry of the Environment for the following:

(a) the management of hazardous wastes;
(b) the use of hazardous wastes in production processes;
(c) the gathering and storage of hazardous wastes generated by third parties;
(d) any activity connected with the management of hazardous waste generated by third parties;

(e) the incineration of hazardous wastes;
(f) the transport of hazardous wastes;
(g) the merging of disposal sites into facilities where hazardous wastes are managed;
(h) the use of thermal treatments of waste by sterilization of thermolysis;
(i) the import and export of hazardous wastes.

422. The Waste Act also establishes the obligation of having a Management Plan. The management plan is defined by section XXI of Article 5 of the Waste Act as an instrument to minimize the generation of waste and maximize its value through actions, procedures, and viable means of producers, importers, exporters, distributors, traders, consumers, users of sub-products, and large generators of waste as well as of the three levels of government. These actions must be guided by criteria of environmental, technological, economic, and social efficiency, and by the principles of shared responsibility and integral management of waste.

423. According to Article 31 of Waste Act, generators of the following waste are required to have a management plan:

I. Used lubricating oils;
II. Organic solvents used;
III. Catalytic converters of motor vehicles;
IV. Accumulators of motor vehicles containing lead;
V. Mercury or nickel-cadmium batteries;
VI. Fluorescent and mercury vapor lamps;
VII. Additions containing mercury, cadmium or lead;
VIII. Drugs;
IX. Pesticides and their packaging containing remnants thereof;
X. Persistent organic compounds such as polychlorinated biphenyls;
XI. Oil-based drilling muds from the extraction of fossil fuels and sludge from wastewater treatment plants when considered hazardous;
XII. Blood and its components, only in their liquid form, as well as their derivatives;
XIII. The strains and cultures of pathogens generated in the diagnostic and research procedures and in the production and control of biological agents;
XIV. Pathological residues consisting of tissues, organs and parts that are removed during necropsies, surgery or any other type of surgery that is not contained in formaldehyde, and
XV. Puncture-staining residues that have been in contact with humans or animals or their biological samples during diagnosis and treatment, including scalpel blades, lancets, integrated needle syringes, hypodermic needles, acupuncture needles and tattoos.

424. In the same vein, the following are obliged to prepare a management plan:

- Whoever uses, produces, sells, or disposes of used, out-of-date, recalled, or disposed of products that are classified as such the Official Mexican Norms NOM-161-SEMARNAT-2014.
- Large generators of hazardous waste, who additionally must submit to the consideration of the Ministry of the Environment said management plan and submit an annual report on the generation and management of their hazardous waste.
- Small generators of hazardous waste, who must subject their waste to management plans, although they do not necessarily have to obtain approval from the Ministry of the Environment.
- Micro-generators of hazardous waste, who must submit to management plans and conditions established by local government authorities, i.e., management plans should not be approved by the Ministry of the Environment, but by local authorities, since, as it has been pointed out previously, the regulation of micro-generators, by virtue of the agreements signed between the Ministry of the Environment and local governments, has been left to the authorities of each local state.

425. Although there is a clearly established obligation to have a management plan, not all generators of hazardous waste have them and still less have obtained approval or approval from the corresponding authority.

426. This is perhaps because there are no specific guidelines that define the content of these management plans.

427. Article 17 of the Regulations of the Waste Act states that management plans must be formulated in accordance with the Waste Act and its Regulations, the corresponding Official Mexican Norms, but even though in 2011, the Draft Official Standard Mexican company PORY-NOM-160-SEMARNAT-2011, almost four years have passed and the standard has not yet been published, so the guidelines for the uniform preparation of hazardous waste management plans are not clear.

428. Finally, the Waste Act considers few authorizations in the field.

429. These authorizations are linked to management activities and not to the generation of hazardous waste. Regarding the generation of hazardous waste, the only obligation that is established is to register with the Ministry of the Environment in the case of large generators or whit the local authorities in the case of small generators.

430. According to Article 50 of the Waste Act conducting the following activities related to the management of hazardous waste need authorization from the Ministry of Environment:

I. Provision of hazardous waste management services;
II. The use of hazardous waste in productive processes;
III. The collection and storage of hazardous waste from third parties;

IV. The performance of any of the activities related to the handling of hazardous waste from third parties;
V. The incineration of hazardous waste;
VI. Transportation of hazardous waste;
VII. Establishment of containments within facilities where hazardous waste is handled;
VIII. The transfer of authorizations issued by the Secretariat;
IX. The use of thermal treatments of residues by sterilization or thermolysis;
X. The import and export of hazardous waste, and
XI. The others that establish by Mexican Laws.

431. The procedure for obtaining the aforementioned authorizations is defined in Third Chapter of Title IV of the Regulation under Waste Act entitled 'Hazardous Wastes', and only makes exceptions regarding the procedure for the import and export of hazardous wastes that are regulated in a different Title.

432. In this case, what is to be done is to submit the application in the format established by the Ministry of Environment, clearly indicate the activity or activities in respect of which the authorization is requested, pay the corresponding rights, present the applicant's identification or the constitutive act which indicates in the corporate purpose that the company can carry out the activity for which authorization is requested as legal administrative documents.

433. It must also present a land-use authorization issued by the corresponding authority that allows it to operate said activity in the requested terms, a plan of the executive project, the flow diagram of the process, and, where appropriate, the authorization of Federal environmental impact. All these as technical data.

434. Finally, they must have a staff-training programme and a programme for the prevention and care of contingencies or environmental emergencies and accidents.

435. In this case, obtaining an authorization depends on the accreditation of the requested requirements, above all, that the technical capacity is demonstrated and that the permits associated with such activity, such as land use and environmental impact, are available.

436. The authorizations issued may be extended whenever requested with forty-five days prior to the expiration of the validity, that the activity developed is the same as that authorized, that the hazardous wastes that were authorized continue to be handled and that the person requesting it is the holder of the authorization that is intended to be extended.

§2. Waste of Special Management and Urban Solid Waste

437. In accordance with section II of Article 10 of the Waste Act, the municipalities are responsible for the integral management of urban solid waste that consists of the gathering, transference, treatment, and final disposition, according to the following responsibilities: to enact regulations and other juridical or administrative dispositions of general observance inside their respective jurisdictions so as to enforce the present Law and the legal dispositions enacted by the states.

438. The Waste Act refers only to wastes requiring special management and urban solid waste in Articles 95–100. In this regard, the Waste Act basically establishes matters on which local and municipal governments can legislate.

439. Regarding incompatible waste, the Waste Act just refers to prohibiting their confining in the same place or cell (Article 67, section VI) and to establish sanctions for mixing incompatible waste (Article 106, section III).

Chapter 5. Soil Pollution

440. Soil pollution is inappropriately ruled by the current environmental legislation because it is associated almost exclusively with the disposal of waste even when it could result from various causes.

441. The Environmental Law contains a chapter called 'Prevention and Control of Soil Pollution', which is composed of Articles 134–144. Almost all these legal precepts are programmatic and only Article 137 states that it is subject to the authorization by municipalities or by the Federal District, the operation of the collection, storage, transportation, accommodation, reuse, treatment, and final disposal of municipal solid waste systems.

442. In the same vein, Article 142 prohibits the import of waste for its spillage, deposit, confinement, storage, incineration, or any treatment for its destruction in the national territory or in the areas in which the nation exercises sovereignty or jurisdiction. However, these two precepts only refer to soil pollution indirectly.

443. Finally, according to Article 141 of the Environmental Act, the Ministry of Environment, in coordination with the Ministries of Economy and Health, shall issue the Official Mexican Norms for the manufacture and use of containers and packages for all kinds of products whose materials make possible the reduction of solid waste generation.

444. The rest of the provisions of this chapter are much more programmatic and refer to the criteria for the prevention and control of soil contamination, the issuance of Official Mexican Norms in this area, and the process of getting into coordination agreements with the states and the municipalities.

445. By contrast, in a different chapter, Article 152*bis* specifically refers to soil pollution and establishes a parameter of soil remediation stating:

> When the generation, management or final disposal of hazardous materials and waste produces soil pollution, those responsible for these operations must carry out the necessary actions to recover and restore the conditions of the soil, so that it can be destined to any of the activities foreseen in the urban development program or of ecological ordinance plan that results applicable for the specific site or area.

446. The Waste Act also contains a chapter on soil pollution called 'liability for contamination and remediation of sites', which includes Articles 68–79.

447. The chapter fundamentally governs five issues: the obligation to repair the damages caused by soil contamination; authorization for the transfer of contaminated sites; abandonment of contaminated sites; identification, inventory, registration, and categorization of sites contaminated with hazardous wastes; and remediation declarations.

448. Transfer of polluted sites is, in principle, banned by Article 71 of the Waste Law, but this prohibition can be lifted by means of the authorization granted by the Ministry of Environment.

449. In the case of sites contaminated by hazardous waste that are abandoned, Article 73 of the Waste Law provides that the Ministry of Environment, in coordination with state and municipal governments, may formulate and execute the corresponding remediation programmes and make effective the guarantees provided by those who abandoned the site in question.

450. Likewise, under Article 75 of the Waste Act, the Ministry of the Environment and local governments are obliged to carry out actions of identification, inventory, registration, and categorization of sites contaminated with hazardous waste, to proceed to its remediation.

451. Finally, according to Article 74 of the Waste Law, the Remediation Declarations may establish modalities to the property right, but the Law does not indicate to whom it corresponds to issue such declarations.

Chapter 6. Noise and Vibrations

452. The issue addressed in this chapter is one of the least treated by Mexican environmental legislation and, because of this also, by jurisprudence.

453. First, the Environmental Act defines noise pollution in Article 3 section VI *ter* as any sound generated by human activities that, due to its intensity, duration or frequency, implies risk, annoyance, damage or harm to people, other living beings or the environment; or those that exceed the levels established by the Official Mexican Norms. The Environmental Act also refers to all these issues from the perspective of jurisdictions between the three levels of government. Article 5, section XV, empowers the federal government to regulate the prevention of environmental pollution caused by noise, vibrations, thermal energy, light, electromagnetic radiation, and odours that could result harmful to the ecological balance and the environment; while in accordance with Article 7, section VII, states have the power to prevent and control pollution generated by such pollutants when they come from fixed and mobile sources that are not of federal jurisdiction. In accordance with Article 8, section VI, municipalities are responsible for enforcing regulations on these matters in the case of commercial facilities and services. Finally, in Article 156 *bis*, the Environmental Act establishes that regarding noise pollution, the Ministry of Environment will issue the Official Mexican Norms for the establishment and operation of noise monitoring systems. The governments of the federal entities, the Municipalities and the territorial districts of Mexico City will carry out the necessary monitoring for the prevention and control of noise pollution.

454. However, Title IV of the Environmental Act contains a Chapter VIII called 'Noise, Vibrations, Thermal and Luminous Energy, Smells and Visual Pollution'. This chapter is integrated by only two precepts that seek to lay the groundwork for the regulation of all forms of pollution to which the nomenclature of the chapter refers, and obviously, it is an incomplete regulation.

455. The regulatory content of Article 155 may be summarized as follows:

(A) Prohibits the emission of noise, vibrations, thermal and light energy and generation of visual pollution, as soon as they exceed the maximum limits established in Official Mexican Norms issue by the Ministry of environment.
(B) The federal or local authorities, according to their field of competence, will take the measures to prevent that these limits are transgressed and, if applicable, apply the corresponding sanctions.
(C) In the construction of works or installations that generate thermal or light energy, noise or vibrations, as well as in the operation or operation of existing ones, preventive and corrective actions must be taken to avoid the harmful effects of such contaminants on the ecological balance and the atmosphere.

456. However, Article 156 of the Environmental Law states the following rules:

A) Official Mexican Norms on noise, vibration, thermal and light energy and the generation of visual pollution shall establish procedures to prevent and control pollution from these causes and shall set up the respective emission limits.
B) The Ministry of Health will carry out the necessary analyses, studies, investigations and surveillance to determine the origin or origin, nature, degree, magnitude and frequency of the emissions to determine when health damages occur.
C) The Ministry of the Environment, in coordination with public or private, national or international organizations, will integrate the information related to this type of pollution, as well as methods and technology to control and treat it.

457. Those who emit smells, gases or solid or liquid particles into the atmosphere, should include them in the processing and obtaining of the licence of operation or unique environmental licence which we have already analysed in the part corresponding to the air pollution, since this precept indicates:

> ARTICLE 111 BIS.- For the operation and operation of fixed sources of federal jurisdiction that emit or can emit smells, gases or solid or liquid particles into the atmosphere, authorization from the Secretariat will be required.

458. By 2008, just four Official Mexican Norms regulating noise pollution had been published by the Ministry of the Environment (NOM-079-SEMARNAT-1994, establishing the maximum permissible limits of noise emissions from new vehicles in factories and their method of measurement; NOM-080-SEMARNAT-1994, establishing the maximum permissible limits of emissions of noise from automobiles and motorcycles on the road; NOM-081-SEMARNAT-1994, establishing the maximum permissible limits of noise from fixed sources and their method of measurement; and NOM-082-SEMARNAT-1994, establishing the maximum permissible limits of noise emissions from new motorcycles in factories and their method of measurement).

459. In addition, a Official Mexican Norms, the NOM-036-SCT3-2000, that establishes the maximum permissible limits of noise emission by subsonic jet aircraft, propeller-driven, supersonic and helicopters, its measurement method, and the requirements to comply with these limits whereas no Official Mexican Norms on vibrations have been passed yet.

460. It is important to mention that in 1982, a regulation under the Federal Act for Environmental Protection on Pollution from Noise Emissions was issued by the Executive. That Regulation is still in force when it does not contradict the Environmental Act. According to the Regulation, the maximum level of noise emissions from fixed sources is sixty-eight decibels from six to twenty-two hours and sixty-five decibels from twenty-two to six hours (Article 11). In cases of mobile sources, the Regulation establishes that the maximum level of emissions is from 79 to 84 decibels (Article 29).

Chapter 7. Luminous Contamination

461. The original text of the Environmental Act that came into force in 1988 did not include the subject of light pollution, but in 2021 a brief reference to it was introduced within Second Chapter of Title Four relating to atmospheric pollution. The new Article 110*bis* states:

> article 110 bis to achieve the prevention, reduction and control of luminous contamination in the atmosphere, the following objectives should be considered:
>
> a) Promote energy efficiency through efficient use of outdoor lighting, without detriment to the safety it should provide to pedestrians, vehicles and property;
> b) To preserve as much as possible the natural conditions of nighttime hours for the benefit of fauna, flora and ecosystems in general;
> c) To prevent, minimize, and correct the effects of light pollution in the night sky and, in particular, in the surroundings of astronomical observatories working in the visible spectrum; and
> d) Reduce light intrusion in areas other than those intended to be illuminated, mainly in natural environments and buildings.

462. According to Article 3, section VI *bis*, luminous contamination is the luminous glow in night-time environments or brightness produced by the diffusion and reflection of light in gases, aerosols and particles suspended in the atmosphere, which alters the natural conditions of luminosity at night and hinders astronomical observations of celestial objects, due to intrusive light, distinguishing natural brightness, attributable to the radiation of celestial sources or objects and the luminescence of the upper layers of the atmosphere.

463. The Environmental Law does not contain any specific regulation on this matter. Instead, the Ministry of the Environment is empowered to issue future regulations. In this sense, Article 111 states:

> The Ministry of the Environment is entitled to:
>
> XV. Issue, in coordination with the Ministry of Energy, the OMNs that establish and certify the maximum permissible levels of artificial light in the environment, including the impact of intrusive light that cause light pollution; and
> XVI. Promote, in coordination with the Ministry of Energy and local governments, the formulation and application of programs to prevent, reduce and control light pollution, aimed at complying with the applicable regulations.

Part II. Nature Conservation and Management

464. Mexico is one of the twelve countries in the world considered to be mega-diverse.[65] According to official data, it ranks fifth in terms of the number of plant species, third in terms of mammals, second in reptiles, and fourth in amphibians.[66]

465. With only 1.4% of the planet's land surface, our country possesses about 10% of the total number of known species in the world. In addition, it stands out for its endemism, which in the case of flora, oscillates between 44% and 63%, while for vertebrates, the proportion is 30% on average.

466. However, as the National Environmental Program 2013–2018 recognizes, 'an important part of the country's biological wealth is at risk'.[67] This document states that according to NOM-059-SEMARNAT-2010, there are 2,606 species in some category of risk, among them many emblematic such as the jaguar, the golden eagle, the quetzal and the vaquita marina. Among the plants, the groups with the most species at risk are cacti, orchids, palms, and agaves. In the case of animals, the groups with the most species at risk are reptiles (54.4% of known species in the country), birds (33.5%), mammals (45.2%), amphibians (53.7%), and fish (7.5%).

467. In fact, one of the environmental problems that is becoming worldwide increasingly important, and to which our country is no stranger, is the constant and growing loss of biological diversity. According to the OECD, the causes of biodiversity loss may be direct or indirect. The direct causes are: destruction or alteration of habitats; exploitation of wild species; homogenization of crops; pollution and climate change. Indirect causes are: consumption and production patterns; population growth and distribution; and the failure of the economic model.[68]

---

65. Mega-diverse countries are a group of nations that contain more than 70% of the Earth's biodiversity, identified by Conservation International (CI), to promote awareness of biodiversity conservation among the nations of the world. Mexico has 12% of the planet's biodiversity with 200,000 different species, ranking 5th in the world. *See*: http://www.biodiversidad.gob.mx/pais/quees.html.
66. This is supported both by a report of the Coordination of Information and External Services of the CONABIO of 2012 and the World Resources Institute of 2014.
67. *See*: Programa Nacional de Medio Ambiente y Recursos Naturales in http://www.semarnat.gob.mx/archivosanteriores/Documents/PROMARNAT%202013-2018.pdf.
68. *See*: OECD, *Savin Biological Diversity. Economic Insentives*. OECD, París, 1976, p. 43.

468. In our opinion, the inefficiency of legal systems in regulating issues such as the ownership and sustainable use of biodiversity resources and habitat conservation contributes significantly to this problem. The following sections analyse this paradigm.

§1. Biodiversity as an Object of Legal Protection in the Mexican Legal System

469. The distinguished environmentalist Michael Prieur has held that one of the fundamental contributions of environmental law is the recognition of the value that nature has as an essential component of the human universe,[69] but as another of the founders of environmental law, Ramón Martín Mateo, points out, 'the concern for the maintenance and intrinsic promotion of biodiversity as a whole is relatively recent, preceded by the protection of singular species, an approach that is obviously maintained but that at least at the national level should be integrated into a general strategy'.[70]

470. In fact, although in Mexico flora and fauna have been the object of legal protection since a long time ago,[71] the integral protection of biodiversity is not yet a reality. Before the Stockholm Summit in 1972,[72] hunting and fishing laws ruled the use of fauna, but not from the perspective of their protection.

471. One of the virtues of the 1988 Environmental Act is that since its original text, this legal body already included in its Title II a series of legal provisions focused on the regulation of protected natural areas, while Title III was dedicated to the rational use of natural elements.

472. It was not until the 1990s when, under the influence of the CBD,[73] the protection of natural resources of wild and aquatic flora and fauna and their habitat took

---

69. Michael Prieur, *Droit de l'environnement.* París, Dalloz, 2001, p. 279.
70. Ramón Martín Mateo, *Tratado de Derecho Ambiental*, vol. III. Madrid, Civitas, 1997, p. 41.
71. The Hunting Act of 1952 and 1940, Fishing Act of the United Mexican States of 1950, Fishing Act of 1947, Fishing Act in Mexican Territorial Waters of the Pacific Ocean and Gulf of California of 1938, Fishing Act of 1932, Maritime and Fluvial Fishing Regulations of the Mexican Republic of 1926 and Fishing Act of 1925.
72. The Stockholm Summit refers to the conference held in Stockholm on 16 Jun. 1972, attended by 110 countries and for the first time the international community discussed environmental issues. The result of this conference was the Stockholm Declaration on the Human Environment with 26 principles to follow.
73. The Convention on Biological Diversity was opened for signature on 5 Jun. 1992 at the Earth Summit in Rio de Janeiro, and entered into force on 29 Dec. 1993. To date, two protocols have been adopted under this convention. The Cartagena Protocol on Biosafety and the Nagoya Protocol on Access and Benefit-sharing. Available at: http://www.un.org/es/events/biodiversityday/convention.shtml.

on a different dimension, due almost everywhere in the world there was a shift from the isolated consideration of these elements to their integral regulation, including that of their habitat.[74]

473. The CBD transforms the paradigm of natural resources protection because it builds all its normative structure based on a new legal category, which is biodiversity. This normative category is defined by the CBD as the variability of life, including terrestrial and aquatic ecosystems, the ecological complexes of which they are part, diversity within species, and among other species (Article 2 of the CBD).

474. However, due to the 1988 Environmental Act did not regulate all aspects contemplated in the CBD, at the beginning of the twenty-first century, a series of new legal bodies were passed: in 2000 the Wildlife Act, in 2003 the General Act on Sustainable Forest Use, in 2007 the General Act on Fishing and Sustainable Aquaculture, and in 2012 the General Act on Climate Change. All these acts deal with diverse aspects related to biodiversity protection. However, the new legal framework built with all these acts is far from being consistent and comprehensive, as it will be analysed in this chapter.

475. The Mexican environmental law deals with biodiversity protection in a non-systematic and incomplete manner. As it will be analysed, this system is based on the establishment of a series of permits, licences and authorizations, taxes with an extra-fiscal purpose, as well as modalities on private property rights.

§2. Biodiversity Property

476. It has been said that 'what belongs to everyone belongs to no one'.[75] This phrase applies very well to the subject we are analysing since, in many jurisdictions, it is claimed that biodiversity resources belong to everyone, and this has led to the weakness of legal structures trying to protect them. In the case of Mexico, neither the Constitution nor secondary legislation establishes a clear criterion in regard to biodiversity ownership. In fact, Article 27 of the Constitution does not refer to the ownership of biodiversity resources. This constitutional provision just focuses on the use of natural elements susceptible of appropriation. In the past, this confusion between ownership and appropriation has led to legislative errors. For example, Article 3 of the now repealed Federal Hunting Act of 1952 stated: 'All wild animal species that subsist in the national territory are the property of the nation and it is up to the Ministry of Agriculture and Livestock to authorize hunting

74. Ramón Martín Mateo, *Tratado de Derecho Ambiental*, vol. III. Madrid, Civitas, 1997, p. 41.
75. Harding Garret, 'The Tragedy of the Commons', en *Science*, núm. 162, pp. 1243–1248, 13 Dec. 1968.

and the appropriation of their products.'[76] It is obvious that such legal precept lacked constitutional foundation; fauna was never considered by the Constitution as a national property.

477. The SCJN has not been very clear on the matter, but in a few rulings, it has distinguished between the direct dominion of the nation over certain natural resources and sovereignty rights over others, as can be observed in the following isolated thesis:

> DIRECT DOMINATION OF THE NATION AND SOVEREIGN RIGHTS OVER NATURAL RESOURCES. ARE SUBJECT TO THE SAME LEGAL REGIME WITHIN THE INTERNAL SPHERE.
> *The amendment to article 27, fourth paragraph, of the Political Constitution of the United Mexican States, published into the DOF on January 20, 1960, incorporated the continental shelf and submarine sockets into Mexican territory, establishing that the Nation does not have absolute sovereignty or full dominion in these areas, unlike any other part of that territory, because while it can explore and exploit all the natural resources of that portion of the continental mass, it is not entitled to affect overlying waters or the airspace above the seabed and subsoil of submarine waters, which is corroborated by article 76 of the United Nations Convention on the Law of the Sea, which uses the word 'exclusive' in the sense that no other State can conduct such exploration and exploitation without the approval of the coastal State that owns or controls such natural resources. For this reason, the Reforming Power assimilated the 'sovereign rights' over natural resources, with the direct dominion of the Nation in relation to them, by virtue of the fact that both concepts presuppose the power to use and dispose of goods, and the recognition that the referred natural resources are theirs, given that the first expression is commonly used in the international sphere because the rights exercised by each State are delimited, and in the second, as the property regime of only one is dealt with, only one direct domain is highlighted, but the two have the same legal connotation in the internal sphere.*[77]

478. However, wild animals have never been the property of the nation not only because the Constitution does not nationalize these natural resources but also because the General Act on National Assets does not include them as such. This Act only considers within the public domain the following goods: (a) Those of common use, (b) Those listed in section II of Article 27 of the Constitution, with the exception of those included in section II of Article 3 of the same Act, and (c) The bed and subsoil of the territorial sea and inland marine waters.

479. However, according to Article 7 of the above-mentioned Act, the following assets are considered of common use:

---

76. The Federal Hunting Act was published in the DOF 5 Jan. 1952.
77. Amparo in revision 288/2010. Esteva Mercantil Mexicana y Asociados, S.A de C.V. 2 Jun. 2010. Five votes. Speaker: José Fernando Franco González Salas, Secretary: Israel Flores Rodríguez.

I. The airspace above the national territory, with the extent and modalities established by international law;
II. Inland marine waters, in accordance with the Federal Sea Act;
III. The territorial sea in the width established by the Federal Sea Act;
IV. The maritime beaches, understood as the parts of land that by virtue of the tide covers and discovers the water, from the limits of greater back-flow to the limits of greater annual flow;
V. The federal terrestrial maritime zone;
VI The ports, bays, roads and coves;
VII. Docks, piers, breakwaters, jetties and other works of the ports, when they are of public use;
VIII. The channels of the currents and the vessels of the lakes, lagoons and estuaries of national property;
IX. The riverbanks and federal zones of the currents;
X. Dams, embankments and their vessels, canals, embankments and ditches, built for irrigation, navigation and other uses of public utility, with their protection zones and rights of way, or banks in the extension that, in each case, the competent agency establishes in the matter, in accordance with the applicable legal provisions;
XI. The roads, highways, bridges and railroads that constitute general means of communication, with their auxiliary services and other integral parts established in the federal act on the subject;
XII. The buildings considered as archaeological monuments according to the act on the subject;
XIII. Squares, promenades and public parks whose construction or conservation is the responsibility of the Federal Government and buildings erected by the Federal Government in public places for ornament or comfort of those who visit them, and
XIV. Other goods considered to be in common use by other laws regulating national goods.

480. According to the aforementioned Act, this type of property may, in principle, be used by all inhabitants of the Republic without any limitations other than those established by the Act, but for special uses a concession is required. Nevertheless, as can be observed, the law does not clarify who owns biodiversity or its elements.

481. This criterion is confirmed by the Federal Civil Code that holds in Article 768: 'Common goods are inalienable and imprescriptible. All inhabitants can use them, with the restrictions established in the Law, but for special uses it is necessary to grant a concession with the requirements established in the respective laws.'[78]

78. The Federal Civil Code entered into force on 1 Oct. 1932.

482. In line with the mentioned provision, we can say that wildlife is considered as *res nullius*, but its appropriation is permitted for harvesting purposes through the issuance of an administrative act that authorizes it. Moreover, the Civil Code itself allows 'special uses' by concession. If this were the case, it would seem that the private ownership of these legal assets is not recognized by the national legal system.

483. In short, the ownership of those natural resources that the Constitution has not reserved to the nation as part of the *demanio* is, in principle, governed by Civil Law, but as we will *see* below, subject to the powers granted to the nation by Article 27 of the Constitution, to modulate the private property right in favour of ecological balance and environmental protection. The Constitution does not refer at any time to the ownership of biodiversity, an issue that is a much more complex issue.

I. The Principle *Accesorium non ducit, sed sequitur suum principale*

484. According to the principle 'the accessory follows the fate of the principal', the ownership of some biodiversity resources such as forests is subject to the ownership regime of the natural resource that supports it. In this regard, Article 5 of the Forest Act states that:

> Ownership of forest resources within the national territory belongs to the ejidos, communities, indigenous peoples and communities, natural or legal persons, the Federation, the States, the Federal District and the municipalities that own the land on which they are located. The procedures established by this Act shall not alter the system of ownership of such land.

485. In other words, forest resources may fall into the private domain or the public domain. It depends on who is the landowner where the forest is located. Since the forest is an accessory of private property, it is subject to private property law and therefore susceptible of the exercise of the powers vested on the nation by the third paragraph of Article 27 of the Constitution to impose modalities on private property.

486. Among the modalities on forest ownership that the Forest Act establishes are the prohibition of forestlands use change that only can be authorized by exception[79] and the authorization of forest use.

487. The exercise of the nation's power to impose modalities on the private property of natural resources has become the foundation of public environmental policies aimed at protecting and promoting the sustainable use of those natural resources that fall within the private domain.

79. Forest Act Art. 58, s. I.

488. Although the General Act on Fishing and Aquaculture does not refer to this matter, the same principle is also applicable to the case of aquatic fauna, and therefore, the resources of the aquatic fauna should be considered as property of the nation. The United Nations Convention on the Law of the Sea and the General Act on National Assets support this criterion, according to which, as we have seen, the living resources of the exclusive economic zone are subject to the Nation's public domain regime.

489. Article 56 of the United Nations Convention on the Law of the Sea points out:

> 1. In the exclusive economic zone, the coastal State has: (a) sovereign rights for the purpose of exploring and exploiting, conserving and managing the natural resources, whether living or non-living, of the waters superjacent to the seabed and of the seabed and its subsoil, and with regard to other activities for the economic exploitation and exploration of the zone, such as the production of energy from the water, currents and winds.

490. The fifth paragraph of Article 27 of the Constitution provides that the territorial seas shall be nationally owned waters to the extent and in terms determined by the international treaties to which Mexico is a party, while the ninth paragraph of the same provision states that:

> The Nation exercises in an exclusive economic zone located outside the territorial sea and adjacent to it, the rights of sovereignty and the jurisdictions determined by the laws of the Congress. The exclusive economic zone shall extend to two hundred nautical miles, measured from the baseline from which the territorial sea is measured. In cases where such an extension would overlap with the exclusive economic zones of other States, the delimitation of the respective zones shall be made to the extent necessary by agreement with those States.

491. According to Article 7, section III of the General Act on National Assets, the territorial sea is considered a national asset of common use.

492. However, the principle is not applicable to terrestrial fauna because the General Act on Wildlife clearly states that the owners of the properties where wildlife is distributed only have sustainable use rights but not property rights.

II. Common-Use Biodiversity Resources (*res nullius*)

493. The third paragraph of Article 27 of the Political Constitution refers to the natural resources susceptible of appropriation, indicating that:

> The nation shall at all times have the right [...] to regulate, for social benefit, the use of natural resources that may be appropriated, with a view to achieving

an equitable distribution of public wealth, taking care of its conservation, achieving the balanced development of the country and improving the living conditions of the rural and urban population.

494. The Constitution does not indicate which are those natural resources that are susceptible of appropriation, but a clear example of this property regime is found in Article 4 of the Wildlife Act, according to which: 'The owners or legitimate possessors of the lands in which the wild life is distributed, will have rights of sustainable use on their specimens, parts and derivatives in the terms prescribed in the present Law and other applicable provisions.'

495. In this case, as can be seen, the owner of the land does not own the wildlife resources that inhabit it, but just a right of use that does not exclude the possibility of use of those resources by people other than the owner, since the Law does not assign to the owner – as in the case of subsoil waters – an exclusive right in such a way that wildlife resources are within the regime of *res nullius*. Therefore, the protection of these resources is materialized in the exercise of the power that the nation has, through secondary legislation, to establish rules on their use, which must be governed by the constitutional principles of sustainability, the right to an adequate environment and the obligation to repair environmental damage.

496. The National Supreme Court pronounces on the matter in the following thesis where it establishes that although it is true that the nation can transmit the original domain of lands and waters to constitute the private property, this does not mean that together with it the property of the natural resources located in them is transmitted and that for the same reason only the nation corresponds to its direct domain, that is to say, that only the nation can dispose of those resources. The National Supreme Court holds that:

> ORIGINAL PROPERTY OF THE NATION AND DIRECT OWNERSHIP OF NATURAL RESOURCES. THEIR DIFFERENCES.
> *Article 27, first paragraph, of the Political Constitution of the United Mexican States expressly states that ownership of lands and waters within the limits of the national territory originally belongs to the Nation, which exercises maximum power over them and, based on it, may transfer them to private individuals to constitute private property, or once their domain has been transferred, if it is necessary to dispose of those through the means provided in the Supreme Law itself, being that both the Constituent Congress of 1916 and the doctrine have called such property as 'absolute property', 'supreme domain', 'full domain' or 'eminent domain', similar to that existing in colonial or virreinal law, currently delimited by international law. Thus, although ownership of land and water may be transferred to private individuals, it does not imply that ownership of the natural resources found in them is always transferred, because the fourth and fifth paragraphs of the aforementioned constitutional precept establish that the Nation has direct control over them, that is to say, only the Nation may dispose of the resources or goods, living or not, described in those paragraphs, but in the use of that sovereignty it authorizes the governed –*

without in these cases private property being constituted – to exploit and temporarily use them through a concession, except in the exceptional cases provided for in the sixth paragraph of Article 27 of the Fundamental Law. [80]

§3. Biodiversity Protection by International Law

497. Mexico has signed several international treaties that commit it to protect wildlife and its habitat, such as: the Convention on Wetlands of International Importance Especially as Waterfowl Habitat (Ramsar Convention);[81] the Convention for the Protection of the World Cultural and Natural Heritage (Paris Convention);[82] the Convention on International Trade in Endangered Species of Wild Fauna and Flora (CITES);[83] the Convention Between the United Mexican States and the United States of America for the Protection of Migratory Birds and Game Mammals and the Convention on the Conservation of Migratory Species.[84] The United Nations Convention on the Law of the Sea (Montego Bay Convention);[85] and the CBD.[86]

498. However, the incorporation of Mexico's commitments into national legislation presents some problems. In fact, it is usual that the provisions contained in international agreements are not self-applicable, so that, despite the fact that in mandatory jurisprudence of the SCJN has granted supremacy to international treaties over federal laws, it is sometimes necessary to issue appropriate national legislation for such agreements to be incorporated into the national legal order. This fact is one of the main factors that explain the relative ineffectiveness of international environmental law since it is normal that the process of adaptation of this legislation takes many years.

499. The following section analyses these issues.

I. The Ramsar Convention

500. The Convention on Wetlands of International Importance, especially as Waterfowl Habitat was signed in Ramsar City, Iran, in 1971 and entered into force

80. Amparo in revision 288/2010. Esteva Mercantil Mexicana y Asociados, S.A. de C.V. 2 Jun. 2010. Five votes. Speaker: José Fernando Franco González Salas. Secretary: Israel Flores Rodríguez.
81. Signed on 2 Feb. 1971. Mexico acceded to this Treaty on 4 Jul. 1986 and was ratified on 20 Dec. 1984.
82. Held in Paris on 16 Nov. 1972. Mexico accepted the Convention on 23 Feb. 1984, ratifying it on 22 Dec. 1983.
83. Signed in Washington, D.C., 3 Mar. 1973. Mexico accepted this Convention on 23 Feb. 1984 and ratified it on 2 Jul. 1991.
84. The first was adopted in Mexico City on 7 Feb. 1936. Mexico ratified this Convention on 27 Nov. 1936 and the second in Bonn in 1983.
85. Signed 10 Dec. 1982. Mexico ratified this Convention on 18 Mar. 1983.
86. This convention was adopted on 5 June in Rio de Janeiro during the Earth Summit in 1992. Mexico ratified this convention on 11 Mar. 1993.

in 1975; it has been amended by the Paris Protocol in 1982[87] and by the Regina amendments in 1987.[88] This Convention is considered to be the first intergovernmental Treaty regulating the conservation and wise use of natural resources, particularly wetlands.[89]

501. The aim of the Ramsar Treaty is to conserve and make wise use of wetlands through local, regional and national actions of international cooperation for sustainable development, which is why it is requested as a membership status that the Contracting Parties must designate at least one site that will be subject to protection under the terms of the Treaty. The Convention currently has 160 Member States.

502. The Treaty also protects the water birds that inhabit the wetlands. To narrow its scope, Article 1 of the Ramsar Convention defines both concepts:

1. For the purpose of this Convention wetlands are areas of marsh, fen, peatland or water, whether natural or artificial, permanent or temporary, with water that is static or flowing, fresh, brackish or salt, including areas of marine water the depth of which at low tide does not exceed six metres.
2. For the purpose of this Convention waterfowl are birds ecologically dependent on wetlands.

503. Mexico currently has 142 sites considered as wetlands of international relevance,[90] making it the country with the highest number of designated sites, after the United Kingdom with 168.[91]

504. In accordance with the provisions of Articles 3–5 of the Convention, the Signatory Parties, in addition to designating suitable sites to be protected, also commit to:

1. formulate and implement their planning so as to promote the conservation of the wetlands included in the List, and as far as possible the wise use of wetlands in their territory.
2. arrange to be informed at the earliest possible time if the ecological character of any wetland in its territory and included in the List has changed, is changing or is likely to change as the result of technological developments, pollution or other human interference.

---

87. The Paris Protocol was adopted by the Extraordinary Conference of the Parties held in the City of Paris from 2 to 3 Dec. 1982 and entered into force on 1 Oct. 1986.
88. The so-called Regina amendments were adopted during the Second Extraordinary Conference of the Contracting Parties on 28 May 1987 and modify Arts 6 and 7 of the Convention.
89. Unlike the other global environmental conventions, the Ramsar Convention is not affiliated with the United Nations system of multilateral environmental agreements but collaborates very closely with the other multilateral agreements and is a full partner among the treaties and agreements of the 'biodiversity group'.
90. *See*: Comisión Nacional de Áreas Naturales Protegidas. Ramsar en México. Available at: intranet.cibnor.mx.
91. *See*: snap, Sitios de referencia internacional. Disponible en: snap.cu.

3. promote the conservation of wetlands and waterfowl by establishing nature reserves on wetlands, whether they are included in the List or not, and provide adequately for their wardening
4. consult with each other about implementing obligations arising from the Convention especially in the case of a wetland extending over the territories of more than one Contracting Party or where a water system is shared by Contracting Parties.

505. This international environmental convention has been implemented in Mexico in the Environmental Act.

II. The Convention for the Protection of the World Cultural and Natural Heritage

506. The Convention for the Protection of the Cultural and Natural Heritage has 191 ratifications and currently protects a heritage that includes 1,073 properties (206 natural properties,[92] 832 cultural properties,[93] and 35 mixed properties[94]) in 145 countries. Its aim is to promote cooperation among nations to protect heritage around the world that is of such extraordinary universal value that its conservation is important for future generations. Mexican legislation has extrapolated the provisions of this Treaty, primarily through the system of protected natural areas established by the Environmental Act and the protection of historical, archaeological, and artistic heritage regulated by the Federal Act on Monuments and Archaeological, Artistic and Historic Zones.

---

92. Article 2 of the Convention provides that the following shall be regarded as natural heritage:
    (a) natural monuments consisting of physical and biological formations or groups of such formations which are of outstanding universal value from the aesthetic or scientific point of view;
    (b) geological and physiographic formations and strictly defined areas constituting the habitat of endangered animal and plant species of outstanding universal value from the aesthetic or scientific point of view;
    (c) natural sites or strictly defined natural areas of outstanding universal value from the point of view of science, conservation or natural beauty.
93. According to Art. 1 of the Convention, monuments, including architectural works, monumental sculptures or paintings, elements or structures of an archaeological nature, inscriptions, caverns and groups of elements, which are of outstanding universal value from the point of view of history, art or science, are considered cultural heritage; ensembles made up of groups of buildings, isolated or assembled, whose architecture, unity and integration into the landscape gives them an outstanding universal value from the point of view of the history of art or science, and to sites, i.e., works of man or joint works of nature and of man, as well as archaeological sites of outstanding universal value from the historical, aesthetic, ethnological or anthropological point of view.
94. Mixed properties are those with both natural and cultural values.

III. The Convention on International Trade in Endangered Species of Wild Fauna and Flora (CITES)

507. This International Convention[95] entered into force after Canada deposited its tenth instrument of ratification on 1 July 1975, in accordance with the provisions of its Clause XXII. To date, 183 countries are members, including Mexico, which approved this international instrument on 2 July 1991.

508. Even though they are not expressly stated by the treaty, the objectives of the CITES are:

1. To conserve the planet's biodiversity on the basis of sustainable development; and
2. To regulate international trade in the species of wild fauna and flora included in its Appendices, guaranteeing their conservation for future generations.

509. In this way, the Convention protects species of wild fauna and flora that are affected both by habitat modification[96] and by human settlements, whether endangered or subject to controlled trade.

510. While the text of the Convention refers primarily to trade in species of wild fauna and flora, the Preamble highlights principles that go beyond trade regulation, which are:

> Recognizing that wild fauna and flora, in their numerous, beautiful and varied forms, constitute an irreplaceable element of the earth's natural systems, must be protected for this and future generations; and Recognizing that peoples and States are and should be the best protectors of their wild fauna and flora.

511. In accordance with these principles, carrying out any works or activities that are intended to develop and may affect the species protected by this Treaty must take into account not only the provisions contained in the CITES on commerce but also the protection of the habitat of species of wild fauna and flora that could be affected by such works or activities.

95. Its website cites.org defines it as an international agreement between governments. It aims to ensure that international trade in specimens of wild animals and plants does not constitute a threat to their survival.
96. About 5,000 animal species and 30,000 plant species are protected by the CITES against over-exploitation due to international trade.

512. CITES refers to species of wild flora and fauna that are under the status of 'endangered or threatened'. However, it does not only protect species that are currently under this status but also those species that, although not in this status, if the relevant measures for their protection are not adopted, could become part of this group.[97]

513. However, although CITES does not refer to the negative impacts that human activities may have on flora and fauna, Mexico's signing of the Convention has provided a foundation for the establishment of a national regime for the protection of threatened or endangered species.

514. In Mexico, the Wildlife Act is the national legal system that regulates this issue, but the list that defines threatened or endangered species is found in NOM 59-SEMARNAT-2010, Environmental Protection – Mexico's Native Species of Wild Flora and Fauna-Risk Categories and Specifications for Inclusion, Exclusion or Change-List of Species at Risk.

515. However, Article 35 of the Environmental Act indicates in its section III, paragraph (b) that the Ministry of the Environment could deny authorization in matters of environmental impact in cases in which the work or activity subject to evaluation could cause one or more species to be declared threatened or in danger of extinction or when one of the said species is affected.

IV. The Convention for the Protection of Migratory Birds and Game Mammals and the Convention on the Conservation of Migratory Species

516. The Convention for the Protection of Migratory Birds and Game Mammals[98] is a bilateral treaty between the governments of the United Mexican States and the US.[99] Although the Convention does not clearly state its objective, it is possible to maintain, in light of the provisions of the preamble, that it consists of the protection of migratory birds from extinction through the rational use of such birds in sport, food, commerce, and industry.

517. In addition to the above, in terms of Article V, the Parties undertake to include the stipulations contained in Article II with respect to the hunting mammals that inhabit their respective countries, which states that the Parties commit themselves to:[100]

---

97. Lists of species offering different levels and types of protection from over-exploitation are available at: https://cites.org/esp/app/index.php.
98. It was signed in Mexico City on 7 Feb. 1936.
99. It was signed by Eduardo Hay who represented the President of the United Mexican States, General Lázaro Cárdenas and Josephus Daniels, representing the President of the United States of America, Flanklin D. Roosevelt.
100. Available at: http://www.conanp.gob.mx.

(…) establish laws, regulations and provisions to satisfy the need set forth in the preceding Article, including:

A) The establishment of close seasons, which will prohibit in certain periods of the year the taking of migratory birds, their nests or eggs, as well as their transportation or sale, alive or dead, their products or parts, except when proceeding, with appropriate authorization, from private game farms or when used for scientific purposes, for propagation or for museums.
B) The establishment of refuge zones in which the taking of such birds will be prohibited.
C) The limitation of their hunting to four months in each year, as a maximum, under permits issued by the respective authorities in each case.
D) The establishment of a close season of wild ducks from the tenth of March to the first of September.
E) The prohibition of the killing of migratory insectivorous birds, except when they become injurious to agriculture and constitute plagues, as well as when they come from reserves or game farms: provided however that such birds may be captured alive and used in conformity with the laws of each contracting country.
F) The prohibition of hunting from aircraft.

518. Likewise, in accordance with Article III of the Convention, the Contracting Parties agree not to permit the transportation over the American-Mexican border of migratory birds, dead or alive, their parts or products, without a permit of authorization provided for that purpose by the government of each country, with the understanding that in the case that the said birds, their parts or products are transported from one country to the other without the stipulated authorization, they will be considered as contraband and treated accordingly.

519. The Environmental Act and the Wildlife Act have introduced some of the commitments set out by the Convention into national law.

520. However, the Convention on the Conservation of Migratory Species or Bonn Convention is a framework convention that aims to conserve fauna through the conservation of its habitat.

521. This Convention provides the basis for regional agreements such as the Convention between Mexico and the US.

522. The convention includes two appendices: the first lists endangered migratory species and the second lists migratory species that need or would benefit from international cooperation.

V. The United Nations Convention on the Law of the Sea

523. The Law of the Sea Convention[101] states that signatory states have an obligation to protect and preserve the marine environment without prejudice to their sovereign right to exploit their natural resources in accordance with their environmental policy. The convention requires States to take such measures as may be necessary to prevent, reduce, and control pollution of the marine environment from any source.

524. They must also take the necessary measures to ensure that activities under their jurisdiction or control are carried out in such a way that they do not cause pollution damage to other states and their environment or to areas beyond the zones where they exercise sovereign rights, i.e., the territorial sea, the contiguous zone, and the exclusive economic zone.[102]

VI. The Convention on Biological Diversity

525. As already mentioned, the CBD was signed in Rio de Janeiro in 1992[103] and aims at the conservation of biological diversity, the sustainable use of its components and the fair and equitable sharing of the benefits derived from the utilization of genetic resources through, among other things, adequate access to those resources and appropriate transfer of relevant technologies, taking into account all rights over those resources and technologies, as well as through appropriate funding.[104]

526. This Convention regulates biological diversity, i.e., the variability of living organisms from all sources, including, among other things, terrestrial, marine, and other aquatic ecosystems and the ecological complexes of which they are part, including diversity within species, between species and ecosystems.

527. In addition to the above, the CBD establishes as obligations of developing countries, the protection of biodiversity, economic and social development, and poverty eradication. The CBD contains three categories of obligations for contracting parties:

(1) Obligations to conserve biological diversity.
(2) Obligations for the sustainable use of components of biological diversity.

---

101. It was signed on 10 Dec. 1982 and approved in Montego Bay, Jamaica. It consists of 17 parts, 320 articles and 9 annexes in total.
102. This Convention gave rise to the following bodies: International Seabed Authority, International Tribunal for the Law of the Sea and Commission on the Limits of the Continental Shelf.
103. Currently 196 are Parties to this Agreement, the USA and the Vatican have yet to ratify.
104. This Convention was open for signature by all States and by any regional economic integration organization from 5 Jun. 1992 to 14 Jun. 1992, and at United Nations Headquarters in New York from 15 Jun. 1992 to 4 Jun. 1993.

(3) Obligations for the fair and equitable sharing of benefits arising out of the utilization of genetic resources.

528. However, when it comes to obligations related to the conservation of biological diversity, the Treaty stipulates that contracting parties must identify and monitor the resources of their biological diversity, as well as conserve it in situ and ex situ. In situ, conservation occurs precisely through protected natural areas.

529. Finally, Article 14 of the Convention refers to the assessment of impact and the minimization of adverse impact, according to this precept, each contracting party, to the extent possible:

a) Will establish appropriate procedures requiring environmental impact assessment of its proposed projects likely to have significant adverse effects on biological diversity with a view to avoiding or minimizing such effects and, where appropriate, permit public participation in such procedures;
b) Will establish appropriate arrangements to ensure that due account is taken of the environmental consequences of its programmes and policies that may have significant adverse effects on biological diversity;
c) Will promote, on a reciprocal basis, notification, exchange of information and consultation on activities under its jurisdiction or control that are expected to have significant adverse effects on the biological diversity of other States or areas not under national jurisdiction, encouraging the conclusion of bilateral, regional or multilateral agreements, as appropriate
d) Wil notify immediately if imminent or serious dangers to biological diversity originate under its jurisdiction or control, or damage to such diversity in the area under the jurisdiction of other States or in areas beyond the limits of national jurisdiction, to States that may be affected by such hazards or damage, in addition to initiating measures to prevent or minimize such hazards or damage; and
e) Will promote national arrangements for emergency measures related to natural or other activities or events involving serious and imminent threats to biological diversity, support international cooperation to complement such national measures and, where appropriate and with the agreement of the States or regional economic integration organizations concerned, establish joint contingency plans.

530. The provisions described above are contained in the Environmental Act. In accordance with Article 28, section XI of that Act, all projects or activities intended to be carried out in protected natural areas under the jurisdiction of the Federation must first be subject to the EIA procedure.

531. In sum, most of the provisions of this Convention, particularly those relating to the identification and monitoring of components of biological diversity, as well as in situ conservation through the establishment of protected natural areas and the establishment of Wildlife Conservation and Management Units and critical habitats have been collected by the Environmental Act and the Wildlife Act.

§4. Biodiversity Protection by National Law

532. Based on the third paragraph of Article 27 of the Constitution, as well as on the principles established by the international treaties adopted by Mexico, environmental legislation establishes various mechanisms aimed at regulating the use of flora and fauna resources that are susceptible of appropriation.

533. In Mexican law, the laws regulating various aspects relating to the ownership and sustainable use of biodiversity are: the Environmental Act, the Wildlife Act, Forest Act, the General Act on Sustainable Fisheries and Aquaculture, the Act on Biosafety and Genetically Modified Organisms and the Federal Act on Plant Varieties,[105] as well as the corresponding local laws which, based on the principle of concurrent competence, have been enacted in these areas by state legislatures.

534. In the following sections, we will analyse each of these laws.

I. The Environmental Act

535. The Environmental Act is neither the only nor the main environmental legal body that deals with biodiversity protection in Mexico. Although Article 82 of that law states that 'The provisions of this law are applicable to the possession, administration, preservation, repopulation, propagation, import, export and development of wild flora and fauna and genetic material, without prejudice to what is established in other legal systems', it only regulates few aspects related to this matter.

536. The Environmental Act establishes the system of protected natural areas as an instrument whose objective is to protect the habitat of flora and fauna species. It also regulates a series of permits and authorizations that refer only to some of the aspects mentioned by the aforementioned Article 82 of that order. In the following sections, we analyse both issues.

105. The Environmental Act was published in the DOF on 28 Jan. 1988, the Wildlife Act was published in the DOF on 3 Jul. 2000, the Forest Act was published in the DOF on 25 Feb. 2003, The General Act on Sustainable Fisheries and Aquaculture was published in the DOF on 24 Jul. 2007, the Act on Biosafety and Genetically Modified Organisms was published in the DOF on 18 Mar. 2005 and the Federal Act on Plant Varieties was published in the DOF on 25 Oct. 1996.

A. Authorizations for the Use of Biodiversity

537. Indeed, Title II of the Environmental Act refers to biodiversity protection from different perspectives. Thus, First Chapter of that Title is devoted to biodiversity habitat protection through the national system of protected natural areas. The Second Chapter of the same Title deals with the restoration of habitats altered or in the process of alteration by desertification or degradation processes. Finally, Chapter Three of the Title that we analyse refers specifically to flora and fauna.

538. However, Title III of the Environmental Act refers to the sustainable use of natural elements, but although it includes aquatic ecosystems among its object of regulation, it does not refer to the elements of biodiversity.

539. Articles 79–87*bis* 2 of the Environmental Act establish very basic instruments for the protection of flora and fauna. Thus, Article 79 establishes ten criteria to which the preservation and use of wild flora and fauna must be subject, while Article 80 states that these criteria must be taken into account during the exercise of various acts of authority relating to the protection of wild flora and fauna.

540. Nevertheless, other provisions of the same chapter lay down additional criteria to those referred to in Article 79 governing the issuing of specific acts of authority, which are as follows:

a) The use of natural resources in areas that are the habitat of species of wild flora or fauna, especially endemic, threatened or endangered species, must be done in such a way that the conditions necessary for the subsistence, development and evolution of such species are not altered (article 83).
b) The use of wild flora and fauna species in economic activities may be authorized when private individuals guarantee their controlled reproduction or development in captivity or semi-captivity or when the rate of exploitation is lower than the natural renewal of the populations, in accordance with the Official Mexican Norms issued for that purpose by the Ministry (Article 87).
c) The exploitation of natural populations of threatened or endangered species may not be authorized, except in cases where their controlled reproduction and the development of populations of the corresponding species are guaranteed (Article 87, second paragraph).
d) Authorization for the sustainable use of endemic species shall be granted in accordance with the Official Mexican Norms issued for that purpose by the Ministry, provided that such use does not threaten or endanger the species (Article 87, third paragraph).

541. However, several precepts of the chapter that we have been analysing grant to the Ministry of the Environment and Natural Resources a series of faculties in the matter, namely: to establish, modify and raise closures of wild flora and fauna (Article 81); to issue Official Mexican Norms for the preservation and sustainable use of wild flora and fauna and other biological resources (Article 84); to issue Official Mexican Norms to which the use of non-timber forest resources and firewood for domestic use shall be subject to the Official Mexican Norms issued by the Ministry and other applicable provisions; to promote before the Ministry of the Economy the establishment of regulatory measures or restrictions, in whole or in part, on the export or import of specimens of native or exotic wild flora and fauna and to impose the necessary restrictions on the circulation or transit through the national territory of species of wild flora and fauna coming from and destined for foreign countries (Article 85); to apply the provisions on preservation and sustainable use of species of wild fauna established by this and other laws, and authorize their use in economic activities, without prejudice to the powers corresponding to other agencies, under other laws (Article 85); to authorize the use of species of wild flora and fauna and other biological resources for purposes of use in biotechnology; and to authorize the collection of species of wild flora and fauna as well as other biological resources for purposes of scientific research (Article 87, fifth paragraph).

542. Finally, the Environmental Act recognizes that although it corresponds to the Ministry of the Environment its authorization, the use of flora and fauna requires the consent of landowners where these resources are located, which is consistent with the provisions of the Wildlife Act in the sense that landowners, where wildlife is distributed have a preferential right of use. Thus, the fourth paragraph of Article 87 states that 'the exploitation of species of wild flora and fauna requires the express consent of the owner or legitimate possessor of the property on which they are located'. In the same way, Article 87*bis* indicates that the authorization for the use of flora and fauna species, as well as other biological resources for purposes of use in biotechnology may only be granted if there is the prior, express and informed consent of the owner or legitimate holder of the property in which the biological resource is found.

543. However, although this chapter does not deal with the establishment of any tax instrument aimed at the protection of wild flora or fauna, if it grants the resources obtained from the collection of those taxes that are established in the corresponding legislation, a proper destination. Thus, Article 87*bis* 1 states that 'The income received by the Federation from the granting of permits, authorizations and licenses for flora and fauna, as determined by the applicable regulations, shall be used to carry out actions for the preservation and restoration of biodiversity in the areas that constitute the habitat of the species of flora and fauna for which permits, licenses or corresponding authorizations were granted.'

544. As can be seen, on the one hand, the precepts that make up this chapter of the Environmental Act do not exhaust the catalogue of subjects that, according to Article 82, should regulate, on the other hand, they also go beyond this scope of application, since in Article 87*bis* 2 it refers to the power of the federal governments, the states, Mexico City and the municipalities, within the scope of their respective competencies, to regulate the dignified and respectful treatment that must be given to animals.

545. The same provision states that it is up to the federal government to issue Official Mexican Norms that determine the basic principles of dignified and respectful treatment provided by this law, including conditions of captivity, exhibition, transportation, feeding, exploitation, training, maintenance, and slaughter of animals, as well as monitoring compliance.

B. Protected Natural Areas

546. The Environmental Act refers to protected natural areas in the First Chapter of their Title II called 'Biodiversity'.[106] The mentioned chapter is composed of Articles 44–77*bis* and has been regulated by the Regulations of the Environmental Act in Matter of Protected Natural Areas.[107]

1. Concept

547. Article 3 section II of the Environmental Act defines protected natural areas as a region within the national territory where the environment has not been significantly affected by human activity or needs to be preserved and restored. However, this definition must be interpreted in line with provisions of the second paragraph of Article 44 and Article 57 of the above-mentioned Act.

548. The first of these articles, as amended in 1996, states that 'The owners, possessors or holders of other rights over lands, waters and forests included within protected natural areas shall be subject to the modalities that, in accordance with this Law, establish the decrees by which such areas are constituted, as well as to the other provisions contained in the management program and in the corresponding ecological ordinance programs', while the second provides that protected natural areas are established by Declaratory (Decree), issued by the Federal or Local Executive.

549. In this way, it can be concluded that the protected natural areas Declarations are acts of Executive nature that impose 'Modalities or limitations' on the property rights of the lands they comprise with the purpose of preserving or restoring the environments that are present in them.

2. Background

550. The 1971 Ramsar Convention was the first in referring to protected natural areas. This Convention entered into force in 1975, and to date, has 165 signatory

106. The name of this title was modified by an amendment published in the DOF on 13 Dec. 1996.
107. DOF, 21 May 2014.

parties and protects 1,782 wetlands around the world covering more than 161 million hectares. The fundamental requirement for membership of the Ramsar Convention is that at least one wetland be registered.

551. The objective of the Treaty is the conservation and appropriate use of all wetlands through local, regional and national actions, as well as international cooperation as a contribution to achieving sustainable development worldwide.

552. According to the latest report of the International Union for Conservation of Nature, protected areas cover 12.7% of the world's land surface and 1.6% of the world's ocean surface.[108] In Mexico, 181 protected natural areas have been declared, representing more than 90.6 million hectares.[109] In 1922, the island of Guadalupe was established as Mexico's first natural reserve, and in 1935, the Iztacíhuatl and Popocatépetl volcanoes were declared the first national parks. However, the protected natural areas system as a mechanism to protect habitat and natural resources was incorporated into Mexican environmental legislation until 1988, when the Environmental Act was approved.

3. Protected Natural Areas Categories

553. According to Article 46 of the Environmental Act, there are the following categories of protected natural areas:

(a) Biosphere reserves.
(b) National Parks.
(c) Natural monuments.
(d) Natural resource protection areas.
(e) Flora and fauna protection areas.
(f) Sanctuaries.
(g) State Parks and Reserves, as well as other categories established by local legislation.
(h) Municipal ecological conservation zones, as well as other categories established by local legislation.
(i) Areas voluntarily destined for conservation.

554. Each of the above categories differs from each other by both the characteristics of the environments present and by the modalities imposed by the corresponding declaration.

---

108. *See*: http://www.cronica.com.mx/notas/2017/1011155.html.
109. *See*: http://www.conanp.gob.mx/.

4. Core Zones and Buffer Zones

555. The protected natural areas define the different uses that can be given to the soil on which they are decreed. The original text of the Environmental Act stated that in the case of biosphere reserves, the limitations to property rights established in the respective Declaratory must be different for the core zone of the area than for the buffer zone.

556. In the core zone, restrictions on land use should be greater, since the natural phenomenon to be protected is found in there, while in the buffer zone, it could withstand greater use, since it is an area that protects the core zone from external impact. However, a subsequent reform was also established for the rest of the protected natural areas of different zoning with different land-use restrictions.

557. Thus, Article 47*bis* of the above-mentioned Act states that:

> To comply with the provisions of this Law, in relation to the establishment of protected natural areas, a division and subdivision shall be made to identify and delimit the portions of the territory that conform it, according to its biological, physical and socioeconomic elements, which constitute an integral and dynamic scheme, so that when the territorial delimitation of activities in protected natural areas is carried out, it shall be carried out through the following zones and their respective subzones, according to their management category:
>
> I. The core zones will have as their main objective the preservation of ecosystems and their functionality in the medium and long term, where activities may be authorized for the preservation of ecosystems and their elements, for research and scientific collection, for environmental education, and to limit or prohibit uses that alter ecosystems. These zones may consist of the following sub-zones:
>
> a) Protection: Those surfaces within the protected natural area that have suffered very little alteration, as well as relevant or fragile ecosystems, or critical habitats, and natural phenomena that require special care to ensure their long-term conservation.
> In the protection subzones, only environmental monitoring activities and non-invasive scientific research under the terms of the corresponding regulations that do not involve the extraction or transfer of specimens or the modification of the habitat will be permitted.
>
> b) Restricted use: Those areas in a good state of conservation where the aim is to maintain the current conditions of the ecosystems, and even improve them in the sites that are required, and in which exceptional use activities may be carried out that do not modify the ecosystems and that are subject to strict control measures.
> In the restricted use subzones, only non-invasive scientific research and environmental monitoring, low environmental impact environmental education and tourism activities that do not involve modification of the original natural characteristics or conditions, and the

construction of support facilities, exclusively for scientific research or environmental monitoring, will be permitted; and

II. The buffer zones will have the main function of orienting the exploitation activities that are carried out there towards sustainable development, creating at the same time the necessary conditions to achieve the conservation of the ecosystems in the long term, and may basically be made up of the following subzones:

a) Preservation: Those areas in a good state of conservation that contain relevant or fragile ecosystems, or relevant natural phenomena, in which the development of activities requires specific management in order to achieve their adequate preservation.
In preservation subzones, only scientific research and environmental monitoring, environmental education activities and productive activities with low environmental impact that do not imply substantial modifications of the original natural characteristics or conditions, promoted by or with the participation of local communities, and that are subject to constant supervision of the possible negative impacts that they cause, in accordance with the provisions of the applicable legal and regulatory systems.

b) Traditional use: Those areas where natural resources have been used in a traditional and continuous manner, without causing significant alterations in the ecosystem. They are particularly related to the satisfaction of the socioeconomic and cultural needs of the inhabitants of the protected area.
No activities may be carried out in those sub-areas which threaten or disturb the natural structure of populations and ecosystems or the mechanisms for their recovery. Only scientific research, environmental education and tourism activities with low environmental impact may be carried out, as well as, where appropriate, artisanal fishing with low environmental impact techniques; as well as the required support infrastructure, using ecotechnics and traditional construction materials typical of the region, use of natural resources to satisfy the basic economic needs and self-consumption of the inhabitants, using traditional methods focused on sustainability, in accordance with the provisions of applicable legal and regulatory provisions.

c) Sustainable use of natural resources: Those areas in which natural resources can be used, and that, for reasons of use and conservation of their ecosystems in the long term, it is necessary that all productive activities are carried out under sustainable use schemes.
In these subzones, only the use and management of renewable natural resources will be allowed, provided that these actions generate benefits preferably for the local population, scientific research, environmental education and the development of tourism activities with low environmental impact.
Likewise, the sustainable use of wildlife may be carried out as long as its controlled reproduction is guaranteed or the populations of the

species used and the habitat on which they depend are maintained or increased; and they are supported by the corresponding plans authorized by the Ministry, in accordance with the applicable legal and regulatory provisions.

d) Sustainable use of ecosystems: Those areas with current agricultural, fishing and livestock uses.
In these sub-zones, low-intensity agricultural, fishing and livestock activities may be carried out on land, or in areas that are suitable for this purpose, and in those where such activities are carried out on a daily basis, and artisanal fishing, agroforestry and silvopastoral activities, provided they are compatible with conservation actions in the area, and where appropriate contribute to erosion control and prevent soil degradation.
The implementation of agricultural, fishing, livestock, agroforestry and silvopastoral practices that are not being carried out in a sustainable manner should be oriented towards sustainability and the reduction of the use of agrochemicals and external inputs for their implementation.

e) Special use: Those areas generally of reduced extension, with the presence of natural resources that are essential for social development, and that must be exploited without deteriorating the ecosystem, substantially modifying the landscape, or causing irreversible environmental impacts on the natural elements that make up.
In these subzones, public or private projects may only be carried out for the installation of infrastructure or the exploitation of natural resources, that generate public benefits, that are in harmony with the landscape, that do not cause serious ecological imbalance, and that are subject to strict regulations for the sustainable use of natural resources, in strict compliance with the management programs issued by the Ministry of the Environment.

f) For public use: Those surfaces that present natural attractions for recreation and enjoyment, where it is possible to maintain concentrations of visitors, within the limits determined based on the carrying capacity of the ecosystems.
In these subzones, only the construction of facilities for the development of services to support tourism, environmental research and monitoring, and environmental education, congruent with the purposes of protection and management of each protected natural area may be carried out.

g) Of human settlements: In those areas where a substantial modification or disappearance of the original ecosystems has taken place, due to the development of human settlements, prior to the declaration of the protected area, and

h) Recovery: Those areas in which the natural resources have been severely altered or modified, and which will be subject to recovery and rehabilitation programs, so that they should not continue the activities that led to such alteration.

In these sub-zones, only species native to the region or, as the case may be, species compatible with the functioning and structure of the original ecosystems may be used for their rehabilitation when it is scientifically proven that the evolution and continuity of natural processes are not affected.
In the buffer zones, consideration should be given to the productive activities carried out by the communities that inhabit them at the time of the issuance of the respective declaration, based on the provisions of both the respective Management Program and the applicable Ecological Management Programs.

5. Protected Natural Area Declaratory

558. Given the system of concurrent jurisdictions governing environmental matters under Article 73, section XXIX-G of the Constitution, protected natural areas can be established by both federal and local governments. According to Article 46 of the Environmental Act, it corresponds to the federal power to declare six different categories of protected natural areas: biosphere reserves, national parks, natural monuments, protected natural resource areas, protected areas of flora and fauna, and sanctuaries, while local governments (states and Mexico City) have the power to establish state parks, reserves, and other categories established by state legislation. Municipalities are responsible for establishing municipal ecological conservation zones, as well as the other categories, in accordance with local legislation.

6. Legal Nature of the 'Modalities' Imposed in the Declarations

559. In light of Article 27 of the Mexican Constitution and the Jurisprudence of the SCJN commented above, protected natural areas declarations can be considered an act of expropriation and the payment of economic compensation should be mandatory.

560. In this line, Article 63 of the Environmental Act states that 'The protected natural areas established by the Federal Executive may include, partially or totally, properties subject to any property regime' but the second paragraph of Article 44 provides that 'The owners, possessors or holders of other rights over lands, waters and forests included within protected natural areas shall be subject to the modalities that in accordance with this Law, establish the decrees by which such areas are constituted, as well as to other provisions contained in the management program and in the corresponding ecological management programs.'

561. However, the Environmental Act does not recognize the government's obligation to pay an economic compensation for imposing limitations on private property through an executive decree. The law tries to avoid the payment of compensation considering that these limitations are 'modalities', despite the fact that these two institutions have a different legal nature. Only the law can impose modalities on private property. Given the general character of the law, no economic compensation to the landowner is required. By contrast, due to an executive Decree having legal effects on specific landowners, 'limitations' on private property require the payment of an economic compensation to those affected by the decree.

In contrast, according to Article 64 *bis* 1, the Federation, the local governments, the municipalities and the territorial districts of Mexico City, within the scope of their respective competencies, may grant concessions, permits or authorizations to owners, possessors, social, public or private organizations, indigenous peoples and other interested persons to carry out works or activities in protected natural areas, per the provisions of this Law, the corresponding declaration and management program. In addition, this article provides that the agrarian nuclei, indigenous peoples and other owners or possessors of the land on which the aforementioned works or activities are to be carried out shall have a preference in obtaining the respective permits, concessions and authorizations.

7. Owners' Participation

562. As mentioned above, protected natural area declarations do not expropriate land ownership, but de facto deprive the owner of several prerogatives inherent in the right of ownership. In this sense, first, the landowners where a protected natural area is decreed lose the right to administer it. This can be seen from the reading of Article 47 of the Environmental Act:

> In the establishment, administration and management of the protected natural areas referred to in the preceding article, the Ministry shall promote the participation of their inhabitants, owners or possessors, local governments, indigenous peoples and other social, public and private organizations, with a purpose of promoting the integral development of the community and ensuring the protection and preservation of ecosystems and their biodiversity.

563. For this purpose, the Ministry of the Environment may sign concertation agreements or coordination agreements with the interested parties.

564. In the same avenue, the second paragraph of Article 65 states that: 'Once a protected natural area under federal jurisdiction has been established, the Ministry shall designate the Director of the area in question, who shall be responsible for coordinating the formulation, execution and evaluation of the corresponding management program, in accordance with the provisions of this Law and the provisions derived therefrom.'

II. The General Act of Wildlife

565. The General Act of Wildlife of 2000 (Wildlife Act) gives municipalities, states, and the federal government concurrent powers to design, implement and coordinate policies relating to the conservation and sustainable use of wildlife resources (Article 1).

Section XLIX of Article 3 of the Wildlife Act defines wildlife as those organisms that exist subject to processes of natural evolution and that develop freely in their habitat. These organisms include minor populations, individuals under human control, and ferals. However, the Wildlife Act does not apply to forest vegetation or species whose complete source of life is water. The Forest Act and the Fishing Act are applicable in these cases. However, this exclusion does not apply to species or populations at risk.

566. The Wildlife Act does not indicate who is the owner of wildlife resources in Mexico, but Article 4 provides that: 'The owners or legitimate possessors of the properties where wildlife is distributed shall have rights of sustainable use on their specimens, parts and derivatives in the terms prescribed by this Act and other applicable provisions.'

567. The Wildlife Act regulates a series of mechanisms aimed at protecting wildlife and its habitat, among them are:

(a) The national wildlife conservation unit management system consisting of wildlife conservation management units and wildlife conservation management units.
(b) Certification of legal provenance.
(c) Critical habitats for wildlife conservation.
(d) Shelter areas to protect aquatic species.
(e) Closings.
(f) Permits and licenses for the sustainable use of wildlife.

A. Critical Habitats

568. According to Article 63 of the Wildlife Act, critical habitats for wildlife conservation are specific terrestrial or aquatic areas, in which biological, physical, and chemical processes are essential, either for the survival of species in risk category, for a specific species or for one of its populations, and which, therefore, require special management and protection.

569. According to this Act, the Ministry of the Environment has the power of establishing critical habitats through a Ministerial Order for the conservation of wildlife when it comes to:

(a) Specific area within the surface in which a species or population at risk is distributed at the time of listing, in which biological processes essential for its conservation are developed.
(b) Specific areas that, due to deterioration processes, have drastically reduced their surface area, but that still host a significant concentration of biodiversity.
(c) Specific areas in which there is an ecosystem at risk of disappearing, if the factors that have led it to reduce its historical area persist.
(d) Specific areas in which essential biological processes are developed, and there are species susceptible to specific risks, such as certain types of pollution, whether physical, chemical or acoustic, or the risk of collisions with land or aquatic vehicles, which may lead to an impact on populations.

570. As a result of a critical habitat declaration, the affected property must be used for wildlife conservation and not for any other use. However, the declaration does not have legal effects on its own. Article 64 of the aforementioned Act states that the Ministry shall agree with the owners or legitimate holders of properties in which there are critical habitats, special management measures, mitigation of impacts, and conservation, so it can be said that the Declaration must be followed by the celebration of an agreement between authority and owner whose content is not defined by law.

571. However, the Act gives the authority two faculties to force the individual not to use the land for purposes other than wildlife conservation. On the one hand, Article 64 states that conducting any public or private work, as well as those activities that may affect the protection, recovery and restoration of natural elements into critical habitats, must be subject to the conditions established as special management and conservation measures in the management plans concerned, as well as the corresponding preventive report, in accordance with regulations.

572. However, the mentioned provision adds that at any time, the Federal Executive may impose limitations on the property rights in the properties that cover such habitat, in accordance with Article 1, section X and Article 2 of the Expropriation Act, in order to comply with the necessary measures for its management and conservation.

573. Consequently, the Declaratory has no legal effect in itself, since it must be materialized in an agreement between the authority and the owner or in a Federal Executive Decree that imposes limitations based on a cause of public utility and through the payment of an indemnity.

574. Finally, the same article gives an account of the scope of the limitations to property rights imposed by critical habitat declarations. This article points out:

> Conducting any public or private project, as well as those activities that may affect the protection, recovery and restoration of natural elements in critical habitats, shall be subject to the conditions established as special management

and conservation measures in the management plans concerned, as well as the corresponding preventive report, in accordance with the provisions of the Regulations.

B. The National Wildlife Conservation Unit's Management System

575. Chapter VIII of the Wildlife Act refers to the National Wildlife Conservation Units Management System. This chapter consists of two sections. The first section regulates the so-called wildlife conservation management units, while the second section regulates the fauna conservation management units.

576. In accordance with Article 3, section XLVIII of the Wildlife Act, wildlife conservation management units are defined as: 'Registered land and facilities operating in accordance with an approved management plan and within which the status of the habitat and of the populations or specimens distributed there are permanently monitored.'

577. Article 39 of the Wildlife Act states that:

> The owners or legitimate possessors of the properties or facilities in which Wildlife conservation activities are carried out must give notice to the Ministry of the Environment, which will proceed to its incorporation into the System of Management Units for the Conservation of Wildlife. In addition, when exploitation activities are carried out, they must request the registration of such properties or facilities as Wildlife Conservation Management Units.

578. As the basic element for the integration of the National Management System, wildlife conservation management units aim to preserve natural habitats, populations, and wildlife specimens.

579. In addition to the above, these management units have specific objectives of restoration, protection, conservation, recovery, reproduction, repopulation, reintroduction, rescue, rehabilitation, exhibition, recreation, environmental education, and sustainable use.

580. The Wildlife Act points out that activities involving the removal of wildlife are only allowed in a registered wildlife conservation management unit and require authorization granted by the Ministry of the Environment.

581. However, unlike in the case of wildlife conservation units, the fauna conservation management units are not defined by Article 3. In fact, the Act does not provide elements to identify the difference that exists between each category of units, but everything seems to indicate that the latter are included within the former.

582. Article 47*bis* 1 states that:

Article 47 bis 1. Management plans for Wildlife Conservation Management Units whose objective, in addition to conservation, is the sustainable use of fauna species shall be prepared by a technical responsible who must register with the Ministry.

C. Legal Origin

583. The Wildlife Act also regulates the traffic of wildlife specimens or any parts of them. In this sense, Article 50 provides that: 'To grant registrations and authorizations related to specimens, parts and derivatives of wild species outside their natural habitat, the authorities shall verify their legal origin.'

584. Legal origin certifies that wildlife specimens or parts thereof have been sustainably exploited, as well as the authorized fee. The legal origin appears on marks or appropriate receipts or invoices. Such marks must comply with the requirements established by the Standardization Act.

585. The receipt or invoice must include the exploitation authorization number; details of where the specimen was authorized to be removed; the species or gender of the specimen, its parts or by-products; the authorized fee; the name of the authorized person; and the proportion of the authorized fee by which the specimen, its parts or by-products represent.

D. Areas for Protection of Aquatic Species

586. Although, in accordance with Article 1, first paragraph of the Wildlife Act, the provisions of the Act are not applicable to aquatic species, Article 65 states that the Ministry of the Environment is empowered to establish through the issuance of a Ministerial Order, areas of refuge to protect native species of wildlife that develop in the aquatic environment, in waters under for federal jurisdiction, federal maritime zones and floodplains, in order to conserve and contribute, through management and conservation measures, to the development of these species, as well as to conserve and protect their habitats, for which it will draw up the corresponding protection programmes.

587. Due to their characteristics, these areas for refuge can duplicate the regulation already established by the Environmental Act in relation to protected natural areas. In fact, Article 68 refers to this problem by stating:

> When the surface of one of the shelter areas to protect aquatic species coincides with the polygon of a protected natural area, the respective protection program must be compatible with the general objectives established in the corresponding declaration and in the management program of the above mentioned protected natural area.

588. However, as in the case of protected natural areas or critical habitats, the declaration of these areas of refuge implies limiting the development of projects or activities. Article 69 of the Wildlife Act deals with this aspect by pointing out:

> The performance of any public or private project, as well as those activities that may affect the protection, recovery and re-establishment of natural elements in shelter areas to protect aquatic species, shall be subject to the conditions established as management and conservation measures in the protection programs in issue, as well as the corresponding preventive report, in accordance with the provisions of the regulations.

589. Since, most of the waters are national property and flora and fauna species are an *accessorium* of the habitat, in the case of aquatic ecosystems, the establishment of these refuge areas does not affect private property rights but still requires adequate justification. In this regard, Article 67 provides:

> Prior to the issuance of the agreement, the Ministry shall prepare the supporting studies, which shall contain, in accordance with the provisions of the regulations, general information, diagnosis, description of the physical characteristics of the area, justification and socioeconomic aspects, for which it may request the opinion of the competent Federal Public Administration agencies.

E. Banned Season

590. In accordance with Article 71 of the Wildlife Act, the Ministry of the Environment is empowered to establish limitations on the use of wildlife populations, including banned seasons and their modification or removal, in accordance with the provisions of Article 81 of the Environment Act. The cited precept clarifies that the establishment of banned seasons may only be invoked when through other measures the conservation or recovery of wildlife populations cannot be achieved.

591. From a reading of Article 71, it can be inferred that the imposition of banned seasons may have three causes:

(1) In case of natural disasters.
(2) Under a request from interested natural or legal persons.
(3) By decision of the Ministry of the Environment.

F. Permits and Licenses for the Exploitation of Wildlife

592. The Wildlife Act does not prohibit the exploitation of wildlife but establishes a series of limitations to this activity. First, Chapter VII of the Act distinguishes between two categories of wildlife use: (1) extractive use and (2) non-extractive use. According to the section I of Article 3 of the Wildlife Act, extractive use involves the use of specimens, parts or derivatives of wild species, through collection, capture or hunting.

593. However, in accordance with section II of that provision, non-extractive use refers to activities directly related to wildlife in its natural habitat that does not involve the removal of specimens, parts or derivatives, and that, if not properly regulated, could cause significant impacts on biological events, populations or habitat of wild species.

594. Article 82 of the Wildlife Act establishes a general rule according to which, extractive use of wildlife may only be done under the conditions of sustainability prescribed in the Act, and Article 83 states that the extractive use of specimens, parts and derivatives of wildlife requires prior authorization from the Ministry of the Environment, which will establish the rate of use and its temporality.

595. In addition, the Wildlife Act provides for a series of special authorizations in the following cases.

1. Species at Risk

596. In this case, Article 85 provides that the exploitation of specimens of species at risk may only be authorized when priority is given to collection and capture for restoration, restocking, reintroduction, and scientific research. This precept also indicates that any other use, in the case of endangered and threatened populations, will be subject to proof that any of the four activities mentioned above have been satisfactorily carried out and that:

i. The specimens are the product of controlled reproduction, which in turn contributes to the development of populations in programs, projects or actions endorsed by the Ministry of the Environment when these exist, in the case of specimens in confinement.
ii. Contribute to the development of populations through controlled reproduction, in the case of specimens of wild species in free life.

2. Species Which Are Not Naturally Distributed Within the National Territory

597. In this case, Article 86 of the Wildlife Act provides that the exploitation of specimens, parts and derivatives of wild species that are not naturally distributed within the national territory and that are in confinement, shall be subject to the submission of a notice to the Secretariat by the interested parties, in accordance with the provisions of the regulations.

3. Use for Subsistence Purposes

598. In accordance with Article 92 of the Wildlife Act, the use for subsistence purposes does not require any authorization. In this sense, the precept in question points out:

> Local people who make use of specimens, parts and derivatives of wildlife for direct consumption, or for sale in quantities that are proportional to the satisfaction of basic needs of these and their economic dependents, will receive support, technical advice and training by the competent authorities for compliance with the provisions of this Act and its regulations, as well as for the achievement of its purposes.

4. Scientific Collection for Teaching Purposes

599. In accordance with Article 97 of the Wildlife Act, the collection of specimens, parts, and derivatives of wildlife for purposes of scientific research and for teaching purposes requires both the authorization of the Ministry of the Environment and the express and informed consent of the owner or legitimate holder of the property where it is carried out.

600. This authorization shall not cover use for commercial purposes or use in biotechnology, which shall be governed by any special provisions that may be applicable. Authorization shall be granted only when it does not affect the viability of populations, species, habitats and ecosystems.

5. Sportive Hunting

601. According to Article 94 of the Wildlife Act, the use of sport hunting can be authorized only in specific seasons. In that sense, the cited precept states:

> The Ministry, according to the geographical area and biological cycles of the species subject to this type of exploitation, may publish calendars of working seasons and must:

1. Determine the means and methods to carry out sport hunting and its temporality, as well as the areas in which it can be carried out; when evaluating the management plans and in its case when granting the corresponding authorizations.
2. Establish specific bans to this type of use, when it is required for the conservation of populations of wild species and their habitat.

602. However, Article 95 of the Wildlife Act establishes a series of regulations on this activity when pointing out:

> Sport hunting is prohibited:
>
> a) By means of poisons, armies, traps, nets, automatic or blast weapons.
> b) From half an hour before sunset to half an hour after sunrise.
> c) In the case of calves, or visibly pregnant females.

603. Finally, it should be noted that in accordance with Article 99 of the Wildlife Act, the non-extractive use also requires authorization by the Ministry of the Environment in order to ensure the welfare of the elements of wildlife, the continuity of their populations and the preservation of their habitat.

III. The Forest Act

604. In 2018, the Federal Congress passed the Forest Act, which, according to Article 1, has the aim of regulating and promoting the conservation, protection, restoration, production, organization, cultivation, management, and exploitation of the country's forest ecosystems and resources. To this end, this law establishes as a mechanism regulating the use of forest ecosystems and their resources various authorizations, permits and notices.

605. This Act grants ownership of the forests to the holders of the lands (communities, towns, private persons, corporations, government, localities, etc.) where forests are located. Article 5 of the Forest Act states that property of forest resources placed in national territory corresponds to ejidos, communities, towns and indigenous communities, natural and juridical persons, federations, estates, Federal districts, and municipalities that own lands where forests are located.

606. Nevertheless, the exploitation of forests is subject to a series of controls established by the Forest Act.

607. First, Article 73 of the Forest Act states that authorization from the Secretariat is required for the use of forest resources timber in forest land.

608. In this regard, Article 69 of the above-mentioned legislation states that it is the responsibility of the Ministry of the Environment to grant the following authorizations:

I. Change of land use in forestlands, by exception;
II. Use of timber resources in forestlands and preferably forest;
III. Establishment of commercial forest plantations on areas greater than 800 hectares, except those on temporary forest land, and
IV. Collection and commercial or research uses of genetic resources

609. Second, Article 75 holds that in the following forest exploitation requires environmental impact authorization:

> The following forest uses require the presentation of an environmental impact statement, in the terms of the General Act on Ecological Balance and Environmental Protection:
>
> I. In tropical forests larger than 20 hectares;
> II. In exploitations of forest species that are difficult to regenerate, and
> III. In protected natural areas.

610. In contrast, under Article 84 of the Forest Act, the use of non-timber resources requires only written notice to the competent authority. However, this provision also adds that the Regulations or Official Mexican Norms will establish the requirements and cases in which authorization and/or presentation of simplified management programmes will be required to carry out this type of exploitation.

611. Authorizations for using timber resources on forest land and preferably forest land shall, in accordance with Article 76 of the same legal ordinance, have a validity corresponding to the cutting cycle and may be countersigned as many times as necessary to achieve the objectives of the respective management programme and until the end of its validity. These authorizations shall be granted only to landowners and persons legally authorized to own and use the land (Article 54).

612. The Forest Act also refers to other types of exploitation:[110] forest plantations and scientific collection. As for forest plantations, the Law is not very clear, but from a reading of Articles 87 and 88, it can be inferred that commercial forest plantations on temporarily forested land or land with an area less than or equal to 800 hectares only require a written notice from the interested party to the Ministry. Consequently, *contrario sensu*, forest plantations on forest land or preferably forest land or land with areas greater than 800 hectares require authorization issued by the Ministry of the Environment.

613. As for the scientific collection, Article 101 of the Forest Act states that the collection and use of forest biological resources for research and/or biotechnology purposes requires authorization from the Ministry, which can only be granted with

110. Second Chapter of Title IV.

the prior, express, and informed written consent of the owner or legitimate holder of the property on which the forest biological resource is located.

614. Besides the traditional methods of direct regulation, Forest Act also refers to several new methods to stimulate forest conservation, such as:

– conservation bonus;
– the market for environmental services; and
– the forest fund.

615. Thus, Article 114 of the Forest Act refers to forest certification as a mechanism to certify adequate forest management, improve the protection of forest ecosystems and make easier access to international and national markets for environmental services.

616. Furthermore, Article 141 adds that within the economic incentives, a bonus may be created that credits the conservation of the forest resource by the Mexican Forest Fund according to the availability of resources, in order to compensate the owners or possessors of forest lands for the environmental commodities and services generated.

617. In addition, Article 133 of the Forest Act establishes that in accordance with international treaties, as well as with national laws, the Ministry of the Environment shall promote the development of markets for environmental commodities and services that reward the benefits generated by the sustainable forest management carried out by the owners and legitimate holders of forest lands.

618. Finally, Article 142 creates the Mexican Forest Fund by stating:

> The Mexican Forest Fund will be the instrument to promote the conservation, growth, sustainable use and restoration of forest resources and their associated resources by facilitating access to financial services in the market, promoting projects that contribute to the integration and competitiveness of the productive chain and developing mechanisms for the collection and payment of environmental goods and services.
>
> The Mexican Forest Fund will operate through a Joint Committee, in which there will be a balanced and proportionate representation of the federal public sector, as well as private and social organizations of forest producers.
>
> The existence of the Fund does not limit the creation of diverse private or social funds that have a direct relationship with forest development.

IV. The Fishing Act

619. The 2007 Fishing Act[111] is not really an environmental law. Article 1 of this legal body states that its general objective is to regulate, promote and manage the use of fishery and aquaculture resources in the national territory and the areas over which the nation exercises its sovereignty and jurisdiction. In the same sense, Article 2 indicates a series of specific objectives. Only one of these objectives deals with the protection of aquatic wildlife. Indeed, Article 2, section III identify has one of these objectives:

> To establish the bases for the management, conservation, protection, repopulation and sustainable use of fishery and aquaculture resources, as well as the protection and rehabilitation of the ecosystems in which these resources are found.

620. Nevertheless, the Act includes very few legal instruments aimed at achieving this objective. Among these instruments, Article 36 states:

> I. Fishing management programs;
> II. Fishery management plans; and
> III. Concessions and permits.

621. However, regulation of these instruments is precarious. For instance, under Fishing Act, the private capture, exploitation, and cultural activities involving the resources referred to in the Fishing Act are possible only through permits or concessions granted by federal authority (Articles 40 and 41 of the Fishing Act). Such permits or concessions may be cancelled if an ecosystem results adversely affected or are in risk of being adversely affected.

V. The General Climate Change Act

622. The General Climate Change Act does not have the direct objective of protecting biodiversity, but it does contain a series of isolated provisions that refer to this matter. For example, in relation to the policy of climate change adaptation, Article 28, section IV states that:

> The Federal government shall define a National Policy for adaptation in the framework of the National System of Climate Change
> The Federal, local and municipal governments, within the scope of their competencies, shall execute actions for the adaptation in the elaboration of the policies, the National Strategy, the Program and the programs in the following areas:

111. DOF, 24 Jun. 2007.

IV. Ecosystems and biodiversity, especially of coastal, marine, high mountain, semi-arid, desert, forest and soil resources […].

623. Similarly, among the objectives of public policies for climate change mitigation, Article 34 section III groups the objectives related to emissions reduction and carbon sequestration in the agriculture sector, forests, and other land uses, as well as the preservation of ecosystems and biodiversity.

624. Finally, in Article 82, this Act establishes the link between climate change mitigation and adaptation with the protection of biodiversity by regulating the allocation of resources from the Climate Change Fund.

VI. Laws on Genetic Resources

625. The regulation of genetic resources[112] is found both in the Biosafety and Genetically Modified Organisms Act of 2005[113] and in the Federal Vegetable Varieties Act of 1996.[114] The objective of Biosafety and Genetically Modified Organisms Act is 'to regulate the activities of contained use, experimental release, pilot release, commercial release, marketing, import and export of genetically modified organisms, in order to prevent, avoid or reduce the possible risks that these activities may cause to human health or the environment and to biological diversity or to animal, plant and aquaculture health' and Federal Plant Variety Act aims 'to lay the foundations and procedures for the protection of the rights of breeders of plant varieties'.

626. The Biosafety and Genetically Modified Organisms Act establishes that the competent authorities in biosafety matters are the Ministry of the Environment, the Ministry of Agriculture, Livestock, Rural Development, Fisheries and Food, and the Ministry of Health. These authorities are empowered to issue various permits and authorizations with respect to various activities related to genetically modified organisms.

627. In accordance with Article 32, the following activities require a permit:

a) The experimental release into the environment, including import for that activity, of one or more genetically modified organisms;
b) The release into the environment in a pilot program, including the import for that activity, of genetically modified organisms; and
c) The commercial release into the environment, including the importation for that activity, of genetically modified organisms.

112. *See*: Rafael Pérez Miranda, *Biotecnología, sociedad y derecho*. México, uam/Miguel Ángel Porrúa, 2001, p. 257.
113. DOF, 18 Mar. 2005.
114. DOF, 25 Oct. 1996.

628. In addition, Article 79 of the Act provides that notification is required in the following cases:

I. Genetically modified organisms that are handled, generated and produced for purposes of teaching and scientific and technological research;
II. The integration of internal biosafety commissions, including the name of the person or persons responsible for such commissions;
III. The first use of laboratories or specific facilities for teaching or scientific and technological research in which genetically modified organisms are handled, generated and produced;
IV. The production of genetically modified organisms used in industrial processes, and
V. The first use of specific facilities where the genetically modified organisms referred to above are produced.

629. However, Article 91 of the Biosafety and Genetically Modified Organisms Act establishes the legal instrument of authorization for the following activities that, due to their relationship with the health sector, must be issued by the Ministry of Health:

> ARTICLE 91.- The genetically modified organisms subject to authorization are the following:
>
> I. Those intended for human use or consumption, including grains;
> II. Those destined to the processing of food for human consumption;
> III. Those with public health purposes, and
> IV. Those intended for bioremediation.

630. Regarding the Federal Vegetable Varieties Act, the competent authority in the matter is the Ministry of Agriculture, Livestock, Rural Development, Fisheries, and Food, and in order to comply with its objective, it establishes a procedure by which a breeder's title is obtained, which, in accordance with Article 2 section VIII, is the document issued by the Ministry recognizing and protecting the breeder's right to a plant variety that is new, distinct, stable, and homogeneous.

631. However, according to Article 4 of the Act, the rights protected by the breeder's title are the following:

I. To be recognized as a breeder of a plant variety. This right is inalienable and imprescriptible, and
II. To use and exploit, exclusively and temporarily, by itself or by others with its consent, a plant variety and its propagating material, for its production, reproduction, distribution or sale, as well as to produce other plant varieties and hybrids for commercial purposes. These rights shall have a duration of:

a) 18 years for perennial species (forest, fruit, vines, ornamentals) and their rootstocks, and
b) 15 years for species not included in the preceding subparagraph.

These periods shall be counted from the date of issue of the breeder's title and, once the plant variety, its use and exploitation have elapsed, shall be placed in the public domain.

632. However, the Act also establishes those cases in which the plant variety may be used without the consent of the breeder, so Article 5 states as follows:

> Article 5.- The consent of the breeder of a plant variety is not required for its use:
>
> I. As a source or research input for the genetic improvement of other plant varieties;
> II. In the multiplication of propagating material, provided that it is for own use as grain for consumption or sowing, in accordance with the regulations of this Law and the Official Mexican Norms established by the Ministry, or
> III. for human or animal consumption, for the exclusive benefit of the person who harvests it.

633. The Federal Plant Variety Act also provides that the Ministry may issue emergency licences permitting a person without a breeder's title to exploit a plant variety already registered. According to Article 25 of the Law, it is understood that there are emergency circumstances when the exploitation of a plant variety is considered indispensable to satisfy the basic needs of a sector of the population, and there is a deficiency in the offer or supply.

634. Finally, in accordance with Article 33 of the studied Act, all applications and the respective breeder's titles deriving therefrom must be entered in the National Register of Plant Varieties.

§5. The Special Regime for Endangered Species

635. The term 'endangered species' refers to those whose areas of distribution or size of their populations in the national territory have drastically decreased putting at risk their biological viability in all their natural habitat, due to factors such as the destruction or drastic modification of habitat, unsustainable use, disease, or depredation, among others.[115]

115. Norma Oficial Mexicana NOM-059-SEMARNAT-2010 2.2.2.

636. Among the endangered species in Mexico are 7 amphibians, 97 birds, 10 fungi, 17 invertebrates, 52 mammals, 81 fish, 187 plants, and 27 reptiles. Some of these species are, for example, the marine otter, the ajolote, the Antillean manatee, the Mexican prairie dog, the volcano rabbit, the Mexican gray wolf, and the jaguar.[116]

637. Neither Mexican legislation nor the regulations derived from it have fully protected endangered species. Only the Wildlife Act, the Environmental Act, the Fisheries Act and the Forest Act contain isolated provisions on the subject.

638. Article 3, section XX of the Wildlife Act defines endangered species and populations as those identified by the Ministry as probably extinct in the wild, endangered, threatened, or subject to special protection. However, the specific regulation of these species is found in Articles 56–62 of that Act. According to Article 58 of the Wildlife Act, among the species and populations at risk are those that are identified as:

a) In danger of extinction, those whose areas of distribution or size of their populations in the national territory have decreased drastically putting at risk their biological viability in all their natural habitat, due to factors such as the destruction or drastic modification of the habitat, unsustainable use, diseases or depredation, among others.
b) Threatened, those that could be in danger of disappearing in the short or medium term, if the factors that have a negative impact on their viability continue to operate, causing the deterioration or modification of their habitat or directly reducing the size of their populations.
c) Subject to special protection, those that could be threatened by factors that negatively affect their viability, thus determining the need to promote their recovery and conservation or the recovery and conservation of populations of associated species.

639. The exploitation of specimens or populations of wild species in danger of extinction is punished with an administrative sanction.[117]

640. The category of biodiversity we are analysing is found in different provisions of the Environmental Act. First, this law alludes to endangered species in Article 35, which refers to the resolution of the environmental impact manifestation; in its section III (b), it foresees that the requested authorization may be denied if the activity causes one or more species to be declared as threatened or endangered or when one of the said species is affected.

116. Norma Oficial Mexicana NOM-059-SEMARNAT-2010. Anexo Normativo III. Lista de especies en riesgo.
117. Article 122 s. IV Wildlife Act.

641. Reference is also made to the category of threatened species in the case of the establishment of protected natural areas (Article 45), and in the case of the establishment of banned seasons, Article 81 establishes that the purpose of banned seasons shall be the preservation, repopulation, propagation, distribution, acclimatization, or refuge of specimens, mainly of those endemic, threatened, or endangered species. And finally, the Act refers to exploitation, which is divided into the exploitation of 'natural resources in areas that are the habitat of species of flora or wild fauna' and the exploitation of 'species of flora and wild fauna in economic activities'. The first establishes that it must be done in such a way that the necessary conditions for the subsistence, development, and evolution of these species are not altered; as for the second, it foresees that it will not be granted to species of flora and wild fauna in economic activities, and when it is granted, it must not threaten or endanger the species with extinction (Articles 83, 87 and 89).[118]

642. The Fishing Act only refers to the subject in its Article 13 that corresponds to local government's powers. Thus, in its section XV (d), the precept stipulates that they must participate with the competent agencies of the Federal Public Administration in the determination of aquatic species subject to special protection, threatened, or endangered.

643. Finally, in the Forest Act, the issue of endangered species is approached from two perspectives. Article 32 establishes the obligatory criteria of forest policy, among which section XI establishes the priority conservation of endemic species, threatened, endangered, or subject to special protection. It should also be noted that the final part of this Act, specifically Article 124 section III, provides that forest closures may be decreed as an exceptional measure when their purpose is the conservation, repopulation, propagation, dissemination, acclimatization, or refuge of endemic forest species that are threatened, endangered, or subject to special protection.[119]

644. However, environmental regulations are not very clear either. Regarding the protection of endangered species of flora and fauna, three Official Mexican Norms have been issued:

(1) the Official Mexican Standard 'NOM-059-ECOL-1994, which determines the species and subspecies of terrestrial and aquatic wild flora and fauna in danger of extinction, threatened, rare and those subject to special protection, and which establishes specifications for their protection', published in the DOF on 16 May 1994.
(2) Official Mexican Standard NOM-059-SEMARNAT-2001, Environmental Protection-Mexican Native Species of Wild Flora and Fauna-Risk Categories and Specifications for Inclusion, Exclusion or Change-List of Species at Risk, published in the DOF on 6 March 2002. This standard replaced the previous one; and

118. Environmental Act.
119. Forest Act.

(3) Official Mexican Standard NOM-059-SEMARNAT-2010, Environmental Protection-Mexican Native Species of Wild Flora and Fauna-Risk Categories and Specifications for Inclusion, Exclusion or Change-List of Species at Risk, published 30 December 2010. This Standard replaced the 2001 Standard.

645. The Official Mexican Standard of 1994, as set forth in its numeral 1, had a dual purpose. On the one hand, to determine the species and subspecies of terrestrial and aquatic wild flora and fauna in danger of extinction, threatened, rare, and those subject to special protection and, on the other hand, to establish specifications for their protection.

646. However, the first objective mentioned above was met with the provisions contained in paragraphs 3.6.1–3.6.4, which established the categorization of flora and fauna in:

(a) endangered species and subspecies;
(b) threatened species and subspecies;
(c) rare species and subspecies; and
(d) species and subspecies subject to special protection.

647. Numeral 5 of the Official Mexican Standard complemented those mentioned above, listing the species present in the national territory and identifying their status in accordance with the classification referred to.

648. However, the establishment of specifications for protecting these species is an issue developed in paragraphs 6.1–6.6.

649. Numeral 6.1 referred to the extraction from the natural environment of specimens, parts, products, by-products or derivatives of species and subspecies of flora and fauna, wild, terrestrial and aquatic in danger of extinction, threatened, rare, and those subject to special protection for purposes of scientific collection, establishing as main regulations two: (1) the necessary authorization and (2) the prohibition of its commercialization.

650. Numeral 6.2 refers to the extraction of specimens or parts of species and subspecies of terrestrial and aquatic wild flora and fauna in danger of extinction, threatened, and those subject to special protection under permanently banned season with the purpose of being used as brood stock, mother plants, seeds, or propagules for the creation of reproductive units. This activity was subject to authorization by the authority. In the same way was the disposition of specimens or parts of species and subspecies of terrestrial and aquatic flora and fauna in danger of extinction, threatened, and those subject to special protection under permanent closure.

651. Numeral 6.3 refers to commercial exploitation, possession or use of species and subspecies, their parts, products and by-products of rare terrestrial and aquatic wild flora and fauna, and those subject to special protection with or without a temporary closure. The regulation that established the norm with respect to these activities consisted that they must be carried out on specimens coming primarily from authorized wild flora and fauna reproduction units.

652. Numeral 6.4 requires authorization for carrying out the following activities: commercial exploitation, possession or use of species and subspecies, their parts, products and by-products of rare terrestrial and aquatic wild flora and fauna, and those subject to special protection without prohibition, in their natural environment. This authorization was subject to availability rates determined by the Ministry.

653. Numeral 6.5 refers to the use of the habitats where the species and subspecies of the terrestrial and aquatic wild flora and fauna are found, which are in danger of extinction, threatened, rare and those subject to special protection and within these categories those endemic to the Mexican Republic, and waters of federal jurisdiction.

654. Numeral 6.6 simply indicated who should grant authorizations for the extraction of the natural environment or the commercialization of specimens, parts, products, by-products, and derivatives of species and subspecies of terrestrial and aquatic wild flora and fauna but did not add any regulation.

655. NOM-059-SEMARNAT-2001 also has a double objective but differs from that of 1994. This norm pursues to:

- Identify the species or populations of wild flora and fauna at risk in the Mexican Republic through the integration of the corresponding lists, as well as,
- Establish the criteria for inclusion, exclusion or change of risk category for species or populations, using a method for assessing their extinction risk.

656. As can be seen, NOM-059-SEMARNAT-2001 no longer dealt with establishing criteria for the protection of the species in issue but only with their classification. Furthermore, in Numeral 2, the Standard states that it is mandatory for 'natural or legal persons who promote the inclusion, exclusion or change of wild species or populations in any of the risk categories in the national territory established by this standard'. Therefore, this norm did not establish any regulation regarding the protection of the species to which it refers, from which it follows that it was the intention of the federal government to repeal this protection regime.

657. Finally, the 'NOM-059-SEMARNAT-2010, Environmental Protection-Mexican Native Species of Wild Flora and Fauna – Risk Categories and Specifications for their Inclusion, Exclusion or Change-List of Species at Risk 2010'[120] has the objective of:

120. In fact, this standard simply constitutes the mandatory update of the 2001 standard, in the terms of the Federal Act on Metrology and Standardization.

> Identifying species or populations of wild flora and fauna that are at risk in the Mexican Republic, by integrating the corresponding lists, as well as to establish the criteria of inclusion, exclusion or change of risk category for the species or populations, through a method of evaluation of their extinction risk and it is obligatory observance in all the National Territory, for the physical or legal persons that promote the inclusion, exclusion or change of the wild species or populations in any of the risk categories, established by this Standard.

658. In other words, like its predecessor in 2001, it no longer refers to specific regulations on flora and fauna species, but only to their classification and integration, where appropriate, within the categories established by it.

659. Consequently, neither Official Mexican Standard NOM- 059-ECOL-1994 nor NOM-059-SEMARNAT-2001 nor NOM-059-SEMARNAT-2010 protects in themselves the species of wild and aquatic flora and fauna 'in danger of extinction, threatened, rare and subject to special protection', with respect to the realization of projects in their habitat, but simply indicate the criteria that regulate the inclusion or exclusion of such species within each of the protection categories that such standards establish, thereby establishing a necessary conceptual basis for subsequent regulations to address the issue, but so far there is no legal provision prohibiting the conduct of productive activities in places where species are located under the status referred to in the standard.

§6. Mangrove Protection

660. Article 60*ter* incorporated into the Wildlife Act states:

> It is prohibited to remove, fill, transplant, prune or any other activity that affects the entire hydrological flow of the mangrove, the ecosystem and its area of influence, its natural productivity, the natural carrying capacity of the ecosystem for tourism projects, nesting areas, breeding, shelter, feeding and spawning, or interactions between the mangrove, rivers, dune, adjacent sea area and corals, or that causes changes in ecological characteristics and services.

661. The cited text has been referred to as the 'mangrove act' because supposedly with the entry into force of that provision, the mangrove habitat would cease to be affected. However, the Wildlife Act does not contain, beyond this prohibition, any other legal instrument that integrally protects this species.

662. The Forest Act prohibits the land-use change in forest lands, which is applicable to the habitat of the mangrove and the Environmental Act, in its Article 28, submits to EIA the performance of works or activities that could affect mangroves.

§7. Species Subject to Specific Protection

663. First Chapter of Title VI deals with establishing an absolute protection regime for a specific species. This act states:

a) No specimen of marine mammal may be subject to extractive exploitation (art. 60 bis).
b) No specimen of sea turtle shall be subject to extractive exploitation (art. 60 bis 1).
c) The exploitation of white shark, whale shark, basking shark, scalloped sawfish and estuarine fish species is prohibited (Article 60a 1).
d) No specimen of the Psittacidae or Psittacidae family may be exploited (art. 60 bis2).
e) It is prohibited to remove, fill, transplant, prune or any other activity that affects the entire hydrological flow of the mangrove, the ecosystem and its area of influence, its natural productivity, the natural carrying capacity of the ecosystem for tourism projects, nesting areas, breeding, shelter, feeding and spawning, or interactions between the mangrove, rivers, dune, adjacent sea area and corals, or that causes changes in ecological characteristics and services (art. 60b).

§8. Tax Regime for the Sustainable Use of Biodiversity

664. Taxation is another of the legal mechanisms through which the Mexican legal regime seeks to guarantee the sustainable use of biodiversity resources. In this case, the tax category used is that of so-called fees or rights. As explained above, fees or rights must be paid by the use or exploitation of goods that pertain to the public domain of the nation.

665. The Federal Act of Fees refers to this issue in its Title II called 'Of the fees for the Use or Advantage of Goods of the Public Domain'. This Title is integrated by the following chapters that tax the use and exploitation of diverse components of biodiversity, under the premise that they are part of the domain:

(1) Forests.
(2) Fishing.
(3) Wildlife.

666. First Chapter of this Title is composed of Articles 196a and 198b, which define different taxable events, the realization of which provides a basis for the obligation to pay the corresponding duties. Thus, Article 196 establishes the right to use national forests on land belonging to the Federal Government. This article states:

> Article 196.- For the use of national forests on land belonging to the Federal Government, fees shall be paid in accordance with the following quotas:

I. For the use of arboreal vegetation:
   a) Woods, per cubic meter, shaft without cortex, authorized of: mahogany, red cedar, spring, Ash tree, walnut, guayacan and other similar species $3,181.59
   b) Wood, per cubic metre fustal roll without cortex, authorized from: chacáguanacastle, ceiba, bojón, cedrillo and similar species $599.43
   c) (Repealed).
   d) (Repealed).
   e) Chicle, per authorized ton. $8,264.20

II. For the use of herbaceous vegetation for grazing, per head-month.
   a) Livestock $20.02
   b) Small livestock $9.66

667. It is important to emphasize that in this case, fees are only caused when it is a question of forests located in lands of national property because only in this case is configured the hypothesis of the use of a good of the public domain of the nation that is a necessary condition for the configuration of the taxable event in that tax category. Therefore, this fee is not caused in the case of the use of forests located in privately owned properties.

668. It should also be noted that this fee to publicly owned forests must be paid prior to the exploitation taking place (Article 197) and that the income collected by it must be allocated to the National Forestry Commission for forest restoration programmes with native species (Article 196, in fine), what gives to this contribution the character of an environmental tribute whose objective, without ceasing to be the tax collection, is of extra-fiscal character since it has a specific destiny.

669. Article 197-A introduced a variable of the fee that we comment on. It is about the 'fee for the exploitation of arboreal forest vegetation in the riverbeds and federal zone of the rivers'. In this case, the fee to be paid will be MXN 173.35 per cubic metre of authorized tree roll, but all the other particularities described above are maintained for the generic fee.

670. In the case of fishing, the Federal Law of Fees charges tax consequences to three different types of activities. First, Article 199 describes the taxable event consisting of fishing activity carried out in the exclusive economic zone with foreign-registered vessels and under the protection of exceptional permits. This precept points out:

> Article 199.- Natural and legal persons who, under the protection of exceptional permits, carry out fishing with foreign-registered vessels within the exclusive economic zone located outside the territorial sea, shall pay the fishing fee per net registered ton or fraction of the vessel, for each trip of up to 60 days, according to the quota of $3,349.11

From the reading of the transcribed legal provision it can be deduced that this fee has the following characteristics:

a) In order for the taxable event to be configured, fishing must take place in the exclusive economic zone but outside the zone known as the 'territorial sea' which, is an integral part of the former, but over which the nation exercises different rights.
b) Fishing must be carried out under exceptional permits.
c) Fishing must be carried out by vessels with foreign registration.

671. Finally, Article 199-B typifies the taxable event consisting of the exploitation of fishing resources in the case of the so-called sport and recreational fishing in the following terms:

Article 199-B.- For the use of fishing resources in sport and recreational fishing, the fee to fish shall be paid, by individual permit, in accordance with the following quotas:

I.	For one day	$155.43
II.	For one week	$389.65
III.	For one month	$584.54
IV.	For one year	$779.59
V.	For sport fishing excursions from abroad, for each member and for trips of more than three days and up to one year	$1.109.01

In the latter case, if they are less than three days, the prescribed fee per day will be paid, multiplied by the number of days of travel.

672. The Federal Fees Act also taxes the sustainable use of wildlife. On the one hand, Article 238 defines the taxable event consisting of the extractive use of wildlife while Article 238-C does the same in relation to non-extractive use. In both cases, since we have held that wildlife is not a national property, it is questionable to tax its use with a 'fee'.

673. As for the extractive use of certain species of fauna that are located on federally owned land, Article 238 of the Federal Fees Act states:

Article 238. For the extractive use of specimens of wild fauna, on federal properties and federal areas, the fee to extractive use shall be paid per specimen or, as the case may be, per lot determined in the rates of use authorized by the Ministry of the Environment and Natural Resources, in accordance with the following quotas:

I.	bighorn sheep	\$583,055.07
II.	Mule Deer in Sonora or Texas Whitetail	\$56,083.47
III.	Puma	\$21,594.61
IV.	Bura Deer Whitetail in the rest of the country and Temazate	\$17,275.68
V.	Collar Pheasant	\$10,797.28
VI.	Ducks, pigeons, quails, teals, geese, partridge, tinamou, Pacific black branta and other birds, by lot	\$31,780.64
VII.	Wild Guajolote and Ocellated Turkey	\$6,478.38
VIII.	Grey vixen and other small mammals	\$6,478.38
IX.	Montane Cat	\$4,318.92
X.	Boar (collared, white lips, European)	\$4,318.92
XI.	Borrego Audat o Berberisco	\$1,079.71

674. In reality, in the cases of exploitation of specimens of wildlife species identified by that legal provision, it is not necessary to pay this contribution but by the issuance of the corresponding authorization since none of these species is considered by the Constitution as a public domain good. This seems to be recognized in Article 238 of the Federal Fees Act when it states that 'the payment of this fee will be made prior to obtaining the corresponding authorization, through a declaration to be submitted to the offices authorized by the Tax Administration Service and will include the cost of the headbands that are used to mark the animals used'.

675. In the case of non-extractive use, Article 238-C states that:

> Article 238-C. For the non-extractive use of terrestrial, freshwater and marine turtles and wildlife in general, originated by the development of observation activities in centers for the protection and conservation of turtles owned by the Nation and in centers for the conservation and research of wildlife, the fee of non-extractive use per person shall be paid, according to the following:
> I. Per person, per day: \$38.05
> You may choose to pay the fee referred to in this article, per person, per year, for all centers for the protection and conservation of turtles owned by the Nation and in centers for the conservation and research of wildlife: \$395.71

676. As can be seen, the taxable event clearly states that this fee is only caused by non-extractive use for carrying out turtle observation activities within centres for protection and conservation owned by the nation, as well as in centres for conservation and research.

677. This fee has a collecting character as well as an environmental one since, according to the precept itself, the income obtained from the collection of the fee referred to in this article will be destined to the NCPNA for programmes of conservation, maintenance, and operation of turtle centres.

678. Moreover, Article 238-C also indicates the subjects who are exempt from the payment of this contribution, specifically:

> Persons under the age of 6, as well as persons with disabilities.
> Persons accessing centres for the protection and conservation of turtles for research purposes, subject to accreditation by the management of such centres, as well as permanent residents of localities adjacent to centres for the protection and conservation of turtles and centres for conservation and research of wildlife, provided that they have the certification of this quality granted by the responsible authority, upon submission of documentation and conduct recreational activities without profit.

679. However, the article that we have been commenting on also indicates that, independently of the characteristics of the passive subject, this contribution is not caused when the non-extractive use is carried out in a Protected Natural Area, but in any case, only the fee foreseen in Article 198 must be paid.

680. Article 198 of the Federal Fees Act refers to the use, or exploitation of natural elements located in the national territory, and is under the public domain of the Federation. The fee is caused when recreational activities, tourism and sports scuba diving, free diving, water skiing, motorized and non-motorized boat tours, observation of marine fauna in general, sport fishing in any of its forms, camping, overnight and navigation in seas, canals, estuaries, and coastal lagoons.

681. The problem is that, as we have already mentioned, in our opinion, there are no natural elements of biodiversity that can be considered public domain, so there is no basis for the establishment of this contribution.

682. Finally, the last paragraph of the mentioned article indicates, 'the residents of the zone of influence of the Protected Natural Areas who carry out some of the activities referred to in this precept, who demonstrate that quality before the competent authority will pay 50% of the quota established in this article'.

Chapter 1. Agricultural Resources

683. The Agrarian Act (AA) regulates matters related to the use of land for agricultural purposes, whereas the Act for Sustainable Rural Development (ASRD) (Rural Development Act) has the objectives of promoting sustainable rural development and of providing a healthy environment, in accordance with Articles 4 and 25 of the Federal Constitution (Article 1°), by promoting the processes of social and economic transformation, recognizing that the vulnerability of rural populations leads to a sustainable and permanent encouragement of acceptable living conditions for these populations.

684. Nevertheless, it is only a statute that establishes the rules for planning actions from Federal and local governments to encourage the sustainability of economic activities for rural development.

685. Conservation and protection of national lands, including those destined for agricultural purposes, are governed by the Rural Development Act. The AA regulates the creation and operation of various forms of agricultural communities, such as ejidos (communal village farmlands) and communities.

686. The Environmental Act establishes the general criteria and policies regulating soil used for the purpose of preserving and restoring the ecological balance. Article 98 sets forth the general principles for soil use regulation and provides that the soil is to be used in a manner compatible with its essential purpose so that its physical integrity and productive capacity are not altered; practices that induce soil erosion, degradation, or other adverse environmental impacts must be avoided; restoration projects in areas of severe erosion or deforestation must be devised; and erosion preventing activities are to be implemented during the construction of public or private works. These principles must be considered by the federal government when adopting support programmes for agricultural activities, including investment, financing, and technical assistance.

687. Article 103 of the Act also requires that soil conservation and restoration practices necessary to prevent soil and environmental deterioration be implemented in connection with all farming activities. In areas of serious desertification and erosion, the Ministry of the Environment, in cooperation with other federal, State, and local authorities, may design and implement special programmes regulating land uses and the exploitation of natural resources, with the aim of restoring the ecological balance. Notice of such programmes must be published in the DOF previously to be implemented.

688. The Rural Development Act is intended to promote Mexico's sustainable rural development and an appropriate environment. The law applies to ejidos and rural communities and associations, as well as to individuals and entities that carry out rural activities.

689. The Act's objectives include the promotion of biodiversity conservation, the improvement of the quality of natural resources, and the furtherance of the Federal government's conservation and improvement of soils and other natural resources.

690. Under the law, support shall be given as needed to change production structures to re-orient land use in cases of high levels of erosion or negative ecosystem impact. In coordination with other sectors, the federal government shall also support the execution of soil and water conservation projects.

Chapter 2. Subsoil and Minerals

691. The Mexican Constitution refers to subsoils and minerals from the following perspectives:

(a) Article 27 grants the Nation direct dominion over all natural resources located in the continental shelf and the submarine foundations of islands; all minerals and substances in veins, the mantle, and masses or deposits that are by nature distinct from the components of the ground; metallic minerals used in industry; precious stones; salts; and materials that may be used as fertilizers.
(b) Under the Mexican Constitution, the Nation has an obligation to promote the conservation of natural resources and the restoration of the ecological balance.
(c) Private parties may only participate in the exploitation and use of these natural resources through concessions granted by the Federal Executive.
(d) In addition, the Mexican Constitution grants the Federal Congress the power to legislate in the area of mining.

692. Mining activities are regulated under the Mining Law and the Regulations of the Mining Law, while wastes resulting from mining activities are governed by the Waste Act. Waste-water discharges resulting from mining activities are governed by the National Waters Law and the Regulations of the Waters Act. Finally, the Foreign Investments Act regulates foreign investor participation in mining concessions.

693. However, Mexican legislation on subsoils and minerals includes the Mining Act (MA) (as amended in 1996), the Regulatory Act of the Constitution in the field of oil (1958), and the Regulatory Act of Article 27 of the Constitution on Nuclear Matters (RACNM) (1989). All of these Acts refer to the exploration and exploitation regimes for subsoil and mineral resources and, in cases where these are allowed, to the manner of granting the concessions for private investments.

694. In general, these Acts contemplate an environmental evaluation system as a mechanism to control negative environmental effects. Consequently, some of them expressly mention the obligation to evaluate the environmental impact of works or activities related to the use and exploitation of mineral and energy resources, while in others, these activities are included in the general obligation of evaluating the environmental impact of any work or activity that can affect the environment in one way or another.

§1. Mining Activities

695. The Mining Law regulates the exploration, exploitation, and benefit of minerals and substances for industrial use, rare metals, mineral gems, rock salt and its by-products, products derived from the decomposition of rocks whose exploitation is mainly carried out through underground works, certain minerals and organic materials that may be used as fertilizers, certain solid fuels, and other resources identified by the Federal Executive.

696. Article 5 of the mentioned Law specifically excludes the following from the jurisdiction of the Mining Law: oil and solid, liquid, or gas hydrocarbons; radioactive minerals; substances in suspension or dissolved in groundwater; rocks or products resulting from their decomposition used as building materials or in construction; products derived from the decomposition of rocks whose exploitation is mainly carried out by means of open-pit works; and salt from salt mines formed in interior basins.

I. Mining Concessions

697. Under Article 10 of the Mining Law, mining activities are carried out under concessions granted by the Ministry of Energy. Such concessions can be granted exclusively to Mexican nationals, ejidos, and agrarian communities, the towns and indigenous communities mentioned in Article 2 of the Mexican Constitution, and Corporations constituted under Mexican laws. There are two types of mining concessions: exploration concessions and exploitation concessions.

698. According to Article 11 of the Mining Law, the following are Corporations eligible to obtain mining concessions under Mexican laws: (a) those whose social objective refers to exploration or exploitation of minerals or substances regulated by the Mining Law, (b) those who have their legal addresses in the Mexican Republic, and (c) those in which participation of foreign investors fulfil legal provisions in that regard.

699. Under Article 13 of the Mining Law, mining exploration concessions are generally granted by the Secretary of Energy to whoever submits the application first. According to Article 15 of the Mining Law, mining concessions are granted for a renewable fifty-year term as of the date that they are registered in the Public Register of Mining.

700. A concession or assignment does not grant property rights over a land surface, but rather the right to explore and exploit minerals and substances that are different from the components of the soil.

701. An amendment in 2022 introduced Article 5 *bis* in the Mining Act, which prohibits granting concessions to private parties to exploit lithium, reserving this activity to the state.

II. Mining Assignments

702. Article 10 of the Mining Law also refers to mining assignments. Mining assignments are issued only to the Mineral Resource Council and strictly for the purpose of identifying and quantifying the potential mineral resources in a given area.

703. Mining assignments are granted for non-committed lots on the free ground and may only be issued by the Ministry of Energy to the Mineral Resource Council. Mining assignments confer rights and obligations and have a non-renewable duration of six years as of the date that the title is published in the DOF.

III. Mining Reserves

704. Finally, Article 10 of the Mining Law points out that, because of causes of public utility or for satisfying future necessities of the country, mining reserves can be established through an Executive decree. In the areas included in mining reserves, no concessions or assignments can be granted. According to Article 17 of the Mining Law, when the circumstances that motivated the incorporation of a given zone into a reserve zone have changed, the Executive shall declare its disincorporation through a decree that shall be published in the DOF.

§2. Radioactive Substances and Minerals

705. Unlike the rights to other natural substances and minerals, the rights to explore, exploit, and use radioactive minerals cannot be granted through concessions or by contract. These activities are reserved exclusively to the State and are regulated under the Law Regulating Article 27 of the Constitution in Regard to Nuclear Matters. Under Article 5 of this Law, the properties of radioactive minerals are vested in the Nation, and the exploration, exploitation, and use of radioactive minerals, including the construction and operation of nuclear plants, is not a matter of concessions or contracts.

706. According to Article 9 of the Nuclear Matters Law, exploration activities may be exclusively carried out by the Mineral Resource Council[121] through assignments from the Ministry of Energy, whereas in accordance with Article 10, exploitation activities may be exclusively carried out by the Commission of Mining Promotion through assignments granted by the Secretary of Energy.

707. Finally, under Article 15 of the Nuclear Matters Law, the generation of electricity from the use of nuclear combustibles corresponds exclusively to the Federal Commission of Electricity. Nuclear energy can be used only for domestic objectives (Article 2).

---

121. In 2005, the Mineral Resources Council changed its name to Mexican Geological Survey.

708. The Ministry of Energy may determine the programme and technical conditions to be fulfilled by the Council in accordance with the relevant National Development Plans.

§3. Hydrocarbons and Petroleum

709. The original text of Article 27 of Mexican Constitution did not nationalize the oil industry. This precept established the principle of the public domain of hydrocarbons that was in force during colonial times[122] but allowed the participation of private investment in the exploitation of oil resources.[123]

710. The fourth paragraph of Article 27 stated that the nation's dominion over hydrocarbon resources was inalienable and imprescriptible, but at the same time, the sixth paragraph of such article authorized the federal government to grant concessions for its exploitation both to individuals and legal entities constituted under Mexican law.[124]

711. The fourth and sixth paragraphs of Article 27 of the original text of the Political Constitution of the United States of Mexico, textually stated:

> The Nation has full ownership over all natural resources of the continental shelf and the seabed and subsoil of the submarine areas of the islands; over all minerals or substances in veins, layers, masses or ore pockets, constituting deposits which nature is different from the components of the land, such as the minerals from which metals and metalloids to be used in industry are extracted; beds of precious stones, rock salt and deposits of salts formed by sea water; the products derived from rock decomposition, when their exploit requires underground work; minerals or organic deposits susceptible to be utilized as fertilizers; solid mineral fuels; petroleum and all solid, liquid or gaseous hydrocarbons; and the space located over national land territory, in the extension and under the terms established by International Law.
>
> In the cases established in the two paragraphs hereinbefore, the Nation's dominion is inalienable and not subject to the statute of limitation and the exploitation, use or enjoyment of the resources in question by private persons or by companies incorporated in accordance with Mexican laws, may not be

---

122. *See*: Casafranca Valencia & Handersson Bady. *Ponencia sobre la propiedad de los recursos naturales en los territorios de pueblos indígenas Perú: La pobreza de los ricos territorios indígenas y recursos naturales* (2008). Available at: www.dar.org.pe/hidrocarburos.
123. In 1910, President Francisco Madero introduced a tax of 3 cents per barrel of oil and another of 20 cents per ton of oil extracted by private companies.
124. According to Raúl Jiménez, Art. 27 of the Mexican Constitution establishes a system of absolute ownership of the nation over hydrocarbons, as well as the direct and exclusive exploitation of these by the nation. Raúl Jiménez, *Historical Elements for the Interpretation of the Constitutional Regime of the Oil of the Mexicans*, in *Oil in the History and Culture of Mexico* 99–118 (Suárez del Real & Jose Alfonso Aguilera eds, PRD Parliamentary Group 2008).

> undertaken save by means of concessions granted by the President of the Republic and in accordance with the rules and conditions set forth by the Laws.

712. In addition to the above, the Regulation of Article 27 of the Constitution in the Field of Oil passed by the Federal Congress in 1925[125] recognized the rights acquired by foreign oil companies based on the principle of non-retroactivity of the Constitution of 1917[126] and detail regulated the regime of concessions that included the exploration, exploitation, and transportation of oil, and other hydrocarbons.[127]

713. In 1934, the Supreme Court of Justice upheld this criterion by recognizing that Article 27 had no retroactive effect. Consequently, the 1925 Act, which established the procedure for private companies to request recognition of their acquired rights was, according to the Supreme Court of Justice's absolute constitutional criteria.[128]

714. The first step on the road to the establishment of the absolute property regime of the oil state was given until 1938, when the Mexican government expropriated the facilities of the oil companies. However, even after the so-called oil expropriation, the absolute ownership principle of the state could not be said to regulate the petroleum property regime.

715. To nationalize the oil sector, it was necessary to introduce another principle in the constitutional text: the principle of the direct and exclusive exploitation of this resource by the nation. With this aim, in 1940, a constitutional reform was approved that modified the sixth paragraph of Article 27 in the following terms:[129]

> In the case of petroleum and solid, liquid, and gaseous hydrocarbons, no concessions or contracts will be issued, and the respective regulatory law will determine the manner in which the Nation will carry out exploitations of those products.

716. Since that moment, the Mexican government constitutionally assumed the monopoly of exploration, exploitation, refining, and distribution of oil and other products derived from it.

717. One year before, granting concessions was forbidden by the second Regulation of Article 27 in the Field of Petroleum. However, in spite of the constitutional reform, that Law was repealed in 1941 by the third Regulation of Article 27 in the Field of Petroleum that allowed the participation of private companies in the

125. DOF, 25 Dec. 1925.
126. For some writers, the enactment of this Law was the result of the 'Treaties of Bucareli' between Mexico and the United States. In these treaties, the United States of America recognized the government emanating from the Mexican revolution with the only condition that Mexico did not apply Art. 27 of the Constitution to the property titles granted by Porfirio Diaz to the oil companies.
127. *See* Arts 7, 8, and 9 of the mentioned Law.
128. *See The Eagle. Mexican Oil Company v. Government of Mexico*, 1934.
129. DOF, 9 Nov. 1940.

oil industry through the so-called contracts of risk. Under the 1941 Act, through these contracts, the exploration and exploitation activities could be carried out by private companies, and the compensation for their services could consist of a cash payment or a percentage of the production obtained.[130]

718. Between 1949 and 1951, several contracts of risk were assigned to foreign companies.[131] These contracts included hydrocarbon resources in an area of 4,000 km^2 of the national territory. The payment to the companies consisted of the total reimbursement of their expenses and investments plus 50% of the value of the hydrocarbons produced by the drilled wells and compensation of between 15% and 18% of the value of the production over a period of twenty-five years.[132]

719. Given that contracts of risk were signed in contravention of the constitutional principles defined in 1940 by the Constitution, in 1958, the Congress of the Union approved a fourth Regulatory Law of Article 27 of the Constitution in the Field of Petroleum. The new law established the nation's ownership system over oil and other hydrocarbons in addition to the monopoly of public monopoly in the sector that included all activities related to the construction and operation of infrastructure.

720. The 1958 Law was an important step towards the configuration of a regime of absolute state ownership over hydrocarbons. This law prohibited, for the second time, private participation in the petroleum industry. Article 2 established: 'only the nation can carry out the different exploitations that constitute the oil industry in the terms of the following article'. Article 3 complemented that provision by noting that the oil industry comprises the exploration, exploitation, refining, transport, storage, distribution, and first-hand sales, and the products obtained from its refining; the exploration, exploitation, processing, and first-hand sales of gas, as well as the transport and storage essential and necessary to interconnect its exploitation and production.

721. A new step towards the nationalization of the oil industry was given in 1960 when the Constitution was amended again to indicate in the sixth paragraph of Article 27 that:[133]

> In the case of petroleum and solid, liquid or gaseous hydrocarbons, no concessions or contracts shall be granted, nor shall any such concessions be granted, and the nation shall carry out the exploitation of those products, in the terms prescribed by the regulatory law Respectively.

---

130. *See*: Mario Alberto Becerra Pocoroba, *Análisis de los aspectos más relevantes de la reforma energética* (2008). Disponible en http://www.senado.gob.mx/reforma_energética/content/foros/docs/20 de mayo2008_7.pdf.
131. In Bolivia, the Capitalization Act of 1996 introduced joint venture contracts for petroleum exploration and production.
132. These contracts were cancelled in 1970 by the General Director of PEMEX, Jesus Reyes Heroles.
133. DOF, 20 Jan. 1960.

722. The 1960 reform also established that the direct domination of the nation over subsoil resources included the continental shelf, the seabed, and the submarine sockets of the islands.

723. Finally, in order to complete the constitutional process of nationalization of the oil industry, in 1982, Articles 25 and 28 of the Constitution were amended to establish that the oil industry is a strategic economic area and consequently a Mexican State monopoly, thus fully recognizing the regime of state ownership over oil and other hydrocarbons.

724. However, on the one hand, in 1995, a constitutional reform explicitly excluded the secondary petrochemicals from the state monopoly over the oil industry; And second, secondary legislation does not follow constitutional principles very closely, since the 1958 Act has been amended several times to allow private sector participation in this sector.

725. In May of 1995, the Federal Congress approved modifications to the Regulation of Article 27 of the Constitutional Act in the Field of Petroleum. This legal reform redefined the gas industry. It allows the private sector to build, operate, and own systems of transport, storage, and distribution of natural gas. These activities were previously reserved to State regulation. The State keeps the power to regulate these activities. It also keeps the ownership of the natural gas itself and the operation of the public sector. As a complement to these modifications, the Regulation of Natural Gas was approved by the Executive. This Regulation defines three types of activities subject to governmental permission: transport, storage, and distribution.

726. By the end of the twentieth century, the oil industry was practically an absolute monopoly of the Mexican State. The only sub-sector of this industry that had been privatized was secondary petrochemicals. This happened by the reformation of the Federal Constitution in 1995. However, in 2008, the Regulation of Article 27, a Constitutional Act in the Field of Petroleum, was substantially modified to allow private investment in several activities regulated by this Act.

727. In 2013, Article 27 of the Mexican Constitution was amended; this amendment preserves the direct, inalienable, and imprescriptible ownership of the nation but allows private participation in the exploration and exploitation of these resources through the signing of contracts. The seventh paragraph of Article 27 of the Mexican Constitution provides as follows:

> In the case of oil and solid hydrocarbons, liquid or gaseous, in the subsoil, the property of the Nation is inalienable and imprescriptible, and no concessions will be granted. In order to obtain income for the State that contributes to the long-term development of the Nation, it will carry out the exploration and extraction of oil and other hydrocarbons through assignments to productive enterprises of the State or through contracts with them or with private corporations, in the terms of the Regulatory Law. In order to comply with the purpose of such assignments or contracts, productive enterprises of the State may

contract with individuals. In any case, the hydrocarbons in the subsoil are owned by the Nation and thus must be affirmed in the assignments or contracts.

728. According to Article Transitory Fourth of the Decree of constitutional reform commented on, the contracts that can be celebrated with the individuals are the following:

(1) Services.
(2) Of shared utility.
(3) Shared production.
(4) Licensing.

729. This brief analysis of the evolution of the constitutional and legal framework of oil and other hydrocarbons leads to conclude that while the reforms to the 1917 Constitution were aimed at establishing the model of absolute state ownership over these resources, subsequent legal reforms were evolving in a sense to recognize a model of national ownership in the terms defined at the beginning of this chapter, allowing private participation.

730. On 11 August 2014, the new Hydrocarbons Law (LH) was published in the DOF, which regulates Articles 25, fourth paragraph; 27, seventh paragraph and 28, fourth paragraph of the Constitution, regarding hydrocarbons. Article 1 of this Law reiterates the constitutional principle according to which: 'The Nation shall be the direct, inalienable and imprescriptible property of all Hydrocarbons found in the subsoil of the national territory, including the continental shelf and the exclusive economic zone Located outside the territorial sea and adjacent to it, in mantles or deposits, whatever their physical state.'

731. For the purposes of this Law, transboundary deposits are those that are within the national jurisdiction and have physical continuity outside it. Also, any deposits or mantles outside national jurisdiction shared with other countries in accordance with the treaties in which Mexico is a party, or under the provisions of UNCLOS, shall be considered as transboundary.

732. In accordance with Article 1, the material scope of application of the LH includes the following activities:

I. The Recognition and Surface Exploration, and the Exploration and Extraction of Hydrocarbons;
II. The Treatment, refining, alienation, commercialization, Transport and Storage of the Oil;
III. The processing, compression, liquefaction, decompression and regasification, as well as the Transport, Storage, Distribution, commercialization and supply to the Public of Natural Gas;
IV. The Transportation, Storage, Distribution, Marketing and Expend to the Public of Petroleum, and

V. Transportation by pipeline and Storage that is linked to Petrochemical pipelines.

733. Pursuant to Article 28 of the Constitution, exploration, and extraction activities for hydrocarbons are considered strategic, and only the nation can carry them out. Article 5 of the LH reiterates this maxim. However, according to the constitutional text, the precept quoted adds that the nation will carry out both activities through assignees and contractors.

734. Accordingly, Title II of the Law entitled 'Exploration and Extraction of Hydrocarbons and Recognition and Surface Exploration' regulates the way assignments are granted and contracts are executed. In addition to the foregoing, the second paragraph of Article 5 of the Law states that 'The activities of Recognition and Surface Exploration, as well as the activities referred to in fractions II to V of Article 2 of this Law, may be carried out by *Petroleos Mexicanos*, any other productive enterprise of the State or parastatal entity, as well as by any person, prior authorization or permission, as appropriate, in the terms of this Law and its regulations.'

Part III. Zoning and Land Use Planning

735. Land use is regulated by both the Environmental Act and the Law on Human Settlements, Land Use Planning and Urban Development of 2016 (Urban Act).[134]

736. The Environmental Law regulates the ecological ordinance of the territory in the Second Section of the First Chapter of the Title I relating to 'Environmental Policy Instruments', whereas the Urban Act rules urban planning.

737. The Environmental Act defines the ecological zoning plan of Mexican territory as 'the instrument of environmental policy that regulates or induces land use to protect the environment and to preserve and to exploit natural resources in a sustainable manner by analysing the deterioration trends and the potentialities for exploiting the land' (Article 3, paragraph XXIV); whereas according to fraction XXVI of Article 3 of the Urban Law, the territorial ordering of human settlements is 'a public policy whose purpose is the occupation and rational use of the territory as the spatial basis of socio-economic development strategies and environmental preservation'.

738. The Environmental Act recognizes four levels of environmental planning: (a) Program of General Ecological Ordinance of the Territory (PGEOT), (b) Regional programmes for the ecological ordinance, (c) Local programmes for the ecological ordinance, and (d) marine zone ecological ordinance programmes.

739. The General Ecology Program of the Territory is issued by the Federal Executive. In accordance with Article 20 of the Environmental Law, it aims to establish:

I. The ecological regionalization of the national territory and of the zones on which the nation exercises sovereignty and jurisdiction, based on the diagnosis of the characteristics, availability and demand of natural resources, as well as of the productive activities that develop in them and of the location and status of existing human settlements, and
II. The ecological guidelines and strategies for the preservation, protection, restoration and sustainable use of natural resources, as well as for the localization of productive activities and human settlements.

134. DOF, 28 Nov. 2016.

740. Article 20*bis* 3 of the Environmental Law states that the Regional programmes for ecological ordinance must contain at least the following:

I. The determination of the area or region to be ordered, describing its physical, biotic and socioeconomic attributes, as well as the diagnosis of its environmental conditions and the technologies used by the inhabitants of the area;
II. The determination of the ecological regulation criteria for the preservation, protection, restoration and sustainable use of the natural resources that are located in the region in question, as well as for the accomplishment of productive activities and the location of human settlements, and
III. The guidelines for its execution, evaluation, monitoring and modification.

741. These programmes must be issued by local state governments. However, in the following cases, participation of the federal government is mandatory:

A) When an ecological region is located in the territory of two or more federative entities, the Federal Government, the respective States and Municipalities, and in the case of the Federal District, within the scope of their competencies, may formulate a regional program for ecological ordering but the Federation will celebrate the agreements or coordination agreements coming with the local governments involved.
B) When a regional Eco regional program includes a protected natural area, or part of the federation's competence, the program must be prepared and approved jointly by the Secretariat and the governments of the States, the Federal District and Municipalities In which it is located, as appropriate.

In accordance with Article 20*bis* 4 and 20*bis* 5 of the Environmental Law, the local ecological ordering programmes are elaborated by the municipal authorities and must have the following objectives:

I. To determine the different ecological areas that are in the area or region concerned, describing their physical, biotic and socio-economic attributes, as well as the diagnosis of their environmental conditions, and the technologies used by the inhabitants of the area.
II. To regulate, outside of the urban areas, the uses of the soil with the purpose of protecting the environment and preserving, restoring and making sustainable use of the respective natural resources, mainly in the accomplishment of productive activities and the location of human settlements, and
III. To establish ecological regulation criteria for the protection, preservation, restoration and sustainable use of natural resources within the urban areas, in order to be considered in the corresponding urban development plans or programs.

Marine zone ecological ordinance programmes are formulated and issued by the Federal Executive and in accordance with Article 20*bis* 7 of the Environmental Law indicates that marine eco-management programmes must contain at least:

I. The precise delimitation of the area that will comprise the program;
II. The determination of the ecological zones based on the characteristics, availability and demand of the natural resources included in them, as well as the type of productive activities that they develop, and
III. Guidelines, strategies and other provisions for the preservation, protection, restoration and sustainable use of natural resources, as well as the carrying out of productive activities and other works or activities that may affect the respective ecosystems.

742. Similarly, the Urban Act establishes the following levels of planning: (a) the National Urban Development Programme, (b) local programmes for urban development, (c) programmes for zoning metropolitan areas, (d) municipal plans and programmes for urban development, (e) programmes for urban development in population centres, and (f) other plans and programmes derived from the aforementioned and considered by local laws.

743. Given that neither the Environmental Law nor the Urban Law are very strict in this regard, it can be argued that both laws are responsible for ordering the same territory, the territory of the country as a whole. Although each of these mechanisms can be interpreted as ordering the national territory from two different points of view, ecological ordering does so from the point of view of productive activities, while urban planning does so from the point of view of human settlements. The fact is that neither law is clear in narrowing its spatial scope of application.

744. However, the reading of Article 22 of the Urban Law allows to assert that the territorial ordering of human settlements is limited to ordering the territory of population centres. When referring to the National System of Planning of Territorial Ordering, Urban and Metropolitan Development, this legal provision states:

> The planning, regulation and evaluation of the Territorial Ordering of Human Settlements and Urban Development of the Population Centres are part of the National Democratic Planning System, as a global, sectorial and regional policy that contributes to the achievement of the Objectives of the National Development Plan, federal programs and state and municipal plans.

745. However, the analysis of the Environmental Law allows to assert that the ecological ordinance of territory has supremacy on the urban order. The above is based on the following reasons:

- The PGEOT establishes guidelines and ecological strategies for locating productive activities and human settlements (Article 20, section I).

- Regional Programs for Ecological Ordinance determine ecological regulation criteria for productive activities and the location of human settlements (Article 20a 3, section II).
- Programmes or Ecological Ordinance establish the ecological regulation criteria to be considered by the corresponding urban development plans or programmes (Article 20*bis* 4, section III).
- The urban planning programmes must be submitted to the EIA procedure (Article 32 of Environmental Act).
- Urban development plans or programmes must take into account the guidelines and strategies contained in the ecological planning programmes of the territory (Article 23, section I).

Part IV. Liability Questions

Chapter 1. Private Law Liability

746. Mexican private law recognizes two types of liability: fault liability and strict liability. Fault liability is based on the existence of three elements: damage, a fault (illegal behaviour), and a link of causation between that conduct and the damage; strict liability, whereas, does not require proof of fault, although causation must still be established.

747. As the strict liability system was established as a link to dangerous activities involving a considerable level of risk, it has the potential to be applied to environmental damage. This explains why most Mexican environmental laws refer to the application of civil liability in cases of environmental damages.

748. For instance, Article 203 of the Environmental Act asserts:

> Independently from the criminal or administrative sanctions that proceed, all persons who contaminate or deteriorate the environment or affect natural resources or biodiversity shall be responsible and shall be forced to repair the caused damages, in accordance with applicable provisions of the Civil Code.

749. In the same way, Article 96*bis* (1) of the Waters Act points out:

> Individuals or Corporations that discharge residual waters, in violation to the legal applicable dispositions, and that cause contamination in a receiving body, shall assume the responsibility of repairing the environmental damage caused, independently of the application of the administrative, criminal, or civil sanctions that proceed, by means of the removal of the pollutants of the receiving affected body and to restore it to the state it was in before the damage took place.

750. Mexican environmental laws also establish a series of rules aimed at adapting the civil law system to the environmental field. Thus, to avoid the problems of proving the link of causation in cases of environmental damage, Mexican environmental laws channel liability to a specific person. For instance, Article 151 of the Environmental Act states:

> Liability for the management and final disposition of hazardous wastes corresponds to those who generate them. In cases for which management services and the final disposition of the dangerous residuals have been hired out to companies authorized by the Secretary and the residuals are given to such companies, liability for the operations will be of these independent from the liability of the generators of the hazardous wastes.

751. In the same way, regarding restoration of damage, environmental laws recognize the priority of remediation over economic compensation. For instance, Article *152bis* of the Environmental Act sets forth the following:

> When the generation, management, or final disposition of dangerous wastes or materials results in soil pollution, those responsible for these operations will carry out the necessary actions to recover and to reestablish the conditions of the soil, so that it can be designated to some of the activities foreseen in the applicable program of urban development plans or of ecological zoning plans for such soils or areas.

752. Finally, although the Waste Act does not establish the obligation of repairing environmental damage, it determines some approaches to carry out the restoration of polluted soils by residuals in Articles 78 and 79, which, respectively, point out:

> The Secretary, in coordination with the Secretary of Health, shall issue the Mexican Official Norms for the characterization of the polluted places, and it shall evaluate the risks to the environment and to health that derive from them, to determine, in conjunction with the risk, the restoration actions that shall proceed (Article 78).
>
> The Regulations on land use and the programs of ecological classification and of urban development shall be considered when determining the level of remediation of polluted places with dangerous residuals, based on the risks that will be avoided (Article 79).

753. In spite of adaptations of traditional civil liability rules by environmental laws, fundamental questions of liability for environmental damages are still unsolved, such as legal standing to bring actions to restore damaged environments. Only the Wildlife Act recognizes that, in cases of damages to wildlife or its habitat, it corresponds to the Environmental Prosecutor to bring actions aimed at restoring the damages. In the rest of the environmental laws, only the directly affected person has legal standing to bring an action.

754. In 2011, the Federal Congress started discussing the bill of Environmental Liability Act that was approved and came into force in 2013.

755. This Law has fifty-six articles organized into three parts or 'Titles'. Title I named 'Of Environmental Liability' is the most important. It is comprised of Article 1 to Article 46. It is also divided into three chapters, as follows:

(1) Chapter One. *General provisions*. This chapter defines environmental damages and distinguishes between environmental and civil liability.
(2) Chapter Two. *Obligations derivate from causing environmental damages*. It states that those who caused environmental damages are obliged to its reparation or when impossible to pay an economic compensation.
(3) Chapter Three. *Judicial procedure of environmental liability*. This chapter regulates: environmental actions; precautionary actions, burden of proof; and the scope of the final ruling. The chapter also creates an environmental compensation Fund.

756. Chapter One defines what is environmental damage and civil damage. Chapter Two is addressed to establish the legal consequence of environmental damage.

757. The Title II of the law regulates the alternative methods of Justice.

758. Finally, the Title III introducing some rules regarding criminal liability for environmental damages. Such rules complement the provision of the Federal Criminal Code in this regard.

Chapter 2. Criminal Law Liability

759. Environmental crimes are regulated by Title XXV of the Federal Criminal Code, called 'Crimes against the Environment and Environmental Management'. This Title contains five chapters, four of which include twenty criminal conducts related to technological dangerous activities; biodiversity, biosafety; and environmental management; whereas Chapter 5 contains general provisions related to innovative penalties and precautionary measures to be adopted by judges when environmental criminal behaviour is committed.

760. The environmental crimes regulated by the Criminal Code include the following:

(a) Article 414 refers to the illicit management of hazardous substances.
(b) Article 415 refers to the illicit emission of pollutants into the air as well as illegal emissions of noise, vibrations, and thermal or light energy.
(c) Article 416 refers to the illicit discharge of pollutants into water or soil.
(d) Article 417 refers to the illegal trafficking of forest materials and flora and fauna.
(e) Article 418 refers to the illegal destruction of natural vegetation, causation of damage to forests, and changing of land use into forest lands.
(f) Article 419 refers to the illegal extraction, transportation, and transformation of timber.
(g) Article 420 refers to the illegal and prohibited means of fishing and hunting; harm caused to marine mammals and sea tortoises; and illegal harm or trafficking of endangered species of flora and fauna, and genetic resources.
(h) Article 420*bis* refers to criminal harm to wetlands and illegal extraction of marine resources.
(i) Article 420 refers to the illegal trafficking and management of genetically modified organisms.
(j) Article 420 refers to the illegal actions against the public management of the environment.

761. Generally, making a person criminally liable implies a complex process. In accordance with the Mexican Constitution and the Federal Code of Criminal Procedure, to indict a person for a criminal violation, the prosecution must acquire enough evidence to sufficiently prove: (a) all of the elements of the specific crime committed, and (b) the probable participation of the person in the commission of the crime.

762. Additionally, environmental crimes contain various elements that must be proven. Pollution crimes are comprised of: (a) a specific action, such as the transport of hazardous wastes or the emission of pollutants into the atmosphere; (b) a harmful result, such as harm to public health, natural resources, wildlife, water quality, or ecosystems; and (c) the violation of an environmental statue, regulation, or legal standard, such as the discharge of pollutants into a river in a quantity that exceeds the statutory limits. Failure to obtain a regulatory permit and the Act of introducing a hazard into the environment may also be considered elements of a crime in some cases.

763. Under Mexican law, to indict a person for the commission of an environmental crime, the government must present evidence enough to demonstrate that a person purposely harmed the environment or possessed knowledge that such harm was possible. Under current regulations, criminal negligence is not enough to present an indictment for the commission of an environmental crime.

Chapter 3. Administrative Liability

764. All Mexican environmental laws have an established system of administrative sanctions to be applied in cases of non-compliance with the provisions of such laws. Thus, according to Article 161 of the Environmental Act, Article 104 of the Wildlife Act, Articles 155–162 of the Forest Act, Articles 101 and 102 of the Waste Act, and Article 86, paragraph V of the Waters Act, environmental authorities shall carry out actions to inspect and verify compliance with the provisions established in these Laws and Regulations. The Environmental Prosecutor and the NWC oversee enforcing environmental laws in two ways: (a) by means of monitoring inspections, and (b) by imposing administrative penalties.

765. The administrative penalties for violations of Mexican environmental laws and regulations include fines, facility closings, and administrative arrests. The fines range from 20 to 50,000 times the minimum wage for the Federal District of Mexico at the time the penalty is imposed. The penalty may result in approximately the equivalent of USD 2,500,000. Sanctions consist of administrative fines, facility closings, arrest, insurance, suspension of authorizations, and so on.

766. A facility may be completely or partially closed through a facility closing or revocation of a business operations permit. An administrative arrest may require the violator to remain under arrest for up to thirty-six hours.

Part V. Juridical Actions of Individuals

Chapter 1. Administrative Remedies

§1. The Right to Access to Information

767. The right to access to environmental information is recognized by Mexican legislation in three ways. First, under the Environmental Act, any person can claim access to environmental information in the procedure of EIA. In this regard, Article 34 of the Environmental Act points out:

> Once the Secretary receives a manifestation of environmental impact and integrates the file referred to by Article 35, it will put the file in the public's disposition so that can be consulted by any person.

768. Second, Articles 159, 159*bis* 1, and 159*bis* 2 oblige the environmental authorities to gather, organize, and make accessible to the public environmental information; whereas Article 159*bis* 3 gives all people the right to access information.

769. Finally, in 2002, the Federal Act of Transparency and Access to Information (Access to Information Act) was passed by the Federal Congress. According to Article 1, this Act has the objective of guaranty to people the right to access to information that governmental offices possess. This Act also created the Federal Institute for Access to Information as an autonomous entity in charge of promoting the right to access to information; to deny requests of information, and to protect personal data that governmental offices possess. Thus, based on this Act, access to information about environmental matters is much more comprehensive.

§2. Public Participation

770. The right of the public to participate in decision-making processes is recognized in three ways as well. First, the Environmental Act contains a specific chapter that addresses the regulation of public participation. According to this chapter, environmental authorities are obliged to promote public participation in the planning, executing, evaluating, and monitoring of public policies on the environment and natural resources.

771. Second, as mentioned in the previous section, public participation is allowed in the procedure of EIA. Article 34 of the Environmental Act sets up the Ministry of the Environment, so that, upon the request of any persons from the affected community where a project is planned to be constructed, it can organize a public consultation so that these persons may propose measures for the prevention or mitigation of environmental impacts that the project could cause.

772. Finally, Mexican environmental law allows public participation in the process of the approval of Mexican Official Norms (MONs).

§3. Access to Justice

773. Administrative decisions issued by environmental authorities can be combated through three mechanisms:

(1) The appeal for review before the environmental authority according to Article 176 of the Environmental Act.
(2) The trial of Nullification before TFJFA.
(3) Injunction actions.

774. As mentioned above, legal standing to file actions to combat environmental authorities' decisions is nowadays widely recognized in Mexico. Neither the Constitution nor legislations require to prove the existence of a direct legal standing, but they recognize the so-called legitimate legal standing to file such actions.

775. By the reform of 2010 Mexican Constitution provided the foundation for collective actions. Third paragraph of Article 17 states:

> The Federal Congress shall to enact laws regulating collective actions. Such Laws shall to define their scope of application, judicial procedures and mechanisms for damage restoration. Federal Judges have exclusive jurisdiction on these procedures and mechanisms.

776. In the same vain, in 2011, Article 107 of the Constitution was reformed to provide a foundation for filing injunctions action to protect not only direct and individual legal interests but also legitimate and direct interests:

> '**Article 107**. All dispute considered under Article 103 shall be subject of the proceeding and formalities established by the law, in accordance with the following bases':
>
> I. 'The amparo trial must always be initiated at instance of injury party, having this character those who argument to have a right or individual or collective legitimate interest, under the condition that the act claimed violets a right recognized by this Constitution and with that it its juridical interest directly or because its especial legal situation.'

777. On its side, the Environmental Act recognizes the legitimate interest in Article 180 when saying:

> ARTICLE 180. – In the case of works or activities that violate the provisions of this Act and those to which it is supplementary applied and regulations and NOMs arising therefrom, ecological management programmes, the declarations protected natural areas or regulations and Official Mexican Standard derived from it, the individuals and entities with a legitimate interest has the right to challenge administrative acts relating thereto and the requirement to carry out the necessary actions to be observed applicable legal provisions, provided that they prove in the process that those works or activities cause or may cause damage to the environment, natural resources, wildlife or public health.
>
> To this end, optionally may lodge administrative review to be in this Chapter or go to the Federal Court of Fiscal and Administrative Justice.
>
> For the purposes of this article, have a legitimate interest individuals or corporations of the communities potentially affected by such works or activities.

§4. Popular Complaint

778. Article 189 of the Environmental Act provides that any individual or group may report to the Environmental Prosecutor, through a *denuncia popular* (popular complaint), any matter that could result in harm to the environment or natural resources, or that violates any environmental law or regulation. According to this Provision:

> Any individual, social group, non-governmental organization, association, and partnership may denounce with the Federal Attorney General's Office or other Authorities, any fact, action, or omission producing or that may produce ecological imbalance or damages to the environment or to natural resources, or in violation of the Provisions of this Law and the other laws regulating matters related to environmental protection and preservation and restoration of ecological balance.
>
> If within the place in question there is no representative of the Federal Environmental Protection Agency, such denunciation may be filed with the municipal authority or, at the option of the complainant, with the closest representative office of such agency.
>
> If the denunciation was filed with a municipal authority and the same falls within Federal jurisdiction, it shall be sent to the Federal Environmental Protection Agency.

Chapter 2. Judicial Remedies

779. The Judiciary Branch participates in enforcing environmental law when people: (a) appeal an EIA authorization, (b) file a constitutional *amparo*, or (c) file a civil suit.

§1. Administrative Motions for Appeal

780. Article 176 of the Environmental Act states:

> The final resolution issued in administrative procedures due to the enforcement of this Law, its Regulations, and provisions derived therein, may be appealed by the affected parties by: (a) filing a motion for review whiting fifteen working days counted from the day of the notice, or (b) through the Nullification action before the Federal Court of Tax and Administrative Justice.

§2. *Amparo*

781. In 1999, the Mexican Constitution was amended to recognize the so-called right to a healthy environment. Since this provision was included in the chapter of fundamental rights, based on such amendment, it was possible to argue that such constitutional reform made it possible to bring an *amparo* action (injunction) in cases for which the Authorities' decisions affect this right.

782. However, the new Law on Amparo, regulating Articles 103 and 107 of the Political Constitution of the Mexican United States (as amended in 2011) recognizes the legitimate interest to file the injunction. Article 5 of the new Law on Amparo establishes that:

> ARTICLE 5. The parties to the injunction: I. The complainant, having such a character who claims to be the holder of a subjective right or a legitimate interest individual or collective, always claiming that the standard, act or omission claimed violated the rights provided in Article 1 of this Act and thereby produce a real and current involvement to their legal rights, either directly or by virtue of their special situation facing the legal system.
>
> Simple interest, in any case, may be invoked as a legitimate concern. The public authority may not invoke legitimate interest.

783. Thus, nowadays, it is clearly possible to file an *amparo* action in defence of the human right to a healthy environment. An *amparo* suit is a legal action, founded in the Mexican Constitution, in which an individual may seek damages for, or the suspension or annulment of, an Act by a government authority that violates the individual's rights. An *amparo* suit may not be brought by an environmental organization on behalf of an affected group, or as a class action on behalf of many similarly situated individuals. Rather, it must be brought by an individual petitioner who can show that he or she has been affected directly and has suffered harm caused by the official action.

§3. Civil Suits

784. During the last years, important changes have occurred in the Mexican legal system aimed at wildly recognizing the legal standing to file actions for environmental damages.

785. First, the Federal Code of Civil Procedure was amended in 2011 to introduce the 'collective actions' to protect collective rights such as the right to a healthy environment.

786. In this regard, Article 578 of the Federal Code of Civil Procedure asserts that protection and defence of collective rights and interests are allowed in environmental matters.

787. Article 585 of the Code recognizes legal standing to file collective actions in environmental matters to:

(a) The Attorney General's Office for Environmental Protection.
(b) A representative of at least thirty people affected by the environmental damage.
(c) NGOs.
(d) The Attorney General.

788. Second, in 2013, a new Federal Environmental Liability Act was passed by the Federal Congress.
This Law is regulatory of Article 4 of the Constitution and, therefore, its objectives are to guarantee the human rights to a healthy environment and the human right to challenge responsibility for environmental damage. To achieve its objectives, the Federal Environmental Liability Law regulates the environmental liability arising from damages caused to the environment, as well as restoration and compensation of such damages (Article 1).

789. Therefore, this Law is applicable only when three circumstances coincide:

(1) the existence of environmental damage; and
(2) liability can be channelled through the federal judicial proceedings provided for by Article 17 of the Constitution – that is to say, through collective actions; alternative dispute resolution mechanisms; administrative procedures; or
(3) environmental damage is the consequence of crimes against the environment or against environmental authorities.

790. The Federal Environmental Liability Act defines environmental damage in Article 2, third fraction as:

> The adverse and measurable loss, change, detriment, impairment, or alteration of habitats, ecosystems, natural elements and resources, their chemical, physical or biological conditions, the interaction relationships between them, and of the environmental services they provide.

791. However, such definition of environmental damage is not entirely clear, since it does not state at what point the adverse change, deterioration, impairment, affectation, or modification becomes damage. Nor is it clear because it confuses the damage that occurs to the environment as a subject of legal protection in itself with the damage that affects the natural elements that make it up. Moreover, it confuses pollution with environmental damage.

792. This lack of legal certainty generated by an inadequate wording of the cited provision may make it more difficult to comply with this Law. In addition, Article 6 states that there is no environmental damage when the impairments, losses, affectations, modifications or deterioration are not adverse, since:

(1) They have been expressly stated by the responsible and explicitly identified, delimited in their scope, evaluated, mitigated and compensated by conditions, and authorized by the Secretariat, prior to carrying out the conduct that originates them, through EIA or its preventive report, the authorization of change of use of forest land or some other similar authorization issued by the Secretariat.
(2) They do not exceed the limits established by Environmental laws and Mexican Official Norms.

793. Consequently, in two cases, although there is, in fact, environmental damage, the system of liability that the Law regulates will not be applicable and, therefore, the restoration will not be possible under the Federal Environmental Liability Act.

794. The exception set forth in section I of Article 6 has another exception, since the last paragraph of this provision states that 'The exception provided for in section I of this article shall not operate, when the terms or conditions of the Authorization issued by the authority.'

795. Disregard for fundamental principles of law reaches its maximum when this law states in Article 7 that:

> In order to grant certainty and to induce economic agents to bear the costs of damages caused to the environment, the Secretariat should gradually issue Mexican Official Mexican Norms, which have the purpose of establishing case by case and subject to the Law of the matter, of deterioration, loss, change, impairment, affectation, modification and contamination, necessary to consider them as adverse and harmful.

796. The criteria established by the quoted provision is wrong. In traditional liability regimes, the plaintiff must prove the evidence of damage whereas the defendant must demonstrate that plaintiff's proofs are not enough to channel liability. It corresponds to the judge to decide on the damage existence. Conversely, this law grants the Ministry the power of defined whether the damage exists.

797. The same legal provision adds that:

> To this end, it will be ensured that these amounts are significant and are considered, among other criteria, the capacity of regeneration of natural elements. Failure to issue the rules referred to in the previous paragraph shall not impede or exempt the person responsible from their obligation to repair the damage to their base state, considering the concept provided for in article 2, section III, of this Law.

798. In other words, the Congress of the Union vested the administrative authority with the power to decide when there is and when there is no environmental damage. This is absurd because environmental damage will exist whenever the balance between the environmental functions deprives the environment of its capacity to be an adequate support of life but not when an administrative authority decides it.

799. One positive aspect is that Article 4 of this law recognizes that environmental damage is different from the civil damage caused to natural resource owners, which is already regulated in the Civil Codes, and also points out that environmental liability is different from administrative or criminal liability. However, it never manages to delimit the borders of environmental damage and, therefore, fails in its objective.

800. The Environmental Liability Act recognizes three mechanisms for environmental damage restoration: (a) reparation *in natura*, (b) substitute reparation *in natura*, and (c) economic compensation, when it states in its Article 10 that any natural or collective person that with its action or omission directly or indirectly causes damage to the environment, will be responsible and will be obliged to repair the damages, or when the repair is not possible to the appropriate environmental compensation.

801. Reparation *in natura* involves returning things to the state they were in before the damage occurred. As stated in Article 13 of the Federal Environmental Liability Act (FELA), reparation of environmental damage will consist of restoring to its base state the habitats, ecosystems, natural elements, and resources, their chemical, physical, or biological conditions and the interaction relations between them, as well as the environmental services they provide.

802. Although this principle is desirable, it is difficult to carry out in practice, for it is necessary to know what the original state of the environment was, and this information is not always available, however, the FELA does not define legal instruments that allow arriving at such certainty.

803. To deal with this problem, the mentioned legal provision states that restoration *in natura* is achieved through restoration, treatment, recovery, or remediation which is obviously tautological and confusing because it leads us to the absurd of asserting that environmental damage is repaired by repairing it.

804. Article 13 indicates a series of principles that govern the reparation of environmental damage. These principles are:

A) The repair must be carried out in the place where the damage was produced.
B) Land owners or possessor of lands where the environment has occurred, must allow restoration, in accordance with this Law. Failure to comply with this obligation will result in the imposition of the means of arrest and the criminal responsibility that Match.
C) Land owners or possessor of lands who are affected by the actions of environmental restoration when damage is caused by third parties, will have the right to file action against the person who is responsible for the damages caused to them.

805. However, *substitute reparation in natura*, consists of repairing environmental damage like the one that is not susceptible of restoration. This mechanism for the restoration of environmental damage is referred to in Article 17 of the Federal Environmental Liability Act. According to this provision, compensation for environmental damage will consist of investments or actions that the responsible party does to generate environmental improvement, replacing total or partial restoration of the damage caused to the environment, as appropriate, and equivalent to the adverse effects caused by the damage. As in the case of *restoration in natura*, the legal provision under analysis also establishes some criteria that govern *substitute restoration in natura*:

A) The investment or actions must be done in the ecosystem or ecological region where the damage has occurred.
B) If this is materially impossible, the investment or actions will be carried out in an alternative location, ecologically, and geographically linked to the damaged site and for the benefit of the affected community.
C) In the latter case, the criteria for priority sites for repair of damages, which the Secretariat may issue in accordance with the provisions of section 5, Chapter Three of this Title, shall apply.
D) The responsible may comply with the obligation set forth in this article, by contracting third parties.

806. The Federal Environmental Liability Act also refers to an economic sanction that, in accordance with Article 19, is not substitute, but an accessory to *restoration in natura* in any of its forms.

807. This pecuniary sanction will consist of the payment of an amount of money equivalent to:

I. From three hundred to fifty thousand days of general minimum wage valid in the Federal District at the time of imposing the sanction, when the person responsible is a natural person, and
II. From one thousand to six hundred thousand days of general minimum wage valid in the Federal District at the time of imposing the sanction, when the person responsible is a moral person.

808. Pursuant to Article 23 of the FELA, the economic penalty will be determined by the judge taking into account the economic capacity of the person responsible for making the payment, as well as the limits, requirements, and guarantees provided in his favour by the Political Constitution of the United States of Mexico, the gravity of the damage caused and the intentional or negligent nature of the violation, ensuring that the economic benefit obtained, if any, is neutralized and the amount of the expenses of the actor or actors that have been necessary to prove responsibility. In each case, the court shall provide that the economic penalty is clearly sufficient to achieve the purposes of inhibition and general and special prevention referred to in Article 2, section XI of this Act.

809. The economic sanction to which we refer also is a mechanism for repairing environmental damage, although Article 2 of the same law states that the economic sanction consists of 'The payment imposed by the judicial authority to penalize unlawful conduct harmful to the purpose To achieve general and special prevention and to inhibit prohibited behaviour in the future', according to Article 46, that economic penalty is allocated to the Environmental Fund. This legal provision states:

> The Fund will be under the supervision, supervision and coordination of the Secretariat, and its patrimony will be integrated with:
>
> I. The economic penalty referred to in section XIV of Article 2. Of this Law, and
> II. The other resources obtained by any other concept, but expressly does not talk about compensation for damage.

810. However, in terms of Article 45 of the Federal Environmental Liability Act, the Environmental Liability Fund will have as its object the payment of compensation for damages caused to the environment, in the cases that the federal environmental authorities decide based on reasons of urgency or importance, as well as to pay for studies and researches requested by judges to the Ministry of the Environment or to the Attorney General's Office during the jurisdictional process of environmental liability. Therefore, the economic penalty is neither pecuniary compensation in the style of civil law nor a fine in terms of administrative law, but a mechanism of general reparation for environmental damage.

811. Article 28 of the new Act grants legal standing to file actions for environmental damages to:

(a) Inhabitants of the community adjacent to the place where the damage occurred.
(b) Mexican non-profit private individuals whose corporate purpose is environmental protection in general, or any of its elements, when acting in representation of some inhabitant of the communities adjacent to the place where the damage occurred.
(c) The Attorney General's Office for Environmental Protection.
(d) Local Environmental Prosecutors.

812. Supreme Court of Justice has ruled that Article 28 is unconstitutional because it reduces the scope of legal standing to non-governmental organizations that only can file actions on behalf of the directly affected communities but not on their own behalf; whereas the Federal Code of Civil Procedure grants standing to such social organization in itself.

Selected Bibliography

Anglés Hernández Marisol. *Instrumentos de política ambiental sobre residuor peligrosos*. México, Porrúa, 2004 (Colección Breviarios Jurídicos).

Amit Ray. 'Waste Management in Developing Asia. Can Trade and Cooperation Help?'. *The Journal of Environment & Development* 17, no. 1 (2008): 3–25.

Raúl Brañes Ballesteros. *Manual de Derecho Ambiental Mexicano*. México: FCE/FUNDEA, 2000.

Patricia Birnie & Alan Boyle. *International Law and the Environment*. New York: Oxford University Press, 1992.

Lucio Cabrera Acevedo. El amparo colectivo protector del derecho al ambiente y de otros derechos humanos. México: Porrúa, 2000.

Lara Carmona. Ley General del Equilibrio Ecológico y la Protección al Ambiente. Comentarios y Concordancias. México: UNAM-PROFEPA, 2003.

Catherine Roche. *Droit de l'environnement*. París: Gualino éditeur, 2001.

Carla De Aceves. *Bases Fundamentales del Derecho Ambiental Mexicano*. México: Porrúa, 2003.

De Cantú Gloria M. Delgado. Estructuras política, económica y social. México, 2ª ed. Ed. Pearson Educación. 2003.

José Juan González Márquez. *Introducción al Derecho Ambiental Mexicano*. México: UAM, 1999.

Raquel Gutierrez Nájera. Introducción al estudio del Derecho Ambiental. México: Porrúa, 1998.

Jímenez Cisneros, Blanca Elena. La contaminación ambiental en México. México: Limusa/Colegio de Ingenieros Ambientales, Instituto de Ingeniería de la UNAM/Femisca, 2001.

José Juste Ruiz. *Protección del Medio Ambiente y Comercio Internacional*. Valencia: Mimeo, 2004.

Kirbi Peter, 'Emissions Trading in the International Context: Kioto Implementation and International Trade Agreements', in Mar Campins Eritja (coord.), *Los retos de la aplicación del Protocolo de Kioto en España y Canadá* Barcelona, Atelier, 2005.

Violeta Mújica Álvarez & Jesús Figueroa Lara. Contaminación Ambiental, causas y control. México: UAM, 1996.

Océano. Atlas Geográfico Universal y de México. Barcelona: Editorial Océano, 2004.

Patricia D. Park. *Energy Law and the Environment*. EUA y Canadá: Taylor and Francis Inc., 2002.

Selected Bibliography

Peter Sands. *The Effectiveness of International Environmental Agreements.* Cambridge: UNCED, 1992.

Philippe Sands. *Principles of International Environmental Law. Frameworks, Standards and Implementation*, vol. 1. Manchester: Manchester University Press, 1995.

Ramón Martín Mateo. *Tratado de Derecho Ambiental*, vol. III. Madrid: Civitas, 1997.

The World Bank. *Fuel for Thought. An Environmental Strategy for Energy Sector.* Washington: The World Bank, 2000.

UNEP. *Register of International Treaties and Other Agreements in the Field of the Environment.* Nairobi: UNEP, 1997.

Yamin Farhana. *Climate Change in Carbón Markets. A Handbook of Emissions Reduction Mechanisms.* RU: Earthscan, 2005.

Yamin Farhana. *The International Rules of the Kioto Protocol and Carbon Markets. A Handbook of Emissions Reduction Mechanism.* UK: Earthscan, 2015.

Table of Legislation

Constitution of the Mexican United States, 1917
Agrarian Act, 1992, as amended in 2008
Act for Sustainable Rural Development, 2001, as amended in 2007
Civil Code of the Federal District as Regards the Common Jurisdiction and for the Whole Republic as Regards the Federal Jurisdiction, 1928 (repealed)
Federal Act to Prevent and to Control Environmental Pollution, 1971 (repealed)
Federal Act of Environmental Protection, 1982 (repealed)
Federal Act of Administrative Procedure, 1994
Federal Duties Act, 1981, as amended in 2008
Federal Act of Metrology and Standardization, 1992, as amended in 2015
Federal Act of the Sea, 1986
Ecological Equilibrium and Environmental Protection General Act, 1987, as amended in 1996
General Act of Wildlife, 2000
General Act of Sustainable Fishing and Aquaculture, 2007
General Act for Sustainable Forest Development, 2003
General Act of Prevention and Integral Management of Waste, 2003
General Act of Human Settlements, 1993, as amended in 1994
Mining Act, 1992, as amended in 2006
National Waters Act, 1992, as amended in 2008
Sanitary Code of the United Mexican States, 1934 (repealed)
Regulation under the Environmental Act in Regard to Environmental Impact, 2000
Regulation Under the Environmental Act in the Field of Prevention and Control of the Pollution Originated by the Emission of Fumes and Powders, 1971
Regulation Under the Environmental Act in the Field of Prevention and Control of Air Pollution, 1988
Regulatory Act of the Constitution on the Oil Branch, 1958, as amended in 2008
Regulatory Act of Article 27 of the Constitution on Nuclear Matters, 1985, as amended in 1998

Judicial Rulings (Jurisprudence)

Ecology – legal standing to file an injunction action against laws on that matter: it corresponds to the community as holder of the collective rights (legislation of the State of Mexico). The notion of legal standing is closely linked with the principle of relativity established by Article 107 of the Political Constitution of the Mexican

United States and with the effects of an injunction decision. Section II of the aforementioned Constitutional precept points out that 'the Judicial Ruling will always be such that it only refers to particular individuals, and it is limited to protect them in the specific case on which the injunction action refers without making a general declaration regarding the law or Act that motivated it'.

In the same way, when protection against a law is granted by the Judiciary, the effect of the decision is to protect the petitioner against the present and future application of such law, with the aforementioned principle of relativity being respected, as has been established by the High Court in the decision entitled 'Injunction Against Laws: The Effects of a Judicial Ruling That Grants the Protection Consists of Protecting the Petitioner Against Its Present and Future Application'. This means that the judicial body that grants the protection of the Justice of the Union will have a relative scope, given that it will be limited to only protect the petitioner that has initiated the respective trial, but not other people, being bound, therefore, to the declaration of unconstitutionality of the law to the specific case.

Article 9o of the Environmental Protection Act of the State of Mexico and Articles 1 section VIII, 15, sections I and II, 18, and 157 of the Environmental Act (effective in February of 1993) contain dispositions in ecological matters that refer to specific communities, establishing rights in favour of natural and juridical persons who integrate it and reside in those places, which could be considered as a collective right that gives to them collective legal standing so that a community by itself or by means of its legitimate representative can initiate the injunction trial.

From that perspective, when the injunction trial is initiated by an association whose existence does not consist of the safeguard of a right granted to it by the law when it is included in the legal hypothesis, but it consists of both the protection of a collectivity that is not represented by such association and of the enactment of a general declaration regarding the refuted law or ordinance, we have the case of the hypothesis described in section V of Article 73 of the Injunction Act; because if the protection is granted, the problem remains to determine the scope of the Judicial Ruling, which could not be other than those mentioned above and which would clearly conflict with section II of Article 107 of the Constitution, and that cannot legally happen. (No. Registro: 198,421. Tesis aislada. Materia(s): Administrativa, Común. Novena Época. Instancia: Pleno. Fuente: Semanario Judicial de la Federación y su Gaceta. Tomo: V, junio de 1997. Tesis: P. CXI/97. Página: 156. Amparo en revisión 435/96. Fundación Mexicana para la Educación Ambiental, A. C. 29 de mayo de 1997. Unanimidad de nueve votos. Ausentes: José de Jesús Gudiño Pelayo y Olga M. Sánchez Cordero. Ponente: Mariano Azuela Güitrón. Secretaria: Mercedes Rodarte Magdaleno.)

Suitable Environment for the Development and Well-Being Concept, and Regulation and Concretion of That Guarantee

Article 4, paragraph 5 of the Political Constitution of the Mexican United States added on 28 June 1999, the consecration of the right of all individuals to an appropriate environment for their development and well-being. In the same way, the preservation and restoration of the ecological balance and the protection of the environment in the National territory are regulated directly by the Constitution, given the great relevance that this matter has. In this sense, the protection of the environment and natural resources has such an importance that it is the 'social interest' of Mexican society, and it implies and justifies, when necessary, restrictions strictly necessary and intended to preserve and maintain that interest, precisely and specifically, in the laws that establish the public order. In this way, the Official Mexican Norms of Emergency MON-EM-136-ECOL-2002, protection of environmental specifications for the conservation of marine mammals in captivity, in paragraphs 5.8.7 and 5.8.7.1, prohibit the temporary or itinerant exhibition of cetaceans. From Articles 40, paragraph 4, 25, paragraph 6, and 73, section XXIX(g) of the Federal Constitution, interpreted in a systematic and causal teleological way, and by principle, it is noted that they protect the right of people to an appropriate environment for their development and well-being, the appropriate use of natural resources, the preservation and restoration of the ecological balance, and sustainable development. The protection of an appropriate environment for development and well-being, as well as the necessity to protect natural resources and the preservation and restoration of the ecological balance, are fundamental principles that the Constitution has tried to protect and, although, this does not define in a concrete and specific way how this protection must occur, the definition of its content should be made based on a systematic, coordinated, and complementary interpretation of the legal provision that tends to meet, to figure out, and to promote the principles and fundamental values that inspired the Reform's power. (No. Registro: 179,544. Tesis aislada. Materia(s): Administrativa. Novena Época. Instancia: Tribunales Colegiados de Circuito. Fuente: Semanario Judicial de la Federación y su Gaceta. Tomo: XXI, enero de 2005. Tesis: I.4o.A.447 A. Página: 1799. Cuarto Tribunal Colegiado en Materia Administrativa del Primer Circuito. Amparo en revisión 28/2004. Convimar, S.A. de C.V. 26 de mayo de 2004. Unan-imidad de votos. Ponente: Jean Claude Tron Petit. Secretaria: Cristina Fuentes Macías. El criterio no es de la Suprema Corte.)

Index

The numbers here refer to paragraph numbers.

Index

www.ingramcontent.com/pod-product-compliance
Ingram Content Group UK Ltd.
Pitfield, Milton Keynes, MK11 3LW, UK
UKHW020142290926
15471UKWH00004B/653

9 789403 502564